A MIRROR OF JAPANESE ORNAMENT

600 TRADITIONAL DESIGNS

DOVER PUBLICATIONS, INC.
MINEOLA, NEW YORK

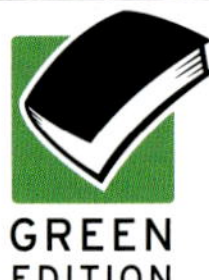

Copyright

Bibliographical Note

A Mirror of Japanese Ornament: 600 Traditional Designs, first published by Dover Publications, Inc. in 2010, is a reprint of one hundred full-color plates from the five-volume collection *Nihon sōshoku taikan*, compiled by Kawanabe Masao and published by Unsōdō, Taishō, Kyoto, in 1915. The original Preface by Masaki Naohiko and the plate notes by Kawanabe Masao have been translated; short descriptive annotations have been added to Kawanabe's text and an Introduction has been provided for the Dover edition.

Library of Congress Cataloging-in-Publication Data

A mirror of Japanese ornament : 600 traditional designs.
p. cm.
"A Mirror of Japanese Ornament: 600 Traditional Designs, first published by Dover Publications, Inc., in 2010, is a reprint of one hundred full-color plates from the five-volume collection Nihon Seishoku Taikan, compiled and edited by Kawanabe Masao and published by Unsōdō, Taishō, Kyoto, in 1915."
Includes bibliographical references.
ISBN-13: 978-0-486-47318-5
ISBN-10: 0-486-47318-X
1. Decoration and ornament—Japan—Themes, motives.

NK1484.A1M57 2010
745.40952—dc22

2010005598

Manufactured in the United States by Courier Corporation
47318X01
www.doverpublications.com

Preface

Each and every surviving example of traditional art continues to exist because of its excellence, and merits study with respectful inquisitiveness. I believe there is a universal truth in the maxim "by exploring the old, one is able to understand the new."[1] This can apply equally to the study of art. Learning from the past forms the basis of new research, which in turn is firmly rooted in the understanding of traditional art. Such scholarship contributes to a greater appreciation of the art objects themselves. Countless and diverse traditional types of art have been collated and catalogued in publications with the aim of learning from traditional arts and crafts. This also applies to decorative patterns and design, which either have not been accurately reproduced, or are presented simply as "reprinted" photographs. As a result, they rarely capture the exquisite designs or the depth of color. The editor of *Great Mirror of Japan's Decoration* [reprinted here as *A Mirror of Japanese Ornament: 600 Traditional Designs*], Kawanabe Masao, has spent many years researching design motifs and has enormous insight into the subject. He selected some 600 outstanding and notable examples of decorative patterns from each period, dating from as early as the ancient Asuka period to the more recent Edo [Tokugawa] period. One hundred superb color plates provide a sense of immediacy in our viewing of the actual artworks. This outstanding compilation offers a good historical overview and broadly covers the main decorative motifs encountered in Japanese art. The plates are reproduced with meticulous attention to color; they are organized in a novel fashion, distinguishing this compendium from other publications and making it an extremely useful reference book of unparalleled clarity. The tireless efforts that this book represents, and its realization, are deserving of high praise. I firmly believe that its publication will mark an important cultural shift for our country and will undoubtedly prove a boon to the world of applied arts as well as the manufacturing (product design) industry. Furthermore, this book will have fully realized its aim, if it in any way serves to strengthen our country.

April 1915
Masaki Naohiko
President, Tokyo School of Fine Arts

[1] The equivalent expression is *onko chishin* (also read as "the discovery of the old in the new") which is referenced in other such design projects, most notably the project (1876–1881) organized by the Japanese government's Bureau of Design to research Western design trends and incorporate them into Japanese export designs. The designs issued by this team are collectively known as the 'Onchi catalogues' (*Onchi zuroku*), the term *onchi* a reference to the expression *onko chishin*. The designs were passed on to Japanese artists and craftsmen who participated in international and domestic exhibitions, as well as to later craft exporters. See Yamamori Yumiko, "Exploring the Old, Understanding the New: The Tradition of Meiji Export Cabinets," in James Bennett and Amy Reigle Newland (eds.), *The Golden Journey: Japanese Art from Australian Collections*. Adelaide: Art Gallery of South Australia, 2009, p. 234, and Moyra Clare Pollard, *Master Potter of Meiji Japan: Makuzu Kōzan (1842–1916) and his Workshop*. New York: Oxford University Press, 2003, p. 100 (Google books online). [Translator's note]

Contents

Chronology

[periods covered in this volume]

Jōmon c. 10,500–c. 300 BC

Yayoi c. 300 BC–AD 300

Kofun or Tomb c. 300–552

Asuka 552–645

Hakuhō 645–710

Nara 710–794

Heian 794–1185

Kamakura 1185–1333

Nanbokuchō 1333–1392

Muromachi 1392–1573

Azuchi-Momoyama 1573–1615

Edo 1615–1868

Meiji 1868–1912

Taishô 1912–1926

Introduction

In his preface to the *Nihon sōshoku taikan (Great Mirror of Japan's Decoration),* Masaki Naohiko (1862–1940), then head of the Tokyo School of Fine Arts,[1] praises this five-volume compilation as one worthy of merit, not only for its richness and accuracy in illustration, but also as an invaluable tool in the understanding of traditional art. A firm grounding in the art of the past, he seems to imply, will inform the art of the future.

Little is known about the compiler of *Great Mirror*, Kawanabe Masao, a fact lamented by author Ōbuchi Takemi in his introduction to the 1975 Japanese reprint of the work. A native of Okayama Prefecture, Kawanabe graduated from the design department of Tokyo School of Fine Arts in 1899, having studied interior design. He is thought to have spent time in New York in the 1910s. It is not clear whether this was before or after the release of *Great Mirror* in 1915.[2] As a student of the Tokyo School of Fine Arts, it is quite possible that Kawanabe knew the author of the preface, Masaki Naohiko, even though Masaki was the head of the Tokyo School of Fine Arts from 1901 to 1932.[3] Sadly, Kawanabe was unable to enjoy any long-term success from the publication with his death in 1918, just three years after the release of *Great Mirror*.

Kawanabe's training at the Tokyo School of Fine Arts corresponded to a period when Japanese "design" witnessed new developments, in the aftermath of the country's opening to extensive trade with the West from the mid-nineteenth century onwards and the resulting increased recognition of Japan on the world stage. The growing international presence of Japanese art—in particular, decorative arts and crafts—was greatly assisted by its inclusion in overseas expositions, most notably, Paris (1867) and Vienna (1873). Crafts became an "economic project for the promotion of international trade."[4] The government supported crafts and the development of design so as to augment revenue in global trade, since Japanese handicrafts represented a substantial portion of the country's export. It reasoned that beautifully designed objects would lead to further possibilities for export trade and exhibition. Even foreigners working in Japan, like the American Ernest F. Fenollosa (1853–1908), perhaps better known as an advocate of traditional Japanese fine art, encouraged the improvement in design for the decorative arts.[5] Such a stance is also echoed in Masaki's preface when he asserts that the publication of *Great Mirror* "will mark an important cultural shift for our country and will undoubtedly prove a boon to the world of applied arts as well as the manufacturing (product design) industry."

---

[1]In 1949, the Tokyo School of Fine Arts later merged with the Tokyo School of Music (Tokyō Ongaku Gakkō) to become the Tokyo University of the Arts (Tōkyō Geijutsu Gakkō).

[2]From explanatory notes by Ōbuchi Takemi in the reprinted *Nihon sōshoku taikan shinhan* (*Great Mirror of Japan's Decoration: New Edition*). Kyoto: Mitsumura Suiko Shoin, 1975, 2 vols., text volume, p. 7.

[3]Masaki was abroad from 1899 to 1901, so may not have known Kawanabe at this time.

[4]For a more detailed discussion on this period and the crafts, Kikuchi Yuko, *Japanese Modernisation and Mingei Theory: Cultural Nationalism and Oriental Orientalism*. London: RoutledgeCurzon, 2004, pp. 84–85 (Google books online).

[5]Moyra Clare Pollard, *Master Potter of Meiji Japan: Makuzu Kōzan (1842–1916) and his Workshop*. New York: Oxford University Press, 2003, p. 86 (Google books online).

Therefore, at a national level, there was considerable effort directed towards the development of *zuan* (a prototypical concept for "design") for the purposes of creating more attractive objects for the export trade.[6] This, in turn, led to the establishment of craft schools and *zuanka,* or departments of design, at trade schools, universities, and manufacturing companies.[7] One such early academic "design" department was established at the Tokyo School of Fine Arts in 1896, where *Great Mirror*'s compiler, Kawanabe Masao, was educated. He would have been among the first graduates in this department in 1899.

Ōbuchi Takemi believes that Kawanabe compiled *Great Mirror* with a designer's eye, and that as a resource for Japanese design its value was as much as a reflection of a designer's understanding about the importance of particular motifs as relates to a "design" aesthetic as it was an historical lexicon of traditional Japanese design motifs.[8] We have little notion of the aesthetic considerations or criteria that led to Kawanabe's selection—their obvious beauty and historical significance aside—since he included no introduction, and the captions to the plates are very brief. Whether the publication was intended for foreign consumption is not entirely clear as the caption texts are in Japanese, but it is clear that the overriding concern was on the imagery, not the accompanying texts.

As a compendium of traditional design motifs, *Great Mirror* follows in the tradition of pattern design books issued from the mid-seventeenth century onwards known as *hinagatabon,* which contained *kimono* designs and were intended mainly as a source-book for copying. These books assisted a client's selection of a garment, and many were commissioned by drapers or cloth merchants. From the seventeenth to the nineteenth centuries, illustrated pattern or design books of other fields and artistic genres were released, making them an important resource for Japanese craftsmen. They depicted designs for lacquerware, ceramics, textiles, sword-fittings, woodcarving, and *netsuke,* to name a few. Even Japanese artists much celebrated in the West, such as the woodblock-print designer Katsushika Hokusai (1760–1849), created illustrations for such publications.[9]

Pattern design books continued to be developed into the Meiji era (1868–1912) and the Taishō period (1912–26) and were a significant aspect of color-printed books from the 1890s until the mid-1930s. They encompassed the tradition of source-books that had a practical application for manufacturing like those in the *hinagatabon* tradition and to the category of which Masaki Naohiko suggests that *Great Mirror* would have great influence. Another feature of design books of this period is the "fine-art" book with lavish color plates. At the forefront of contemporary *and* traditional design books (also known as *zuanshū,* or "design compendiums," by this time) was the publisher of *Great Mirror*, the Kyoto-based company Unsōdō.[10] From its establishment in 1891 until the 1930s, the company produced many woodblock-printed fine-art and deluxe pattern and design books that are characterized by an extremely high level of block-cutting and printing. They marketed their stock both in Japan and abroad.[11] Their publications of contemporary artists and designers

---

[6]Nōtomi Kaijirō (1844–1918) is credited with creating the term "*zuan*" as with the term "design" *(dezain)* used after WWII in Japan; see Kikuchi (2004), p. 83.

[7]*Ibid.*, pp. 83–84, and Pollard (2003), p. 86.

[8]Ōbuchi (1975), pp. 5–6.

[9]Included among Hokusai's pattern books, for example, were his *Modern Patterns for Combs* (*Imayō kushi kiseru hinagata*, 1823), and *A Picture-book of New Patterns for All Kinds of Trades* (*Shōsoku ehon Katsushika shin hinagata*, 1836), which was devoted largely to wooden architectural structures and carvings.

[10]It is operated today by the third-generation head Yamada Teiichi; Yamada Naosaburō was the first manager, followed by Yamada Enji. As listed in the colophon of the 1915 edition, the store still operates from Kyoto's Teramachi Nijō-minami, Kamigyō Ward; it also has a branch in Tokyo.

[11]They are known to have released catalogues in English, for example, therefore catering to a foreign clientele. An equally significant consequence of the Unsōdō productions was the continued employment of highly skilled block-cutters and printers, thus keeping the tradition of the woodblock-printed image buoyant.

included the "Neo-Rinpa" artists Kamisaka Sekka (1866–1942) and his pupil Furuya Kōrin (1875–1910), who was especially instrumental in the development of Japanese "modern" design in the early twentieth century.[12]

Great Mirror is clearly a product of this vogue for beautifully crafted design books, and similar traditional design books served as a complement to the more "modern" designs issued by the Unsōdō books such as Sekka's *Momoyogusa* (*Worlds of Things*, 1909), or Kōrin's *Kōrin moyō* (*Kōrin*'s *Designs*, 1907).[13] While a product that could be appreciated on a purely aesthetic level or as a sumptuous resource of decorative motifs, *Great Mirror* also expresses pride in Japan's own art historical past, not only as a validation of its own rich artistic traditions but also in making this known on the international stage. Masaki Naohiko's preface—as well as the colophons in *Great Mirror*, such as those prefacing volumes 2 and 3—*ekiko shūkin* ("unravel the old/cultivate the new") or *kōko shōki* ("cherish the old/appreciate the unusual")—remind the reader that one must appreciate the old as the new is explored. Such introspection is not surprising if we consider the climate in Japan from the Meiji era onwards. With the government's move towards modernization and industrialization along Western lines at this time, society and culture had been exposed to dramatic change. It was the government's stand, voiced in slogans like *wakon yōsai* ("Japanese mind with Occidental knowledge"), that this change could be effected through a synthesis of Japanese thought and modernization.[14] However, questions about the viability or efficacy of such a stance—with some seeing modernization (Westernization) at the cost of Japanese traditions—awakened in some quarters a nationalist sentiment, with many looking to the past for guidance in the search for a national identity.[15] A staunch advocate of traditional arts, Masaki Naohiko's obvious pride in traditional art and design bubbles over in his concluding words in the preface: "this book will have fully realized its aim, if it in any way serves to strengthen our country." [16]

* * * * *

Comprising some 600 designs drawn from both secular and sacred objects spanning the Asuka (552–645) to Edo (1615–1868) periods, the artistic techniques represented by the designs in *A Mirror of Japanese Ornament* are diverse, and the range of media broad, including metalwork, textiles, lacquer, painting, and carved wood. Yet as a "mirror" of design, *A Mirror of Japanese Ornament* is neither exhaustive nor comprehensive in its art historical scope. It does include designs from a number of objects that are today considered significant national treasures, such as those on Plates 52 and 53, or from complexes designated as UNESCO World Heritage sites, such as the Shōsōin (see Plates 12–19). But not included, for example, are designs from objects pre-dating the Asuka period, namely from Japan's pre-historic Jōmon (c. 10,500–c. 300 BC) and Yayoi (c. 300 BC–AD 300) periods to the ornamented artifacts and mural paintings of the Kofun or Tomb period (c. 300–552). Perhaps this omission can be explained by the fact that at the time of the compilation the comparatively fewer

[12]See Yokoya Kenichirō, *Zuanchō in Kyoto: Textile Design Books for the Kimono Trade*. Stanford: Stanford University Libraries, 2007.

[13]A black-and-white precursor to Kawanabe's work can be seen in *Narumikata* by Odagiri Harue, a multi-volume compendium of designs based on Japanese shrine and temple decoration; it was reprinted from the original blocks as *Narumikata zokuhen* (*Narumikata: The Sequel*) by the Unsōdō in around 1910.

[14]Kikuchi (2004), p. 76.

[15]It is not the intent in this brief introduction to discuss the socio-political circumstances of Japan at this time, which also would have an influence. For an overview of the period, see Elise K. Tipton, *Modern Japan: A Social and Political History*, Nissan Institute/Routledge Japanese Studies. London: Routledge, 2002.

[16]Masaki firmly believed in the superiority of Japanese national culture, which may explain his somewhat nationalistic tone here; see also Aida Yuen Wong, *Parting the Mists: Discovering Japan and the Rise of National-Style Painting in Modern China,* Asian Interactions and Comparisons, published jointly with the Association for Asian Studies/University of Hawai'i Press, 2006, p. 84 (Google books online).

objects of these eras were seen more as archaeology than art history and may have held little interest for designers of the period. Noteworthy, too, is the fact that Kawanabe does not include the artistic developments in the Meiji era, when Japanese crafts, in particular, were making great strides in the development of design. Nevertheless, Ōbuchi suggests that *Great Mirror* is a testimony to Kawanabe's pioneering spirit in the introduction of traditional Japanese design to new fields. Whatever its intent, however, design books such as *A Mirror of Japanese Ornament* are, to borrow the words of the late Japanese book scholar Jack Hillier, objects that can be appreciated as "an expensive gift in thoroughly good taste, admired as a splendid product of the publishers."[17]

---

[17]Jack Hillier, *The Art of the Japanese Book.* London: Sotheby's Publications, 2 vols./1987, vol. 2, pp. 975–986.

Plate Notes

The following catalogue reproduces the original text by Kawanabe Masao, with short descriptive annotations added for a number of the Plates. In the 1975 reprint of *Great Mirror of Japan's Decoration*, Ōbuchi Takemi remarked upon the numerous discrepancies in the original, and these have been noted wherever relevant. However, it is not the intent of this edition to verify each of Kawanabe and Ōbuchi's notations. All Japanese names appear in traditional order—last name preceding first name—and all Japanese terms and names that have entered into English usage appear in the anglicized form, unless in original Japanese citations (e.g., Tokyo, not Tōkyō). The original text was divided into five sections, arranged chronologically, and introduced by colophons by Japanese cognoscenti such as the Imperial Household minister, Hijikata Hisamoto (Shinzan, 1833–1918) and the celebrated literati painter Tomioka Tessai (1836–1924). [Translator's note]

***Volume 1. Suiko* [552–645] *to Tenpyō* [729–749] *eras*[1]**

Calligraphic inscription: *shūhō* ("the fragrance of many flowers"), dated Spring 1915 and signed "the 83-year-old Shinzan" (Shinzan is the art name of Hijikata Hisamoto)

Plate 1. (right to left, top to bottom): a–b. Designs from low-relief (*usunikubori*) tile decorations from the time of Empress Suiko (two designs across top); c. Designs from applied low-relief decoration on Buddhist halo and canopy (*tengai*), Hōryūji (three designs, second row right); d–f. Low-relief design on halo for Buddhist statue, Hōryūji (two designs, second row left; third row); g. Painted sections from board placed under the eaves (*noki-ita*) of a canopy (*tengai*), Hōryūji; h–i. Applied openworked designs, one section of a Buddhist banner (*kanjōban*), Hōryūji
Plate 2. Designs from metal fittings, Tamamushi (no) zushi, Hōryūji (various examples)
Plate 3. Designs from Buddhist gilt bronze altar fittings and implements, Tōdaiji (various examples)
Plate 4. Patterns from gilt-bronze banner(s), listed in the register of Imperial treasures (*gomotsu*), formerly at Hōryūji (nine examples)
Plate 5. Designs from halos (nimbus) of Buddhist statues, listed in the register of Imperial treasures (*gomotsu*), formerly at Hōryūji (four examples)

Plates 1–5 focus on design elements associated with Buddhism dating to the Asuka period. Plates 1, 2, 4 and 5 illustrate design motifs found on tiles, halos on Buddhist figures (*kōhai*), canopies above Buddhist statues (*tengai*), metalwork, and other Buddhist implements from the Hōryūji. Located in Ikaruga, Nara Prefecture, the oldest buildings of the temple, Hōryūji, date to between 670 and 711. Plate 3 has taken elements from the Tōdaiji in Nara, which was established in 752, and, like other temples, demonstrates the wealth and power held by Buddhist clergy at that time.

[1] "Suiko era" is the archaic name used for the Asuka period (552–645); it is taken from the name of Empress Suiko (reigned 592–628). The beginning of the Tenpyō era (710–94) marks the transfer of the capital from Fujiwara to Nara (Heiankyō); it ends with the move of the capital to Kyoto in 794. This period is also referred to as the Late Nara.

Plate 1 depicts various floral and vine motifs (lotus, honeysuckle, etc.) on objects at the Hōryūji, including the halos of the famous triad of the Historical Buddha and his two attendants, the Buddha of Healing, the canopy in the temple's Golden Hall (Kondō), as well as tiles and open-work banners (*kanjōban*) made in fabric and covered with gilt bronze that were used in canopies. Plate 2 shows stylized honeysuckle (*nindō*) and arabesque (*karakusa*, literally "Chinese grass"; see Plates 20–21) designs from the Tamamushi (no) zushi, or "Jewel Beetle Wing Shrine," a portable shrine in the shape of a miniature golden hall, at the Hōryūji. The shrine is so-named because the bronze filigree bands adorning the pedestal and architectural members were once inlaid with the iridescent *tamamushi* beetle wings. The form of this wooden structure offers valuable evidence regarding seventh-century architectural styles.

The designs in Plate 3 show diverse decorative elements, including diamond-shaped floral, circular vine, and cloud motifs, while Plate 4 exhibits honeysuckle patterns, among others, from objects such as open-work banners or flags. Plate 5 shows sections from the halos that appear behind Buddhist statues such as Kannon, the Bodhisattva of Mercy; the decoration on these objects includes images of celestial beings in flight (*asparas*), Bodhisattvas, and flame, honeysuckle and lotus motifs. The term *gomotsu* (also read *gyobutsu*, or "emperor's or imperial property") is a reference to objects listed in the register of Imperial treasures (*gomotsu daichō*), perhaps the most famous of which are those housed in the Shōsōin storehouse at the Tōdaiji (see notes for Plates 12–19).

Plate 6. Designs from wall paintings (*hekiga*), Hōryūji (various examples)
Plate 7. Designs from wall paintings (*hekiga*), Hōryūji (various examples)
Plate 8. Selection of *mitsuda-e* designs from dais of Buddhist statues, Hōryūji[2]

The Hōryūji suffered a devastating fire in 1949 that damaged much of the Golden Hall (Kondō), including its murals. The publication of *Great Mirror of Japan's Decoration* in 1915, therefore, is a useful resource regarding some of the mural design motifs. Plates 6 and 7 display various patterns, ranging from repetitive geometric patterns to honeysuckle, lotus, "precious or auspicious flowers" (*hōsōge*; see notes for Plates 41–46), and pearl-like forms in circular configurations (*renjumon*).

Plate 8 illustrates *mitsuda-e* (literally, "litharge painting"), a modern art historical term for a type of painting that uses the natural mineral form of lead oxide (*mitsudasō*) as a drying agent. To make *mitsuda-e*, powdered pigments are mixed with an oil base and lead oxide. The technique is believed to have been transmitted from China to Japan sometime in the seventh century and was employed on wood and leather objects. It was relatively common in the Nara period, since white painting, not possible at the time in lacquer painting, could be produced with this technique.

Plate 9. (right to left, top to bottom): a–c. *Mitsuda-e* designs; d. Low-relief (*usunikubori*) on Buddha dais, Tōshōdaiji; e. Hairline engraving (*kebori*) on silver objects, Tōdaiji; f. Low-relief design on Buddha dais, Tōshōdaiji; g–h. Open-work metal ornamentation for Buddhist statues; i. Buddhist statue designs, Kōfukuji

The Buddhist temples Hōryūji, Kōfukuji, Tōdaiji, and Tōshōdaiji, whose treasures serve as the inspiration for designs in the first two volumes of *Great Mirror of Japan's Decoration*, were included at various times in Japan's history as the "seven great" temples and were popular pilgrimage destinations.

---

[2]Detailed as from the "Tamamushi (no) zushi, Hōryūji" (see Plate 2 above) in the 1975 reprint.

In the 1975 Japanese reprint of *Great Mirror*, Ōbuchi Takemi deleted the detailed caption, substituting simply the notation "Designs of Chinese grasses (*karakusa*)" (see notes for Plates 20–21 for an explanation of *karakusa*).

Plate 10. Design from mirror boxes/silver against a black ground, Tōdaiji (three examples)

This plate illustrates three designs from mirror boxes housed in the Shōsōin at the Tōdaiji. The circular design in the upper left is most likely from the back of a mirror with mother-of-pearl and amber inlay. The designs in the upper right and the bottom illustrate the technique of silver *heidatsu* (or *hyōmon*), for which thin metal sheets, such as those of gold or silver, are cut into decorative shapes—here bird and floral motifs—and set into a base. The surface is then covered with lacquer; the metal design is exposed when the lacquer is polished or carved away in "hairline engraving." Inside the edges of the bottom-left design are three groups of eight-petalled floral motifs, with a centrally placed peacock. It reportedly was part of the ornamentation on a box used for an eight-sided mirror.

Plate 11. (top to bottom) Both listed in the register of Imperial treasures (*gomotsu*), formerly at Hōryūji: a. Design of the patterned weave "*Shitennō*" banner (cloth), formerly Hōryūji; b. Designs illustrating animal hunt (from ancient textiles)

Here "*Shitennō*" refers to the "Four Guardian Kings," the defenders of the Buddha's teaching, easily identified by their armored appearance. The images here are from textiles showing hunting scenes in a circular cartouche, with animals like Chinese lions (*shishi*) (top/bottom) and deer (top), and other decorative motifs. Overall, the ornamentation is reminiscent of Persian art.

Plate 12. Textile designs, Tōdaiji (four examples)
Plate 13. Textile designs, Tōdaiji (five examples)
Plate 14. Textile designs, Tōdaiji (four examples)
Plate 15. Textile designs from small banners, Tōdaiji (six examples)[3]
Plate 16. Tenpyō-period textile designs (three examples)
Plate 17. Listed in the register of Imperial treasures (*gomotsu*), Shōsōin (top to bottom): a. Carved board clamped resist-dyed (*kyōkechi*) designs; b. Wax resist-dyed (*rōkechi*) designs (two examples)
Plate 18. Wax resist-dyed (*rōkechi*) designs (two examples)
Plate 19. Wax resist-dyed (*rōkechi*),[4] listed in the register of Imperial treasures (*gomotsu*), Shōsōin (three examples) [These plates have been turned horizontally]

The Shōsōin is a raised-floor storehouse at the Tōdaiji in Nara. Erected in the Heian period, it contains hundreds of rare treasures dedicated to the temple by Empress Kōmyō (701–760) following the death of Emperor Shōmu (701–756). Among the collections of the Shōsōin are a sizeable group of diverse textile types such as brocades, gossamers, and plain silks, which display decorative techniques ranging from embroidered to printed patterns. They are an invaluable source in our understanding of Japanese Asuka- and Nara-period textile history.

[3]The term "small banners" has been deleted in the 1975 reprint.
[4]*Kyōkechi* and *rōkechi* are both listed in the 1975 reprint.

The decorative cycle on these textiles includes numerous motifs from the natural world, as evinced in the examples here. Particularly elegant are Plates 17 to 19. They showcase designs executed with the resist-dye techniques *kyōkechi* and *rōkechi*, which were initially imported from China but produced domestically, it is believed, from the Nara period onwards. For *rōkechi*, the cloth is patterned with wax before dyeing; the wax is removed after the dye is applied. For *kyōkechi,* thin cloth was sandwiched between thick mirror-image boards, then clamped and dyed.

***Volume 2: Tenpyō* [729–749] *to Kōnin* [810–824] *eras*[5]**
Colophon: *ekiko shūkin* ("unravel the old/cultivate the new"), dated and signed by the "great senile" Tessai Gaishi (Tomioka Tessai, 1836–1924)

Plate 20. (top and bottom): a. Carved wood with applied gold, halo for Buddhist statue,[6] Tōshōdaiji, Nara; b. Low-relief (*usunikubori*) bronze, halo of *nenjibutsu* of Kusunoki family Buddhist image, Hōryūji
Plate 21. Designs for open-worked carved wood decoration on halo of Buddhist image (ten examples)

Design elements in Plate 20a are taken from various Buddhist dais and altars at the Hōryūji and Tōshōdaiji, respectively. They exhibit patterns such as honeysuckle, arabesque (*karakusa*), lotus, vine, and *hōsōge* ("precious or auspicious flowers," see notes for Plates 41–46) frequently seen in art from the Asuka to Nara periods. The *nenjibutsu* in Plate 20b is a Buddhist image for personal worship, in this case associated with the powerful Kusunoki family. The dominant motif in both is the central lotus blossom. The Tōshōdaiji was founded around 759 as a private temple for the Chinese monk Jianzhen (Jp: Ganjin).

The term *karakusa* ("Chinese grasses"), or arabesque, refers to exotic plant motifs imported to Japan from China, even though many of the motifs are thought to have originated from more distant lands, such as Central Asia, Persia, and perhaps even Greece and Egypt. *Karakusa* does not refer to any particular floral element and is typically a flower and leaf design linked by continuous scrolling tendrils or vines. There are numerous variations: it can be a combination of imaginary flowers and vines, or adapted to Japanese taste with the use of known flowers such as peonies, grapevines, bamboo, and chrysanthemums. *Karakusa* were used extensively in Japanese design.

Plate 22. Auspicious/sacred animal motifs, Tenpyō to Fujiwara periods (twelve examples)

Depicted in Plate 22 are sacred animals associated with Buddhist decoration, such as the phoenix, dragon, flying horses and birds, auspicious birds, the winged *karyōbinga* (see Plate 50), *kirin* (composite creature with a deer body and tail of an ox), Chinese lions (*shishi*), and animals connected with the four cardinal directions (see Plate 24) taken from objects such as those found at the Shōsōin and Hōryūji (see notes for Plates 12–19 and 1–5, respectively).

Plate 23. Ancient mirrors, Shōsōin (two examples)
Plate 24. (top to bottom) a. Ancient mirror, verso, twelve animals of the zodiac; b. Designs of

[5]Eras within the later Nara (710–94) and early Heian (794–897) periods.
[6]The term "applied gold" or "gold appliqué" has been deleted in the 1975 reprint.

Chinese mythical animals connected with the four cardinal directions on Buddhist dais, low-relief (*usunikubori*) metal fittings

The spectacular eight-lobed bronze mirror in Plate 23 (top) is ornately decorated: the central zone of four mountains and seashore patterns surround a knob symbolizing Mount Hōrai (Chinese: Mount Penglai; mythical mountain of the Eight Chinese Immortals), with various figures, coiled dragons, and phoenixes; the middle zone has patterns of floral scrolls with peacocks, phoenixes, and birds; the outer zone contains the eight symbols of Chinese divination at each cusp and a poem of eight five-character phrases. The central design elements in Plate 24 are, along the top, the twelve animals of the zodiac (right to left: tiger, ox, rat, snake, dragon, rabbit, monkey, sheep, horse, boar, dog, and rooster) and the animals of the four cardinal directions. The latter are the green/blue dragon of the East; the white tiger of the West; the red phoenix of the South; and the black warrior (tortoise-like creature with head/tail serpent) of the North. These are clearly recognizable in two zones in the bottom image of Plate 23.

Plate 25. Views of sections of the top and side, *mitsuda-e* lacquer box, listed in the register of Imperial treasures (*gomotsu*), Shōsōin

For a definition of the technique of *mitsuda-e*, see note for Plate 8. The dominant design elements on this black-lacquered wooden box in the Shōsōin are honeysuckle vines, phoenixes, and fire-spitting birds.

Plate 26. Ancient textiles, listed in the register of Imperial treasures (*gomotsu*), Shōsōin (two examples)
Plate 27. Designs from a small box, listed in the register of Imperial treasures (*gomotsu*), Shōsōin
Plate 28. Designs from small painted box, listed in the register of Imperial treasures (*gomotsu*), Shōsōin; (bottom), copy, Tokyo Imperial Museum[7]

In the 1975 Japanese reprint of *Great Mirror,* Ōbuchi Takemi notes that these two design patterns are from small boxes in the Shōsōin.[8] Plate 27 illustrates a technique known as *kingindei*, in which gold and silver powders are mixed with glue to decorate an object. The cover (bottom image) and side (upper image) include floral motifs; the central motif on the cover is surrounded by eight birds and four butterflies. Plate 28 displays a stylized arrangement of red, blue, and green floral and grass motifs; the Tokyo Imperial Museum (Household Museum of Art) is the present-day Tokyo National Museum.

Plate 29. Designs for *kin* soundboard, Shōsoin, Tōdaiji (various examples)

Designs taken from section of the top, back, and sides of a lacquered seven-stringed *kin* zither, illustrating three figures drinking and playing music, birds, phoenixes, floral motifs, clouds, and so forth in the *heidatsu* technique (see note for Plate 10). This *kin* is thought to have been of Chinese manufacture.

Plate 30. Rosewood *go* board with pictorial representation, listed in the register of Imperial treasures (*gomotsu*), Shōsōin

---

[7]"Copy, Tokyo Imperial Museum" is deleted in the 1975 reprint.
[8]Ōbuchi (1975), pp. 31–32.

Plate 31. (top to bottom) Both listed in the register of Imperial treasures (*gomotsu*), Shōsōin: a. Rosewood *go* board with pictorial representation (eight examples); b. Silver (*heidatsu*) lidded container (*gōshi*) and ivory tusk *go* board pieces

The designs in Plates 30 and 31a are described in the original text as "wood pictures" (*mokuga*), which used various inlaid materials to create decorative details and ornamentation. In Plate 30, a board with open side panels, ivory has been used to illustrate a hunting scene, camels, birds, and floral motifs (*karakusa*); the red strip to the left illustrates the decorative base piece of the board. Plate 31 depicts various details from the *go* board, including the decoration on the small side drawers, interlocking motifs, and the stained ivory *go* pieces (see notes for Plate 10 for an explanation on the technique of *heidatsu*).

Plate 32. Red- and green-stained ivory foot-rules, listed in the register of Imperial treasures (*gomotsu*), Shōsōin (two examples)

Stained ivory foot-rules (approximately one foot in length) were presented annually to the imperial court. Here, the decorated top, bottom, and side pieces are illustrated. They were stained and carved with decorative patterns in the *bachiru* technique, which involves the carving of design elements on a stained ivory object and then tinting; some motifs are left in reserve in the white ivory.

Plate 33. Long sword (*tachi*) fittings, listed in the register of Imperial treasures (*gomotsu*), Shōsōin

This plate displays various parts of a decorative *tachi* sword, such as the scabbard fittings, and *tsuba*, executed in an open-worked, gilt silver and low-relief design of tendril scrolls, flower-shaped studs, and cloud and animal motifs. Particularly striking are the inset beads of blue and green glass and crystal (red paint under crystal inlay) on the body and ferrule of the scabbard.

Plate 34. Designs for Buddhist imagery, Sangatsudō, Tōdaiji (five examples)
Plate 35. Buddhist motifs, Kōfukuji (six examples)

The Sangatsudō is a temple hall whose plan allows for circumambulation of a statue or statues; the purpose of the circumambulation is to encourage meditation on the *Lotus Sutra* (*Hokekyō*). The Sangatsudō, or Hokkedō (mid-eighth century) at the Tōdaiji in Nara is particularly celebrated. Decorations on Buddhist images of this period were particularly rich, and, according to Ōbuchi Takemi, the design motifs here are taken from the Buddhist statues of the *Shūkongōjin* (also *Kongōshu*), the "Four Guardian Kings" (*Shitennō*) of the Tōdaiji, and *Ashura,* one of the eight guardians of Buddha, at Kōfukuji.[9] They include Chinese floral motifs (*karakusa*; see notes for Plates 20–21) and a combination of *hōsōge* ("precious or auspicious flowers," see notes for Plates 41–46).

Plate 36. Designs on a "Chinese chest" (*karabitsu*), Tōdaiji

[9]Ōbuchi (1975), pp. 34–35.

A lacquered *karabitsu* (Chinese chest) is used to store valuables, including sutra scrolls. It can be made of plain wood or lacquered, as the example here. The designs here, executed in the *mitsuda-e* technique (see note for Plate 8), depict lions (perhaps *karashishi*, or "Chinese lions") amidst cloud, vine, and lotus motifs against a black lacquer ground.

Plate 37. (top to bottom) Multi-colored lotiforms for a *kōinza*, Tōdaiji collection (four examples)
Plate 38. Kanshinji, Kawauchi (-Nagano, Osaka), lotiforms for the pedestal of the principle Buddha image [Nyorin Kannon] worshipped at the temple (two examples)

The caption for Plate 37 in the *Great Mirror* states that this is a *kōinza*, a dais for a tray used in burning incense before a Buddhist image. Lotiform petals are affixed in alternating tiers to a base and, as here, decorated in various patterns in a color scheme known as "rainbow coloring," in which distinct bands of color are placed adjacent to each other to give the impression of shading. The design is so-named because of its resemblance to a rainbow. The Kanshinji is an esoteric (Shingon sect) Buddhist temple located on Mount Hino, and the petals on the pedestal on the ninth-century statue illustrate a *hōsōge* pattern.

Plate 39. (top to bottom): a. Ceiling motifs, Tōshōdaiji; b. Hōōdō, Byōdōin (three examples)

See notes Plates 20–21 and 41–46 for notes on the Tōshōdaiji and Hōōdō, respectively.

Plate 40. (top to bottom): a. Textiles, Tōdaiji (three examples); b. Ancient embroidery (*shishū*)

Volume 3. Fujiwara to Heishi Periods[10]
Colophon: *kōko shōki* ("cherish the old/appreciate the unusual"), dated February 1915 and signed (signature unreadable)

Plate 41. Hōōdō, Byōdōin: a. (top) Selection of carved gilt wood with "Chinese grass" (*karakusa*) designs; b. (bottom seven) Decoration for carved wooden beams and metal fittings
Plate 42. Carved curved wooden tie beam (*kōryō*) with decoration in gold appliqué, Hōōdō, Byōdōin (four examples)
Plate 43. Designs on decorative lintel (*nageshi*), Hōōdō, Byōdōin
Plate 44. Designs on decorative lintel, Hōōdō, Byōdōin (two examples)
Plate 45. Frame and fascia board motifs from canopy structure (*tengai*), Hōōdō, Byōdōin
Plate 46. Decoration on interior door jamb, Hōōdō, Byōdōin (two examples)

The Hōōdō is the central hall of the Byōdōin monastery in Uji, Kyoto Prefecture. It was originally constructed as a villa by the powerful Fujiwara family, but was converted into a Buddhist temple in 1053. Viewed from above, the Hōōdō resembles a phoenix with outstretched wings, thus its name "Phoenix (*hōō*) Hall" (*dō*). The ceiling of the hall is coffered with intricate lattice work (see also Plates 39 and 48). The decorative elements in Plates 41 to 46 are dominated by the *hōsōge* ("precious or

[10]A reference to the later ninth century to 1185, thus part of the Heian period. The Fujiwara and the Taira (or Heishi) were two of the most powerful families at that time.

auspicious flowers"), a reference to a floral pattern that combines flowers such as the lotus, peony, and others in a complex arrangement. It is frequently included as a variation of the arabesque *karakusa*, or "Chinese grasses" (see notes for Plates 20–21). Motifs in Plate 45 are recorded as from *tengai*, a type of canopy hung over Buddhist statues; the eleventh-century example of the Amida Buddha at the Hōōdō is particularly famous.

Plate 47. Metal fittings, Chūsonji (seven examples)
Plate 48. Examples of designs using *raden*, Chūsonji and Hōōdō, Byōdōin (five examples)

The Chūsonji, located in Hiraizumi in southern Iwate Prefecture, is a significant example of late Heian-period regional architecture. It was not unusual for Heian-period temple halls to be opulently ornamented with elaborate techniques and precious materials so as to create the sense of an other-worldly paradise. The small Buddhist mausoleum and worship hall, the Konjikidō ("Gold-Colored Hall"), at Chūsonji, and the Hōōdō, were no exception. Plate 47 features elaborate metal fittings and Plate 48 designs executed with *raden*, a type of shell inlay technique—in particular, mother-of-pearl—in which the shells are ground to the desired thickness, inlaid or pasted into a wood or lacquered surface and then polished. The overriding decorative elements depicted are *karakusa* and *hōsōge* (see notes for Plates 20–21 and 41–46, respectively).

Plate 49. Section of painted leather *keman*, Tōdaiji
Plate 50. Section of open-worked metal *keman*, Chūsonji

A *keman* is a pendant disc used in architectural decoration; some scholars believe that they originated as floral wreaths hung as Buddhist offerings. Plate 49 shows the frequently encountered motif of the period, the *hōsōge* (see Plates 41–46). This floral motif also appears on the gilt-bronze *keman* from the Konjikidō at the Chūsonji in Plate 50 along with a *karyōbinga*, a sacred creature with the head of a bodhisattva, winged bird body, and a tail that resembles a phoenix. The *karyōbinga* is believed to live in the paradise of the Amida Buddha.

Plate 51. (top to bottom): a. Designs from the *Kenda kokushi kesa* (Buddhist surplice) storage box, Tōji (Kyōōgokuji); b. Mount Hiei sutra case[11]

The ornamentation in this plate is taken from a box for a *kesa*, a Buddhist surplice (a) reportedly brought back from China by the Buddhist monk Kūkai (774–835),[12] and a sutra case (b). The compositions show auspicious motifs of fish, turtles, birds in flight, and *hōsōge* in gold and silver pigments; during the earlier Heian period, design motifs from the continent were undergoing a transition towards a more native aesthetic, as seen in the freely executed compositions illustrated here.

Plate 52. Nishi Honganji (National Treasure), *jigami* (fan paper) from the *Anthology of Thirty-six Immortal Poets* (*Nishi Honganji [hon] sanjūroku ninkashū*) (five examples)

---

[11]The designation of Mount Hiei is deleted in the 1975 revision; perhaps, in the original, compiler Kawanabe is referring to the famous eleventh-century sutra case now in the collection of the Enryakuji.

[12]See Jan Mrázek and Morgan Pitelka, *What's the Use of Art?: Asian Visual and Material Culture in Context*. Honolulu: University of Hawai'i Press, 2007, p. 161, for an explanation of the name *Kenda kokushi kesa*.

Plate 53. Nishi Honganji (National Treasure), *jigami* (fan paper) from the *Anthology of Thirty-six Immortal Poets* (*Nishi Honganji* [*hon*] *sanjūroku ninkashū*) (five examples)

Located in Kyoto, the Nishi Honganji is associated with the early twelfth-century anthology of Japanese-style poetry (*waka*) known as the *Anthology of Thirty-six Immortal Poets*. The lavishly decorated papers—painted with gold/silver foil, or printed with mica—and calligraphy of this compendium (some thirty-seven albums pre-dating the modern period) make it a significant example of Heian design. (The selections in *Great Mirror* are illustrated without the calligraphy.) The appellation "thirty-six immortal poets" (*sanjūrokkasen*) refers to the thirty-six noted poets of the seventh to tenth centuries chosen by Fujiwara no Kintō (966–1041).

Plate 54. Fittings for the *Heike nōkyō* scrolls, Itsukushima Jinja (ten examples)
Plate 55. Decorative (cover) designs for the "Belief and Understanding" chapter (*Shinge-hon*) from the *Heike nōkyō* scrolls, Itsukushima Jinja (five examples)
Plate 56. Decorative (cover) designs, *Heike nōkyō* scrolls, Itsukushima Jinja (three examples)
Plate 57. *Mikaeshi*, *Heike nōkyō* scrolls, Itsukushima Jinja (two examples)
Plate 58. *Mikaeshi*, the "Bestowal of Prophecy" chapter (*Juki-hon*) from the *Heike nōkyō* scrolls, Itsukushima Jinja (two examples)
Plate 59. Decorative details from *Heike nōkyō* scrolls, Itsukushima Jinja (five examples)
Plate 60. Decorative details from *Heike nōkyō* scrolls, Itsukushima Jinja (five examples)

During the Heian period, aristocrats often had Buddhist sutras copied as religious offerings. The thirty-three richly illustrated scrolls of the *Lotus Sutra* (*Hokekyō*), which were commissioned by the Taira (Heike) clan and dedicated to the principal deity of the shrine Itsukushima Jinja in 1164, are known as the *Heike Dedicatory Sutra* (*Heike nōkyō*). The scrolls are exquisitely mounted and illustrated with rich pigments, silver, and gold. Plate 54 shows various designs from the metal and crystal mount fittings (roller and end-piece knobs), which are adorned with open-worked designs associated with Buddhism, such as the child attendants and lotus (fourth from left) or dragon and the esoteric Buddhist implement known as a "thunderbolt" (*vajra*; third from left). The chapters illustrated in Plates 55 and 58 are the fourth and sixth chapters, respectively, and depict lotus, floral, and arabesque patterns. The term *mikaeshi* refers to an "endpaper" or "frontispiece," which can be either paper or fabric.

It is said that the Shinto Itsukushima Jinja in Hiroshima was established in the sixth century, even though its main building was first designed in the twelfth century. It was the tutelary shrine of the powerful Taira (Heike) clan.

Volume 4: Kamakura* [1185–1392] *to Ashikaga* [Muromachi, 1392–1568] *periods
Colophon: *Momo sakura/iro to iro to no/yosooi wa/sumeramikuni no/kagami narikeri* (The blossom of spring/the myriad array/a mirror of the imperial reign) Viscount Sugawara Chōgen

Plate 61. Ornamental designs, three-storied pagoda (Sanjū-no-tō), Kōfukuji (six designs)

The tutelary Buddhist temple of the powerful Fujiwara family, the Kōfukuji, is located in Nara and dates to the seventh century. Its three-storied pagoda dates much later, to the earlier twelfth century (see also Plate 82).

Plate 62. Metal sword fittings, Ise Jingū

The refined ornamentation illustrated here are most likely for *chokutō*, a type of straight, single-edged sword that most probably had a ceremonial purpose and was thus a symbol of imperial power. The plant motifs are principally "Chinese grasses" (*karakusa*; see notes for Plates 20–21). The Ise Jingū in Mie Prefecture is one of the most significant early Shinto sites in Japan. Although the exact date of its initial construction is unclear, some believe that the earliest complex therein (the Inner Shrine) was built in the third century. The shrine is dedicated to the sun goddess Amaterasu Ōmikami, the legendary ancestor of Japan's imperial family.

Plate 63. (right to left, top to bottom): a. Design with bees; b. Patterns repeated along diagonals, which can be read in interlocking groups of two, Kumano Jinja; c. Design on the unstarched outer robe (*nōshi*), from the *Takayoshi Genji* (i.e., reference to early twelfth-century, *Illustrated Handscrolls of the Tale of Genji* [*Genji monogatari emaki*]); d. Falling blossoms (on cotton); e. Imperial ox carriage (on brocade), Daijingū
Plate 64. Textile designs, from the shrine Hachimangū, Kamakura (four designs)
Plate 65. Designs for Bugaku theater *hakama* (a type of divided skirt) (two designs)

The three plates shown here are examples of *yūsoku mon*, a general reference to traditional motifs—initially influenced by Tang Chinese designs—which were utilized by the imperial family for items employed in both public and private functions. Such motifs appeared singly or in repeated patterns and were employed for the decoration of diverse media, including textiles (brocades, dyed fabrics, etc.), wood, gold, leather, and paper. Plates 63 and 64 illustrate *yūsoku mon* appearing on objects that have come down through two Shinto shrines (see also Plates 75–78).

Plate 66. Designs from the "Masako" *maki-e* cosmetic box, Mishima Taisha collection. [The plate has been turned horizontally.]
Plate 67. Designs from the "Masako" *maki-e* cosmetic box, Mishima Taisha collection. [The plate has been turned horizontally.]

These designs are from a scene of trees and geese illustrated on the c. mid-thirteenth century cosmetic box in the collection of the Mishima Taisha in Shizuoka Prefecture.[13] The Unsōdō caption lists this as the "Masako" cosmetic box, a reference to Hōjō Masako (1156–1225), the wife of the first shogun of the Kamakura period, Minamoto no Yoritomo (1147–1199), and the donor of this box to the shrine. The *maki-e*, or "sprinkled picture," technique of lacquerware decoration entails the scattering or sprinkling of adhesive metal or colored powders, such as gold, silver, and tin, over soft lacquer.

[13]See Nakasato Toshikatsu, "Kamakura jidai shitsugei gihō shiryō I – ume makie tebako, Mishima taisha zō" (Materials on the Techniques used in Lacquer Craftsmanship in the Kamakura Period, Part I – The Cosmetics Box with a Plum Blossom Pattern in makie, in the possession of the Mishima Shrine), *Hōzon kagaku,* no. 25 (March 1986).

Plate 68. (right column, top to bottom; left column, top to bottom) (all tanned leather): a. Nail-shaped iris; b. Duckweed with leaves; c. *Komon* water plantain; d. Facing mountain ferns; e. Duckweed and iris; f. Maple, deer, and iris; g. Butterflies and birds; h. Iris, turtles, and cranes
Plate 69. (right column, top to bottom; left column, top to bottom) (all tanned leather): a. Pattern with enclosing honeycomb-shaped borders; b. Pattern with enclosing tortoiseshell borders; c. Dove and diamond shapes; d. Dragon amidst waves; e. Fūdō Myōō; f. Miscellaneous motif; g. Sacred gem (*hōju*)
Plate 70. (right to left, top to bottom) (all tanned leather): a. *Komon* "Chinese lions" (in the style known as "Tenpyō leather"); b. "Chinese lion" mask; c. Sanskrit character and Chinese lion (in the style known as "Tenpyō leather"); d. *Komon* motifs with honeycomb-shaped patterns; e. Floral motifs; f. Six roundel patterns with comma-shaped motifs; g. Waves and rabbits

The publication of *hinagatabon* (pattern books), picture books of designs used to assist clients in the selection of kimono, became popular during the Edo period (1615–1868). Pattern books also included designs for objects such as lacquerware, ceramics and porcelains, textiles, sword-fittings, woodcarvings, and netsuke. Many were produced by craftsmen, as well as designed by *ukiyo-e* artists, and are important records for the study of kimono fashion. According to Ōbuchi Takemi,[14] the motifs here resemble such *hinagatabon* designs. A few of the plates include the term *komon* ("small pattern")—a reference to repetitive design patterns—their production enabled by the introduction of paper rather than wood stencils. The Japanese characters seen in the examples above would not have been included on the original object.

Plate 71. Patterns taken from the *Kasuga kenki* [*Kasuga gongen kenki emaki*] (six examples)

The Illustrated Miracles of the Kasuga Deity (*Kasuga gongen kenki emaki*) is an illustrated handscroll completed by the painter Takashina Takakane (active 1309–1330) in the early fourteenth century. The twenty fascicles depict the miracles of the Kasuga deity, the tutelary god of the Fujiwara clan worshipped at the Kasuga Taisha (Kasuga Grand Shrine) in Nara. The shrine exercised enormous political and cultural influence at this time, together with the Kōfukuji, with which the shrine was united. Masaki Naohiko, the author of the preface to *Great Mirror of Japan's Decoration*, acted as a consultant in the research of these scrolls in the Taishō period.

Plate 72. Mid-Tokugawa period dyed patterns (eight examples)
Plate 73. Patterns from the pictorial biography of Priest Ippen (Ippen Shōnin) and designs from the *Kasuga kenki* [*Kasuga gongen kenki emaki*] (six examples)

Priest Shōnin, commonly known as Ippen Shōnin (1234–1289), founded the Jishū sect of Buddhism, which placed importance on the recitation of the name of the Amida Buddha (*nenbutsu*). Ippen's insistence on constant traveling and the abandonment of family and possessions led to his nickname of the "traveling saint." The designs here are reportedly from the twelve illustrated narrative handscrolls painted by the artist En'i and other artists in 1299 that depict Ippen's journey around Japan. See notes for Plate 71 regarding the *Kasuga kenki*.

[14] Ōbuchi (1975), p. 42.

Plate 74. From the Kamakura to Ashikaga (Muromachi) periods:[15] textile (clothing) designs from illustrated scrolls (*emakimono*) (nine examples)
Plate 75. *Yūsoku mon,* traditional design motifs (seventeen examples)
Plate 76. *Yūsoku mon,* traditional design motifs (twenty-four examples)
Plate 77. *Yūsoku mon,* traditional design motifs (six examples)
Plate 78. *Yūsoku mon,* traditional design motifs (six examples)

As in Plates 63 to 65 above, Plates 75 to 78 illustrate a few of the many variations of *yūsoku mon*, a broad reference to traditional design motifs. Plate 76, for example, illustrates circular designs (*marumon*) such as comma and floral motifs; such designs were employed on textiles and family crests by all classes of society. Plate 77 displays *tasukimon*, a design motif characterized by crossed diagonal patterns that was used in textiles from early in Japan's history. The *tatewaku* pattern in Plate 78 consists of vertical flora and vine patterns (e.g., clouds and chrysanthemums) positioned inside curvilinear lines that create an hourglass effect.

***Volume 5: The Era of Toyotomi Hideyoshi* [1536–98] *to the Tokugawa [Edo] period* [1615–1868]**
Preface (see above)

Plate 79. Chrysanthemum designs, *surihaku* technique, on Konparu-school Nō robes[16]

The motifs used here represent the technique of *surihaku* (see notes to Plates 90–93), frequently used to decorate the robes of Nō theater actors.

Plate 80. Cherry-blossom motifs against a purple ground

The pattern here has most likely been executed using *tsujigahana*, a hybrid stitch-resist technique in which designs in color are given hand-painted details and, occasionally, details in embroidery.

Plate 81. Embroidery designs for waist belts (*ateobi*) on Konparu-school Nō robes
Plate 82. Kobori Enshū, favorite designs of *ranma* open-work carvings (twelve examples)
Plate 83. Decorative architectural carvings (eighteen examples)

Kobori Enshū (1579–1647) was an influential tea master, talented calligrapher and poet, and garden designer. In Plate 82, compiler Kawanabe links him with designs for *ranma* (transom), an architectural design element constructed between lintels, as frames for sliding doors and ceilings, or between verandahs and the interior of a building, under gate ridges, on fences or above entrances. The decoration on *ranma* was diverse, including, as here, open-worked designs of differing motifs. Plate 83 illustrates various carved wooden architectural nosings (*kibana*), which found full expression from the Muromachi to Edo periods; the creatures here include Chinese lions (*shishi*), dragons, or tusked elephant-like beasts (*zōbana*).

[15]Period designations have been deleted from the 1975 reprint.
[16]The terms "Konparu," one of the major schools of Nō theater, and "gold" are deleted in the 1975 new edition.

Plate 84. Two designs of the cloth used as mounts for *waka* death poems (*jisei*) of the mistresses of Hidetsugu, Zuisenji
Plate 85. Two designs of the cloth used as mounts for *waka* death poems of the mistresses of Hidetsugu, Zuisenji

Popular history tells us that following the death of warlord Toyotomi Hideyoshi's nephew, Toyotomi Hidetsugu (1568–1595), a number—by some accounts thirty-four—of his mistresses met on the banks of the Kamo River in Kyoto, where they gathered together their death poems (*jisei*) and used the cloth from their robes as mounts. Hidetsugu's mistresses were executed following his ritual suicide. These poems are still housed in the temple of Zuisenji in Kyoto.

Plate 86. a. Designs for corridor bracket/transom (*ranma*), Nikkō Tōshōgū
Plate 87. Corridor pillar designs, Nikkō Tōshōgū
Plate 88. Corridor designs, Nikkō Tōshōgū (six examples)
Plate 89. Corridor designs, Nikkō Tōshōgū (six examples)

The Nikkō Tōshōgū is a Shinto shrine located in Tochigi Prefecture. Built in 1617 in dedication to the founder of the Tokugawa shogunate, Tokugawa Ieyasu (1542–1616), the shrine is celebrated for its elaborate, ornate architectural carvings, which depict creatures like the phoenix (Plate 86, left) and arabesque/auspicious floral patterns (Plate 86, right).

Plate 90. Designs for Nō theater robes (*nōshōzoku*), Maeda family (two examples)
Plate 91. Designs for Nō theater robes (*nōshōzoku*), Maeda family (two examples)
Plate 92. Designs for Nō theater robes (*nōshōzoku*), Maeda family
(four examples)
Plate 93. Designs for Nō theater robes (*nōshōzoku*), Maeda family (four examples)

These designs—principally plants and animals—illustrate techniques such as *surihaku* ("rubbed metal foil") found on Nō theater robes of the Maeda family. For *surihaku*, a technique dating to Nara period, stencilled designs of gold or silver foil are applied to cloth with paste. Gold or silver leaf is laid on this. The Maeda family were wealthy daimyo in Kaga Province (present-day Ishikawa Prefecture) and patrons of the Nō theater (see also Plates 79 and 81).

Plate 94. Kōami Nagashige (Chōjū) X (1599–1651), furnishings (shelves), "The First Song of Warbler," top view

This design is taken from the wedding set, dating to 1639 and today in the collection of the Tokugawa Art Museum, for Princess Chiyo, known as *Hatsune no chōdo* ("First Song of the Warbler Furnishings"). As seen here, each item is decorated with designs inspired by the poem in Chapter 23 of the eleventh-century tale of romance, *The Tale of Genji* (*Genji monogatari*): "The old one's gaze rests a long time on the seedling pine/Waiting to hear the song of the first warbler."[17] *Hatsune* designs were popular for their auspicious symbolism.

[17]Murasaki Shikibu, *The Tale of Genji,* translated by Edward G. Seidensticker. New York, Alfred A. Knopf, 1992, p. 432.

Plate 95. Various design elements from scrolls dating to around the Genroku (1688–1704) and Kyōhō (1716–36) eras (six examples)
Plate 96. Garment designs from scrolls by Miyagawa Chōshun (1682–1754) (eight examples)
Plate 97. Various designs for *kosode* (a robe with small sleeves) from scrolls dating to around the Genroku [1688–1704] and Kyōhō [1716–36] eras (six examples)
Plate 98. Designs from scrolls by Miyagawa Chōshun (seven examples)
Plate 99. Clothing designs from scrolls by Miyagawa Chōshun (eight examples)

Miyagawa Chōshun (1682–1754) was the foremost *ukiyo-e* ("pictures of the floating world") painter in the first half of the eighteenth century, and he was the progenitor of an artistic lineage that would become the influential Katsukawa school of *ukiyo-e* artists. Chōshun produced many paintings of single courtesans, and genre scenes, as well as scenes from the Kabuki and puppet theaters. The designs are taken from his genre scrolls, similar to examples today housed in institutions such as the Tokyo National Museum.

Plate 100. Textile designs from the mid-Tokugawa period (seven examples)

Selected Bibliography

Books

Allen, Jeanne. *Designer's Guide to Japanese Patterns.* San Francisco: Chronicle Books, 1984.

Hibi, Sadao and Niwa Motoji. *Snow, Wave, Pine: Traditional Patterns in Japanese Design.* Tokyo: Kodansha International Ltd., 2001.

Hida, Toyojirō and Yokomizu Hiroko. *Meiji, Taishō zuanshū no kenkyū. Kindai ni ikasareta Edo no dezain* (*The Research of Meiji and Taishō Design Books. Giving Life to the Pre-modern Age through Edo Design*). Tokyo: Kokusho Kankōkai, 2004.

Hillier, Jack. *The Art of the Japanese Book.* 2 vols. London: Sotheby's Publications, 1987.

Kikuchi, Yuko. *Japanese Modernisation and Mingei Theory: Cultural Nationalism and Oriental Orientalism.* London: RoutledgeCurzon, 2004.

Lillehoj, Elizabeth. *Critical Perspectives On Classicism In Japanese Painting, 1600–1700.* Honolulu: University of Hawai'i Press, 2004.

Marra, Michael F. (ed.). *A History of Modern Japanese Aesthetics.* Honolulu: University of Hawai'i Press, 2001.

Mrázek, Jan and Morgan Pitelka. *What's the Use of Art?: Asian Visual and Material Culture in Context.* Honolulu: University of Hawai'i Press, 2007.

Noma, Seiroku. *The Arts of Japan: Ancient and Medieval,* vol. 1. Translated and adapted by John Rosenfield. Tokyo/New York: Kodansha International, c. 1966/1978.

Noma, Seiroku. *The Arts of Japan: Late Medieval to Modern,* vol. 2. Translated and adapted by Glenn T. Webb. Tokyo: Kodansha International, 2003.

Ōbuchi, Takemi. *Nihon sōshoku taikan shinhan* (*Great Mirror of Japan's Decoration: New Edition*). 2 vols. Kyoto: Mitsumura Suiko Shoin, 1975.

Pollard, Moyra Clare. *Master Potter of Meiji Japan: Makuzu Kōzan (1842–1916) and his Workshop.* New York: Oxford University Press, 2003.

Rathburn, William Jay (ed.). *Beyond the Tanabata Bridge: Traditional Japanese Textiles.* London: Thames and Hudson in association with the Seattle Art Museum, 1993.

Sadao, Tsuneko S. and Stephanie Wada. *Discovering the Arts of Japan: A Historical Overview.* Tokyo/ New York/London: Kodansha International, 2003.

Shosoin Office (ed.). *Treasures of the Shosoin.* Tokyo: Asahi Shimbun Publishing Co., 1965.

Yokoya, Kenichirō. *Zuanchō in Kyoto: Textile Design Books for the Kimono Trade.* Stanford: Stanford University Libraries, 2007.

Web site

http://www.aisf.or.jp/~jaanus/

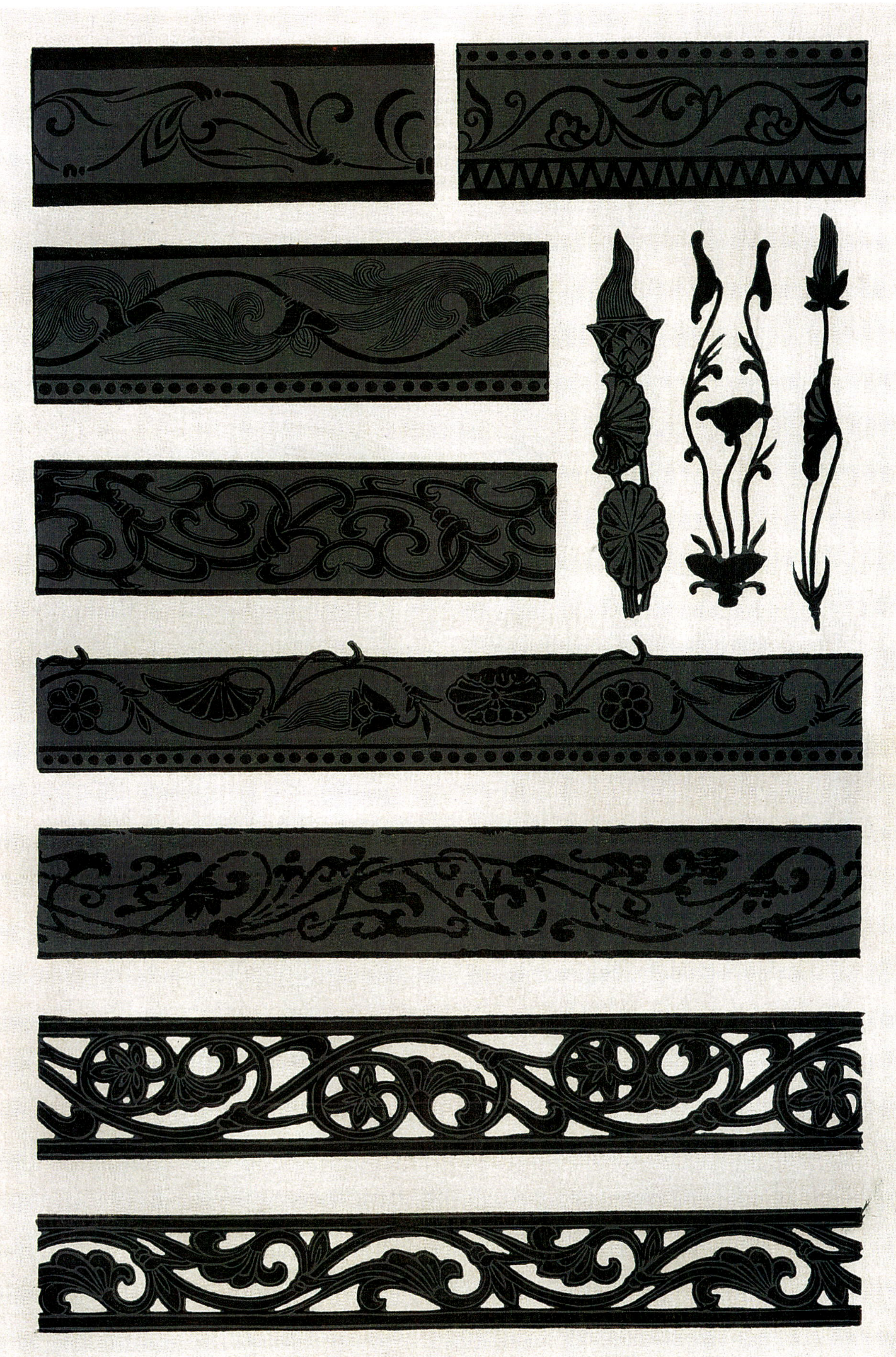

Plate 1

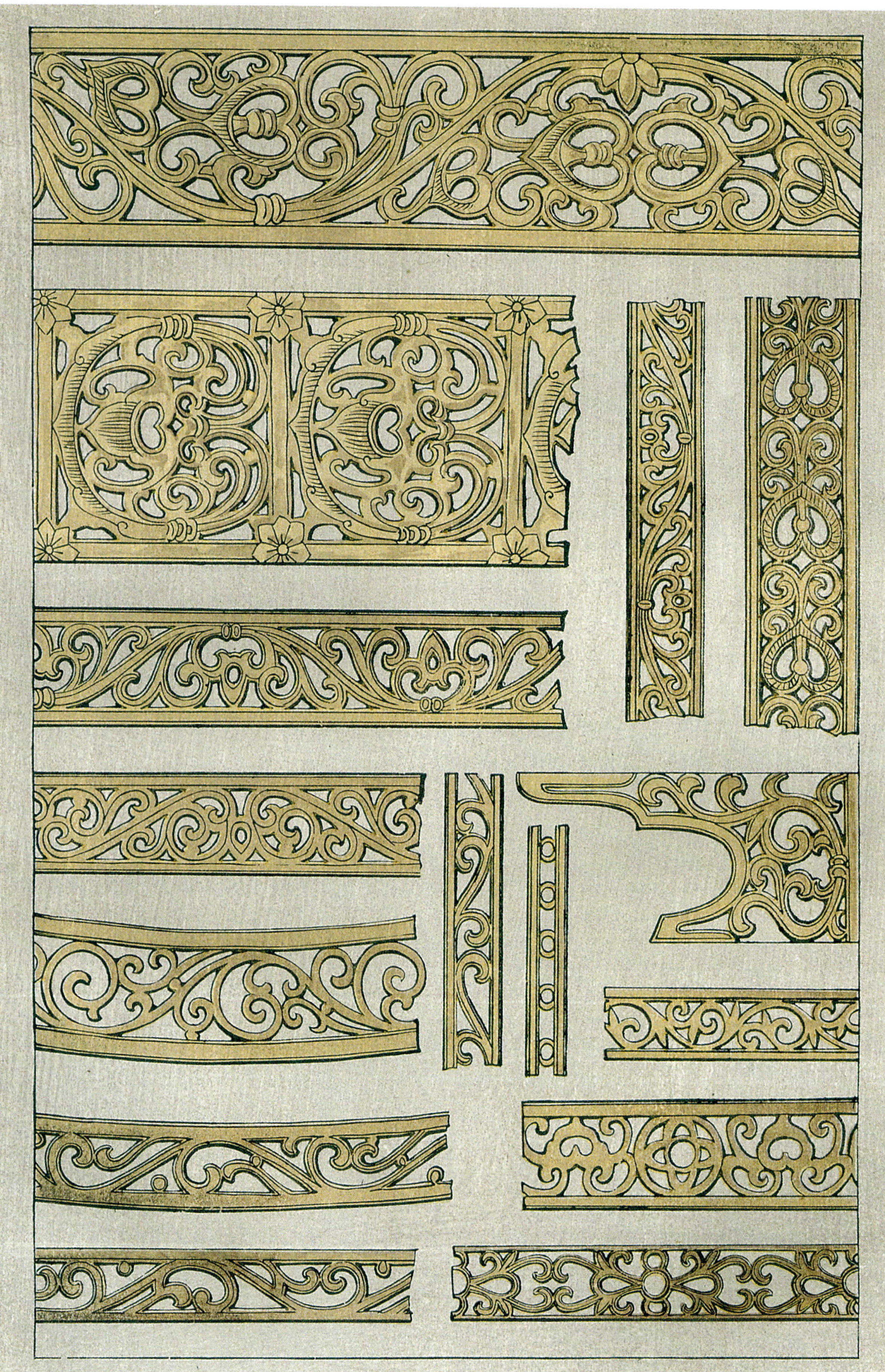

Plate 2

Plate 3

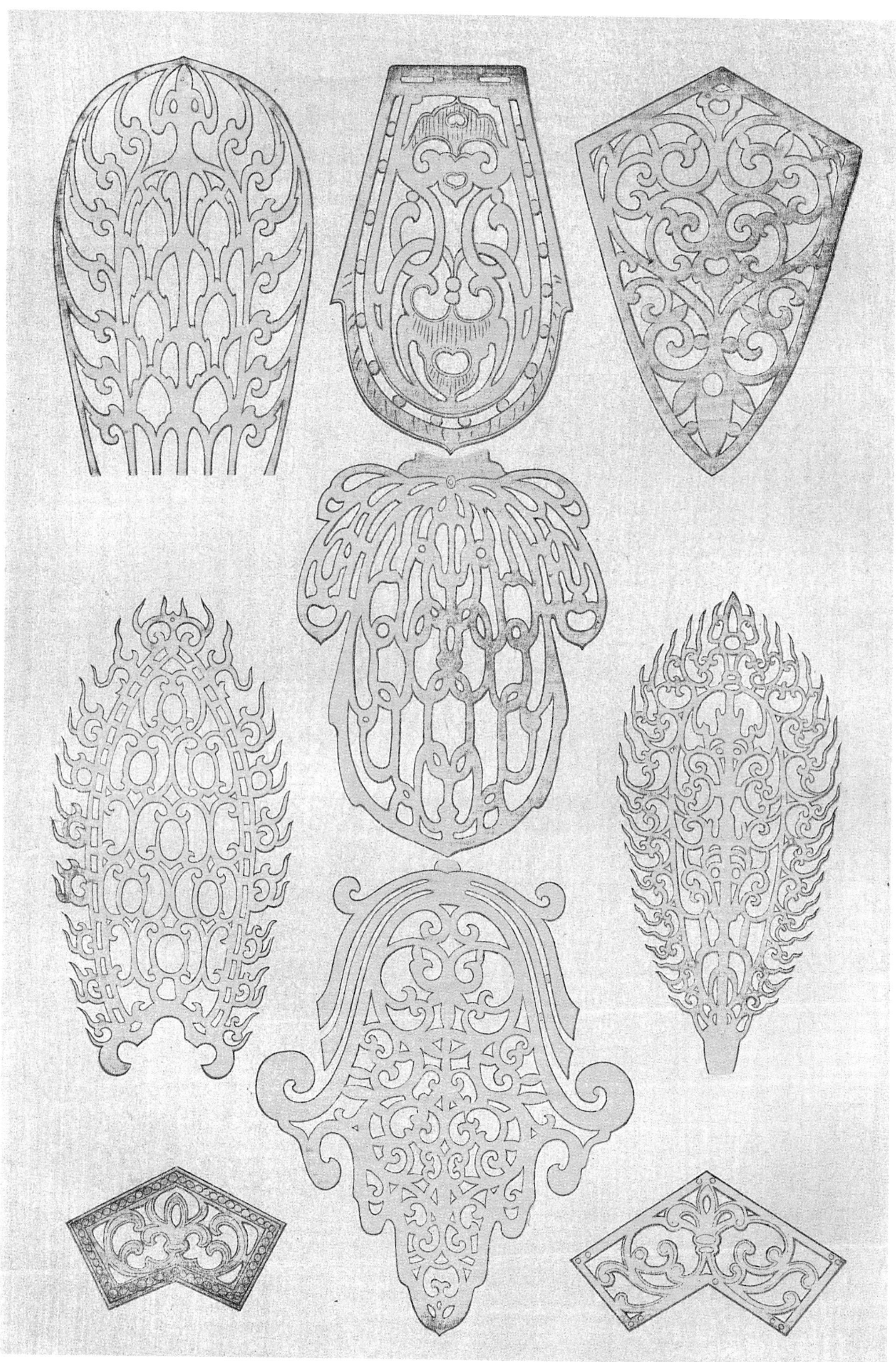

Plate 4

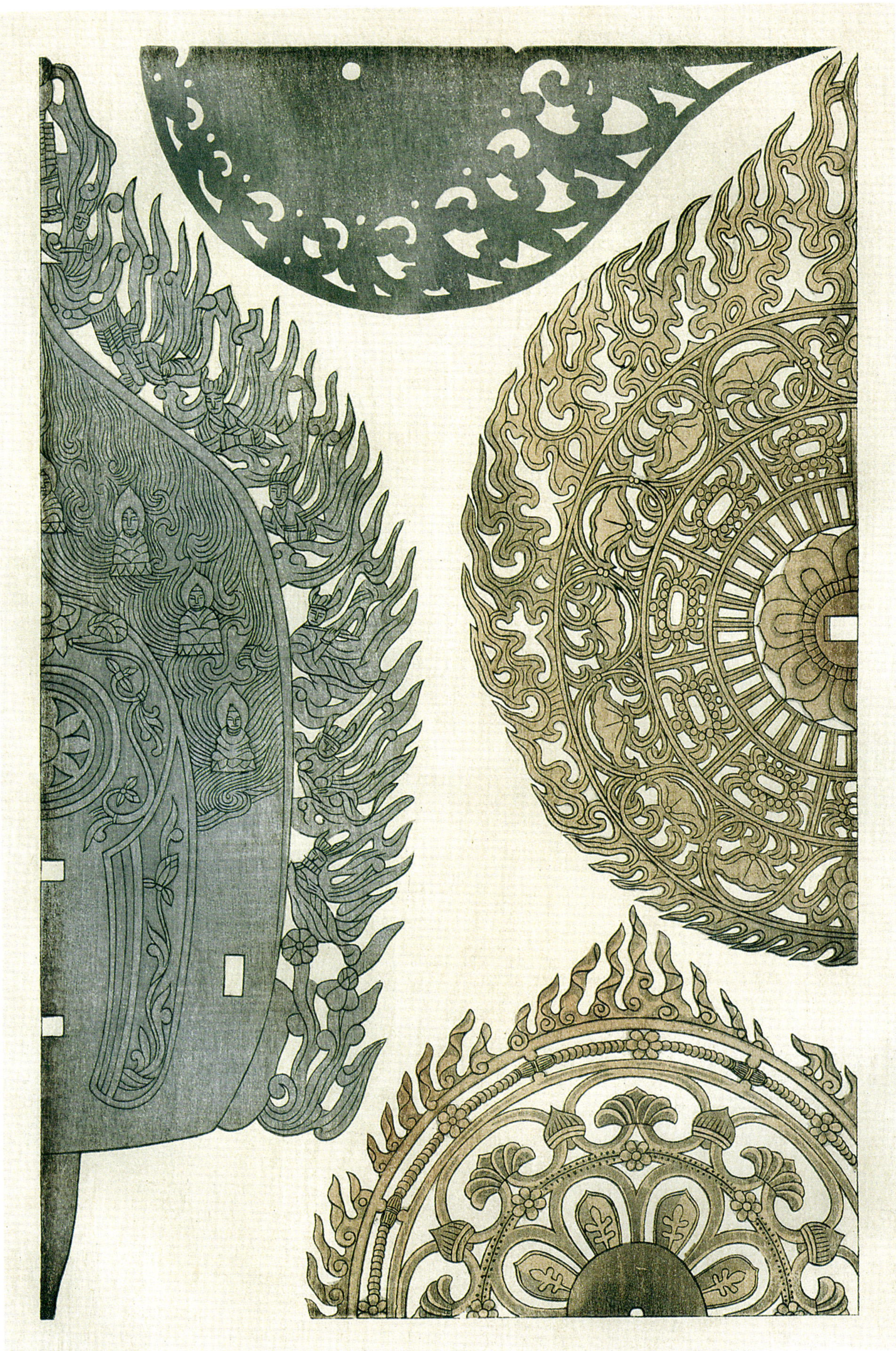

Plate 5

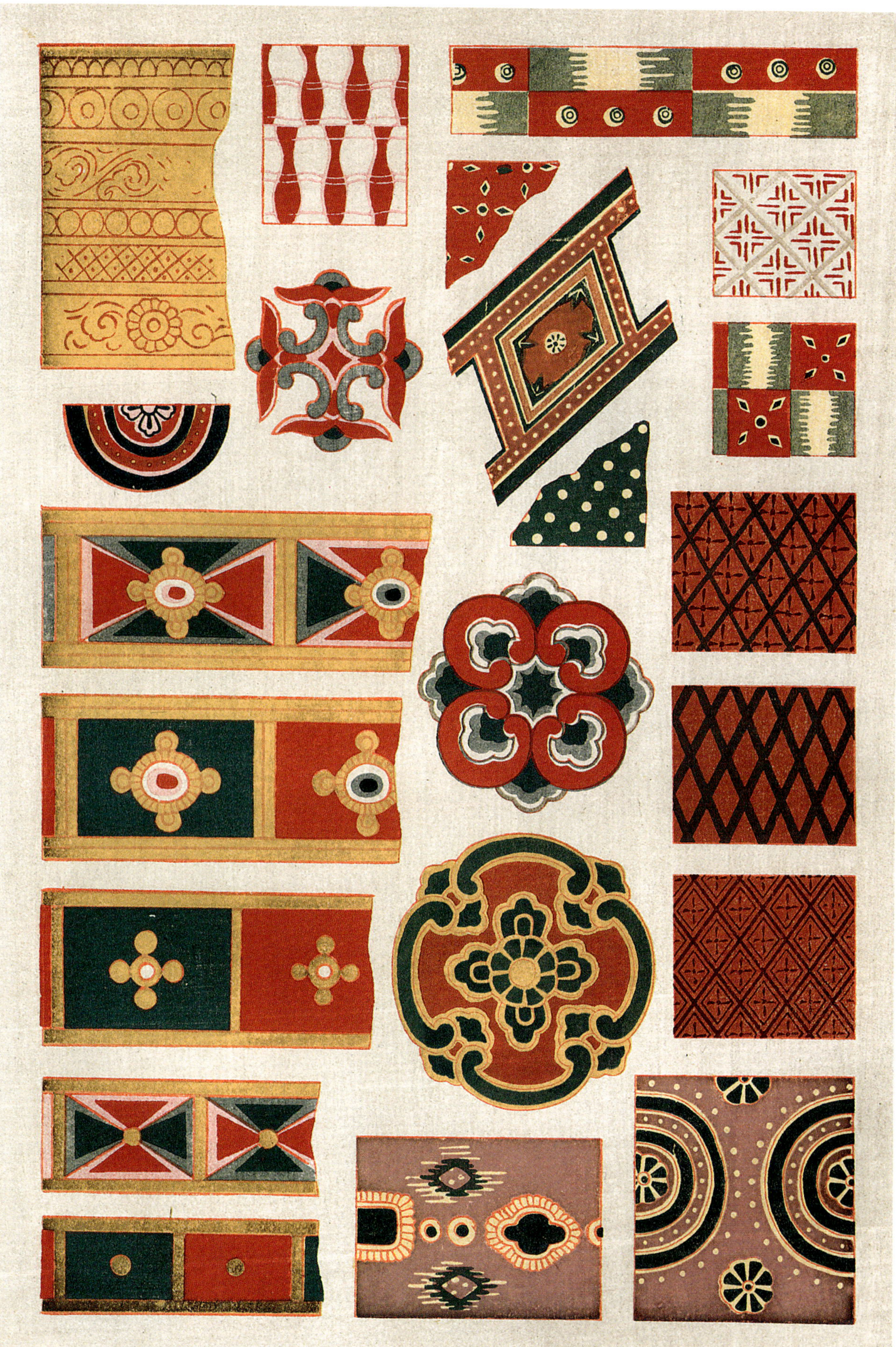

Plate 6

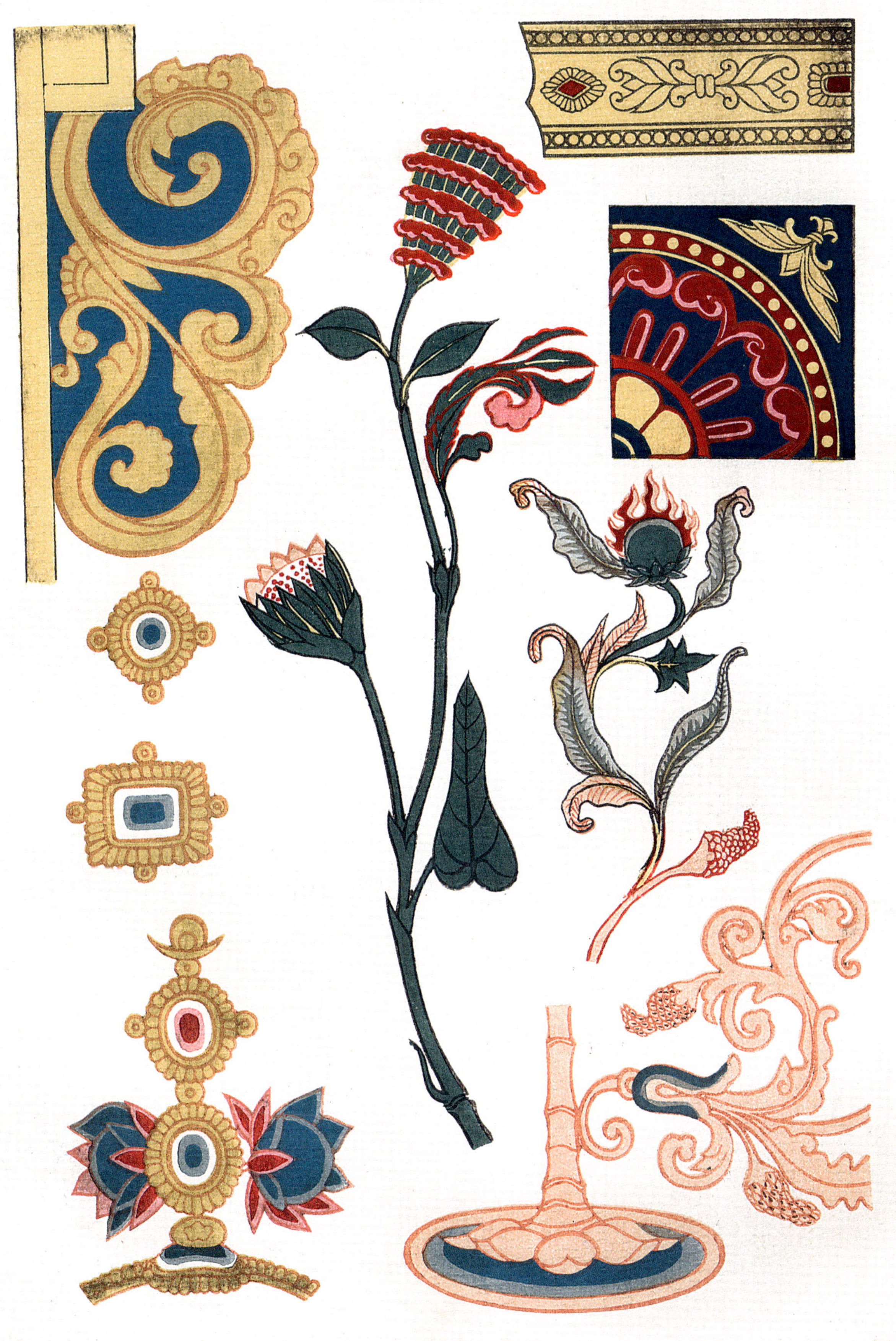

Plate 7

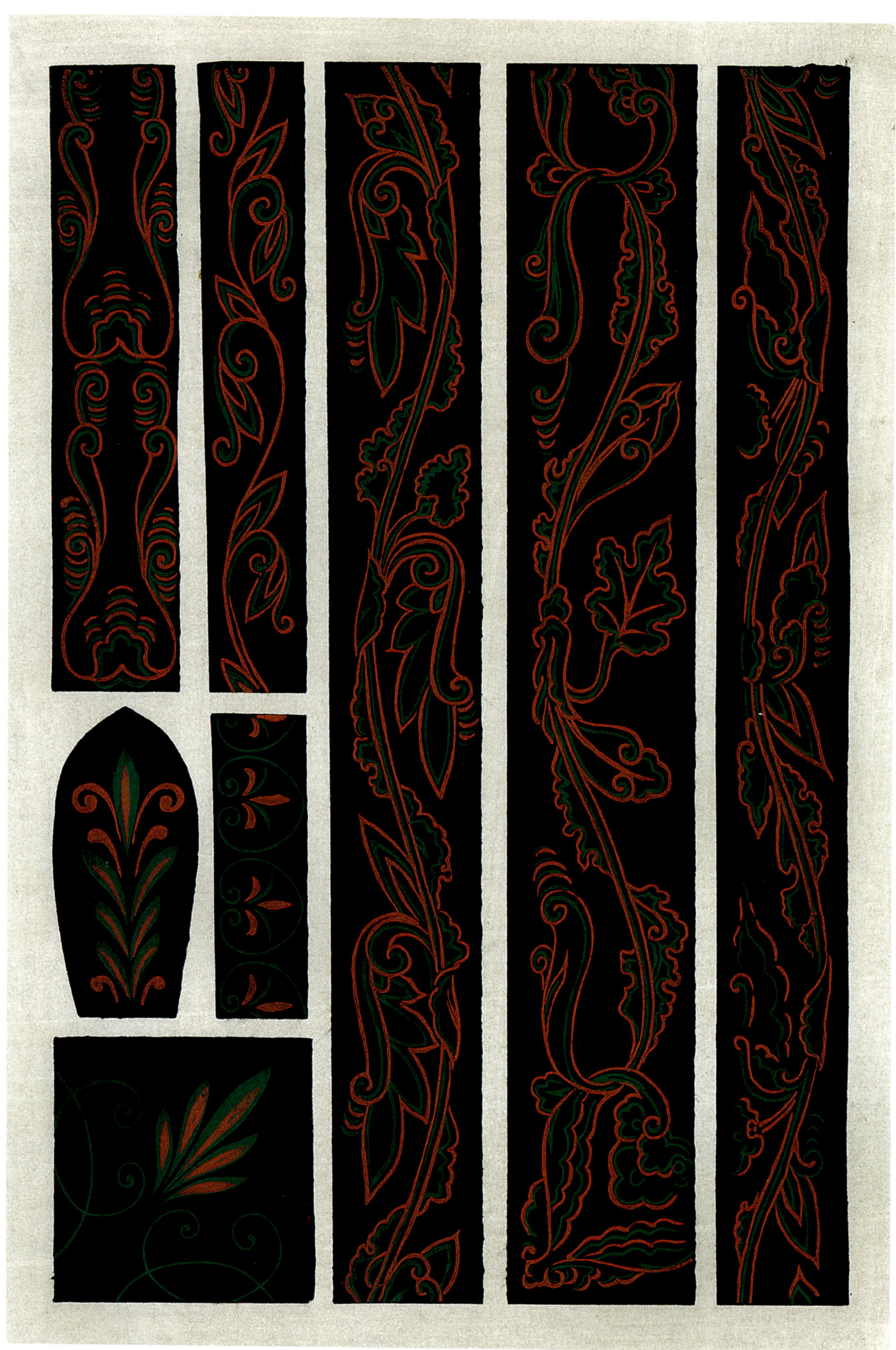

PLATE 8

Plate 9

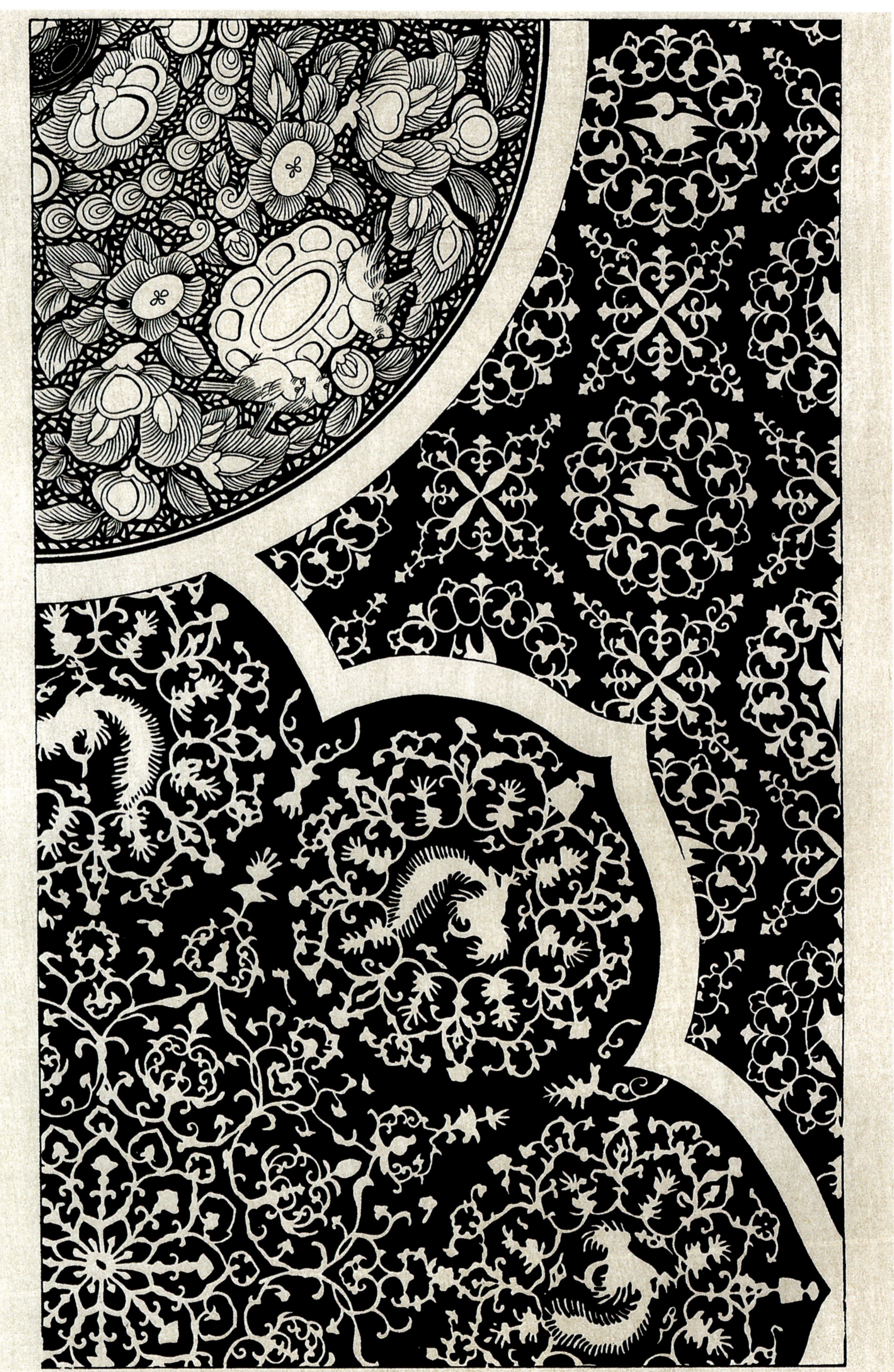

Plate 10

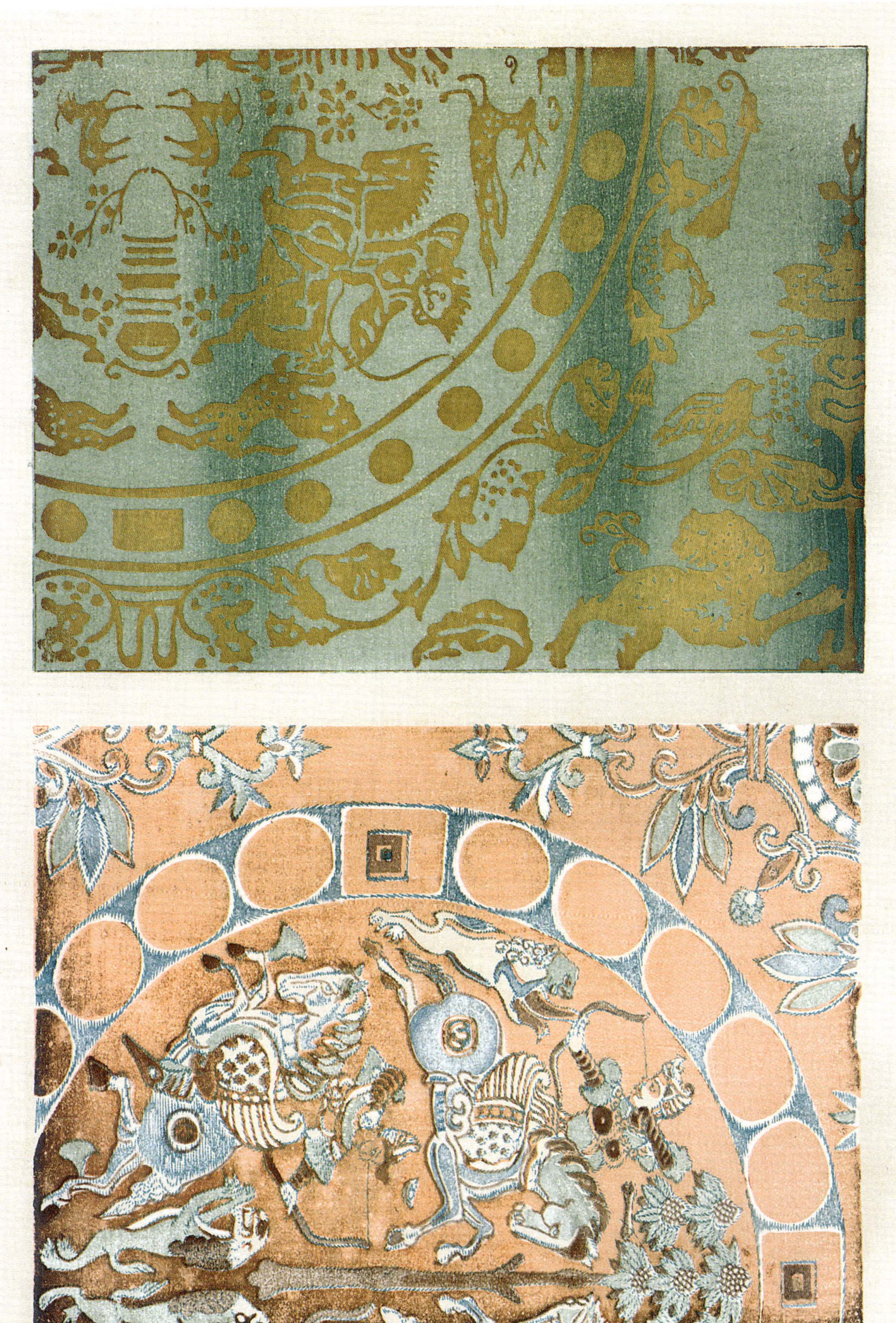

PLATE 11

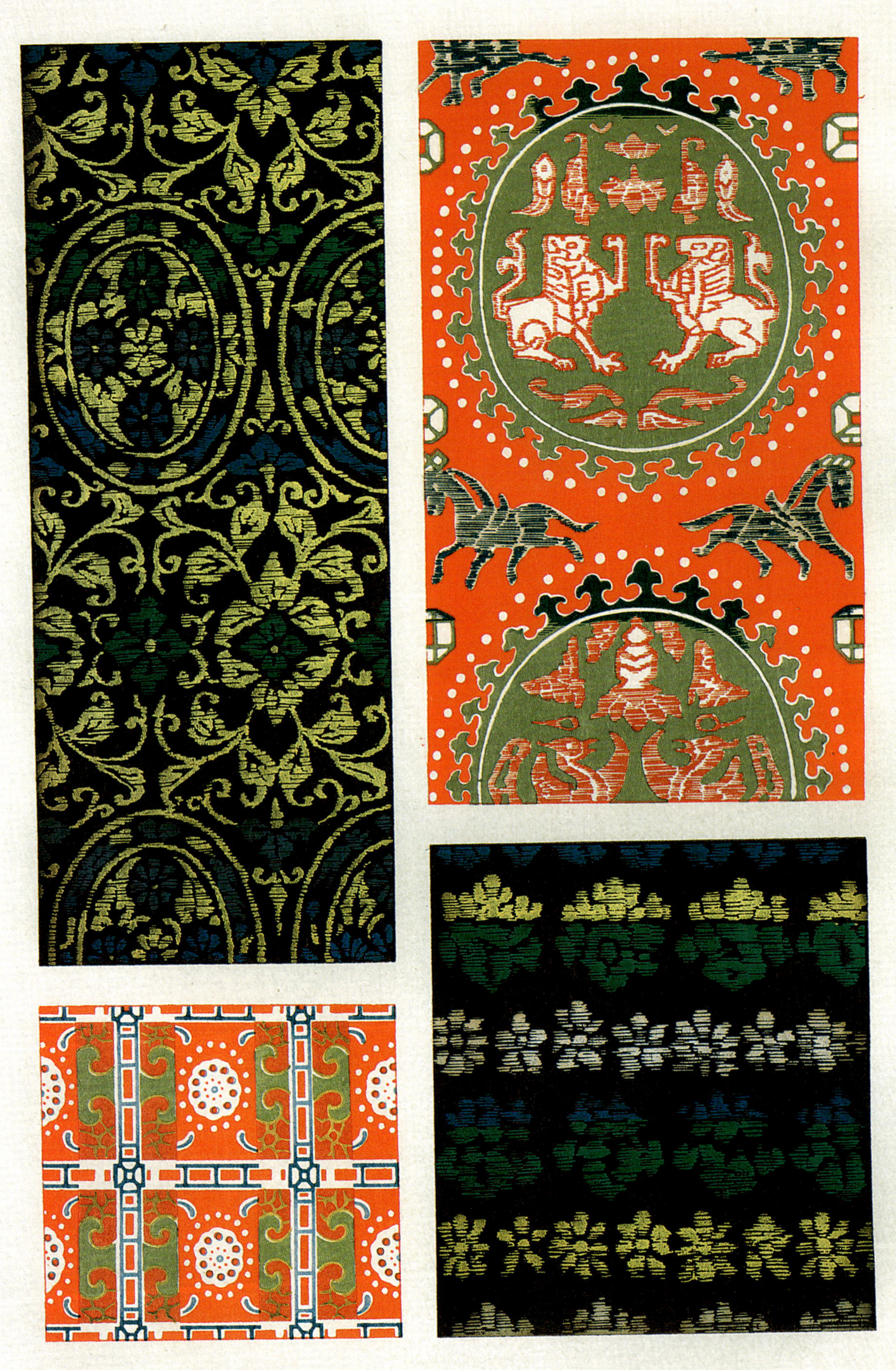

PLATE 12

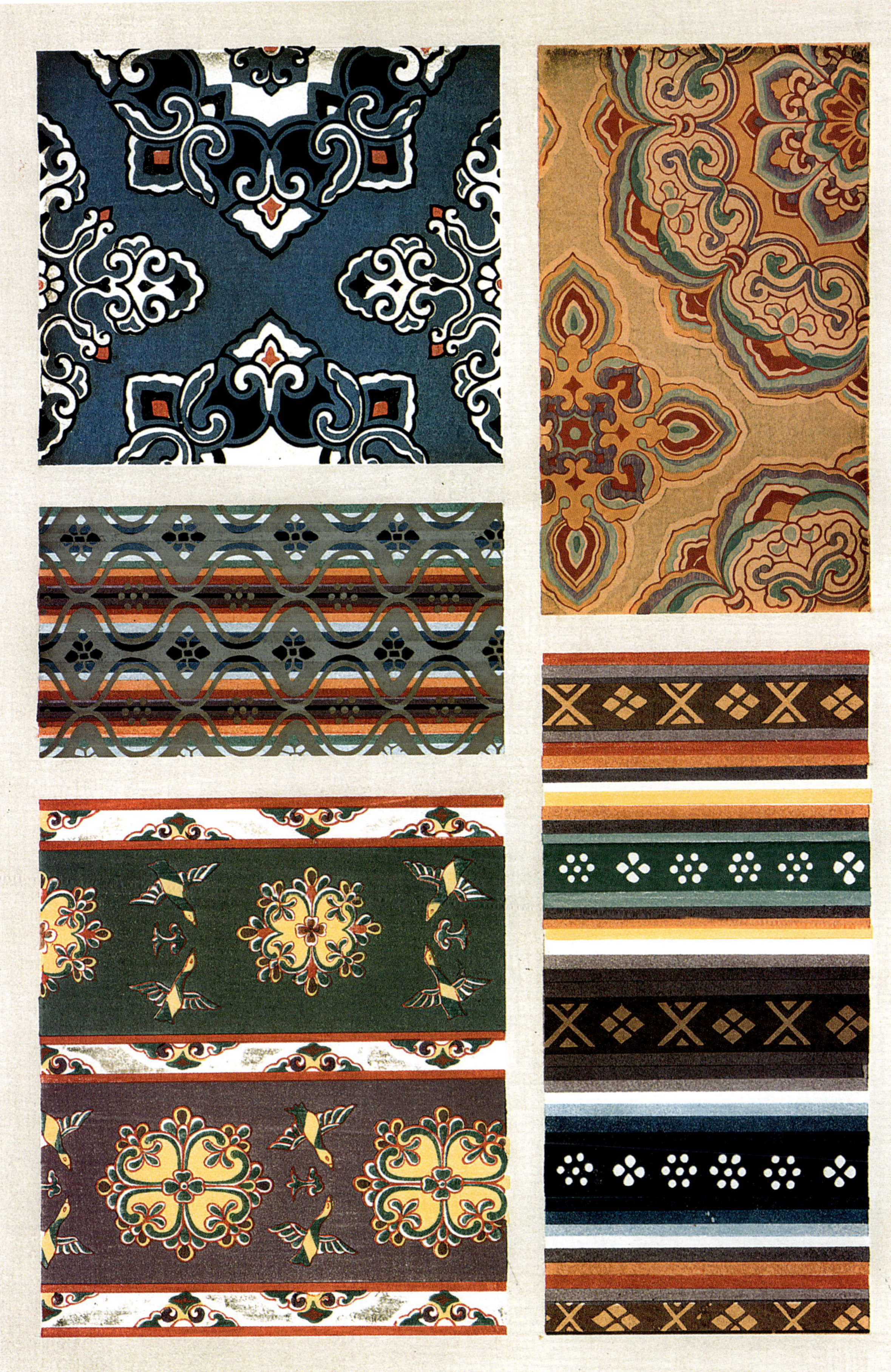

Plate 13

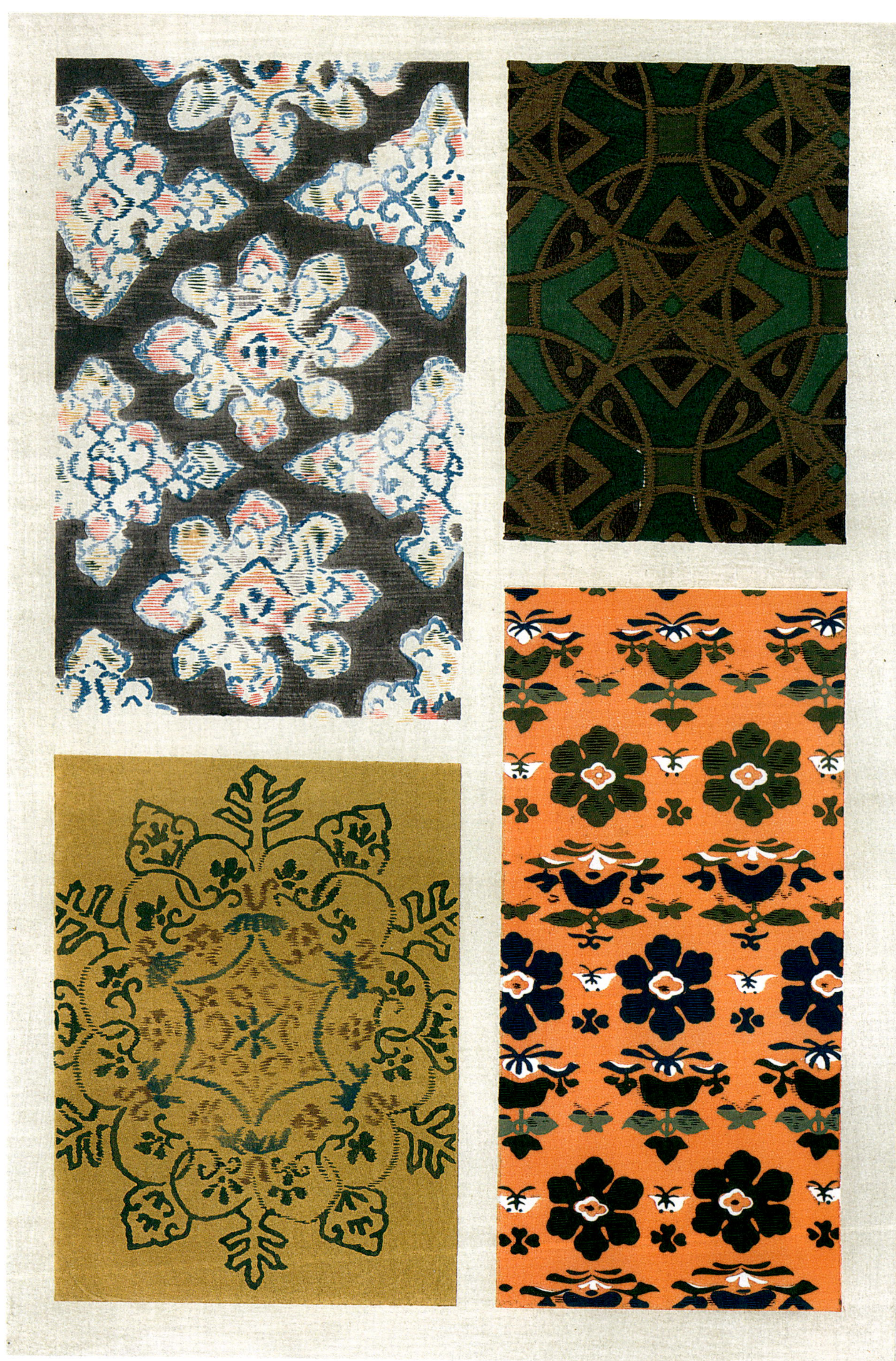

Plate 14

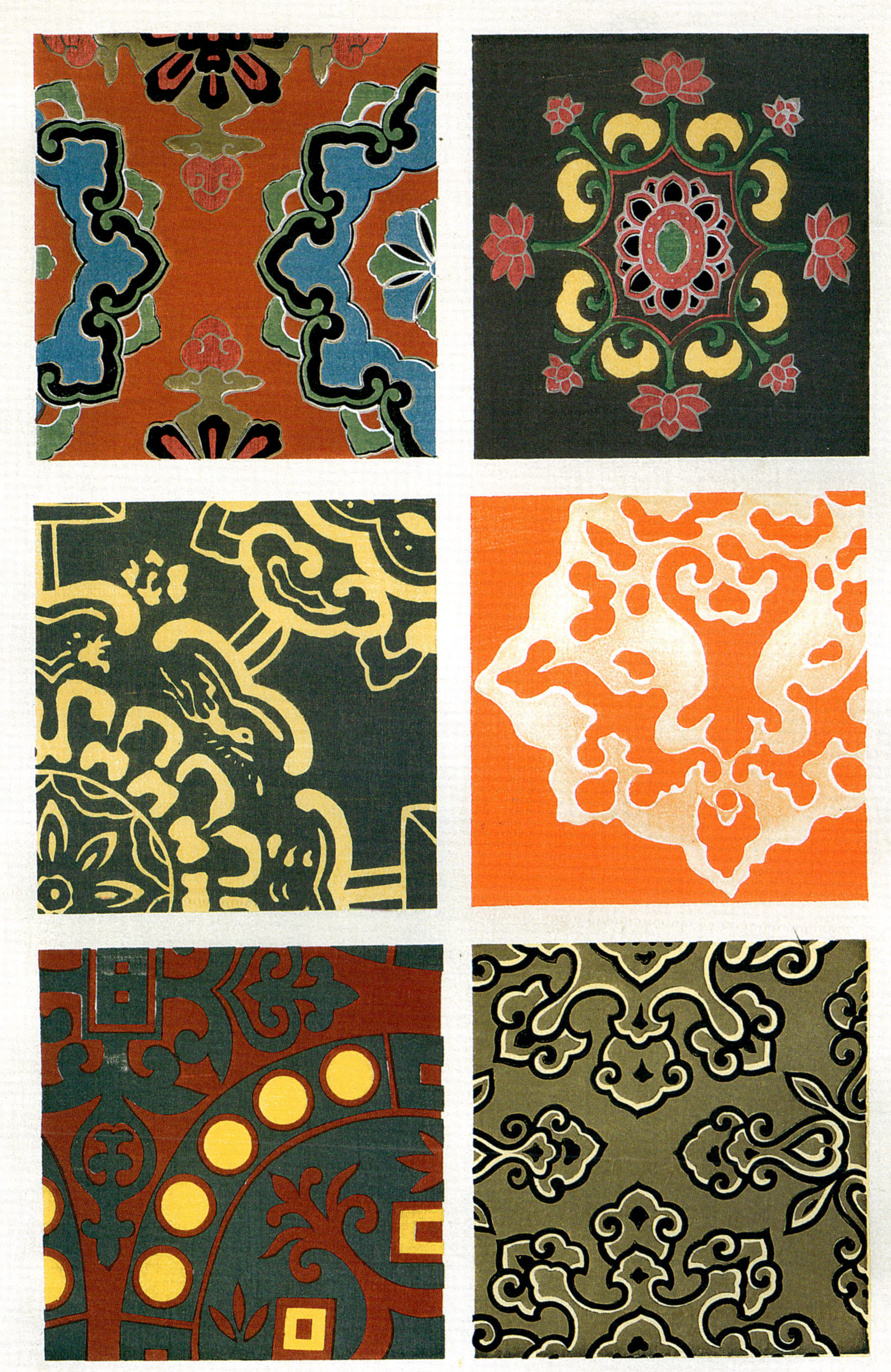

Plate 15

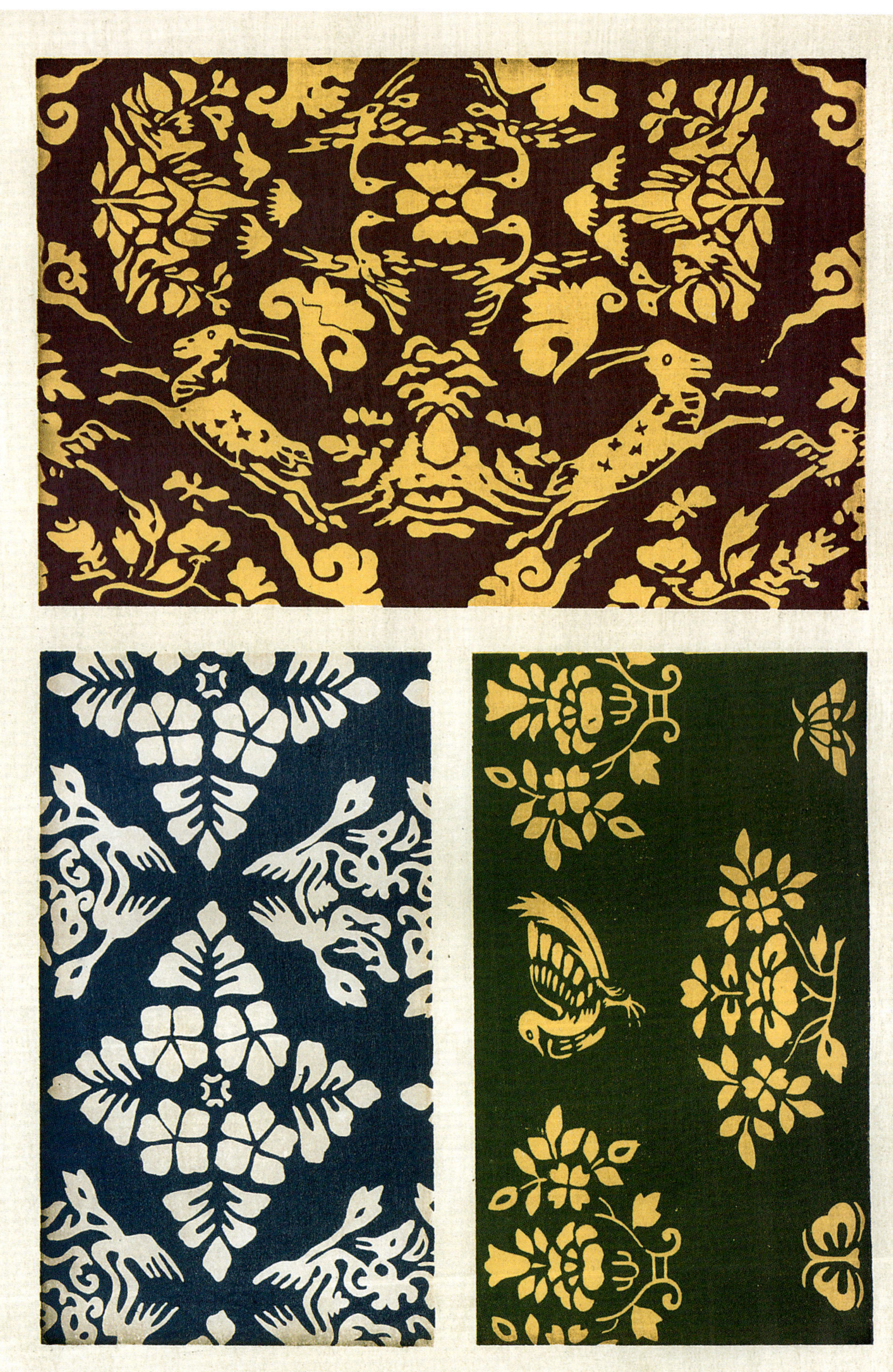

PLATE 16

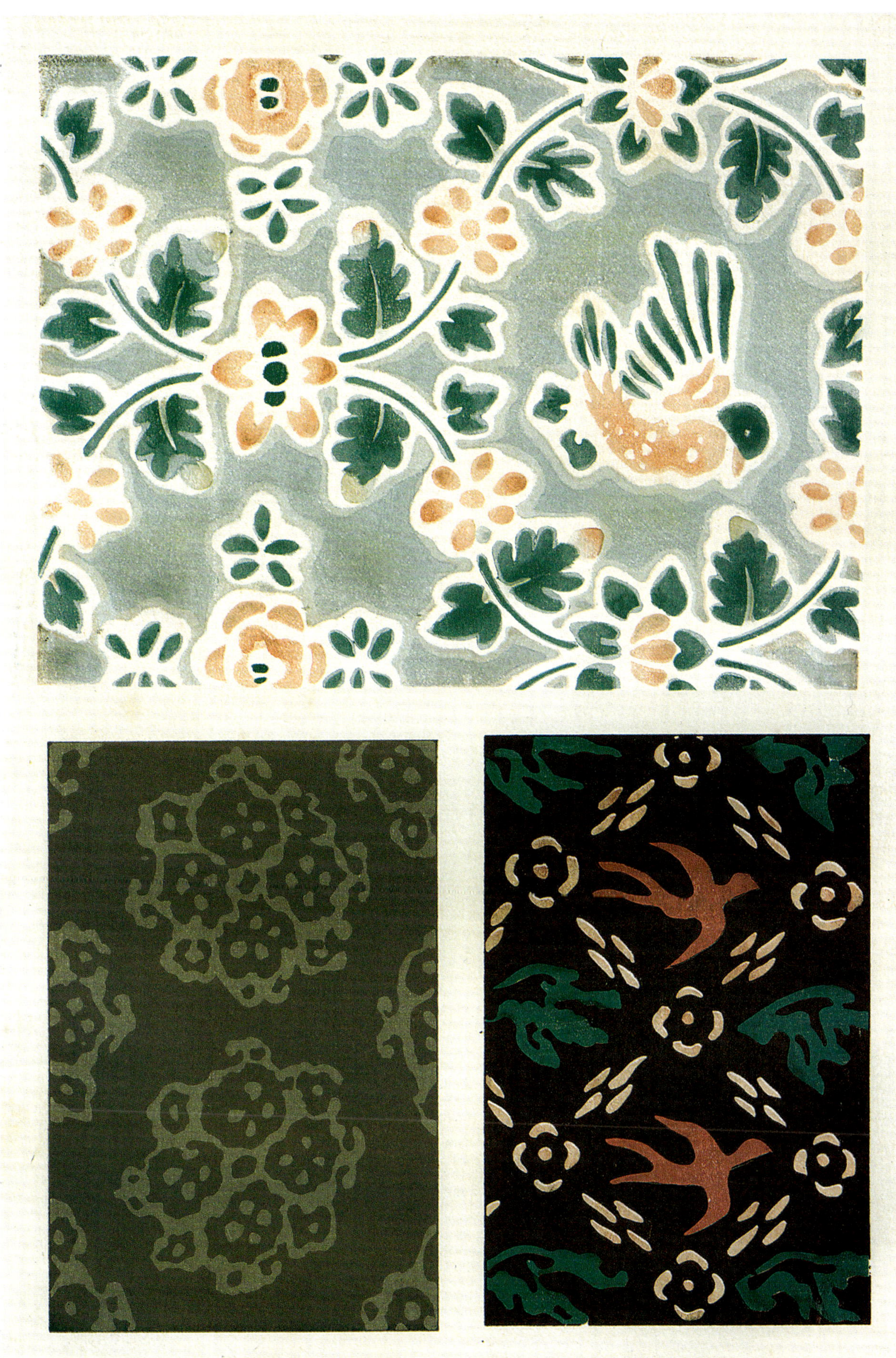

Plate 17

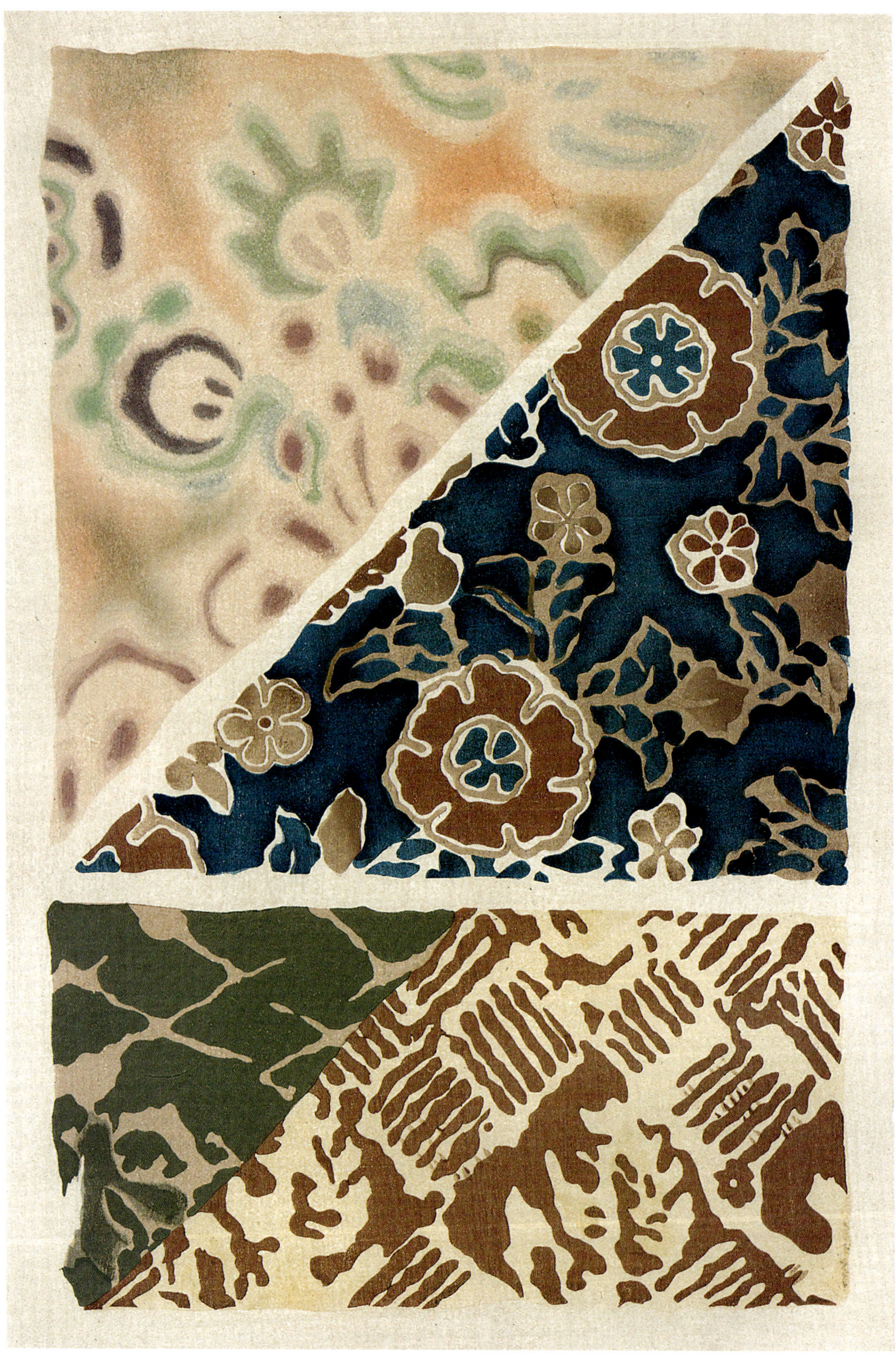

Plate 18

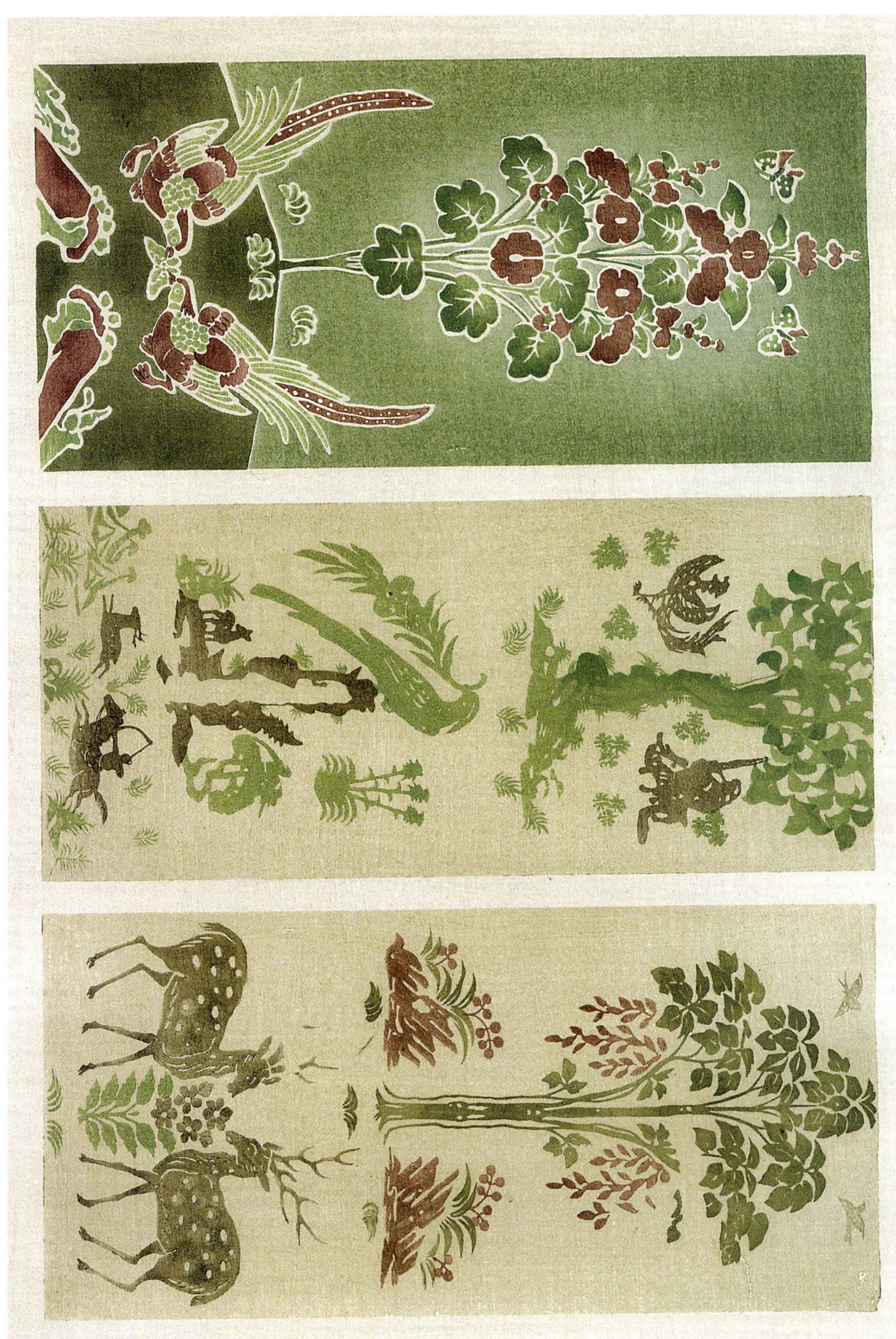

Plate 19

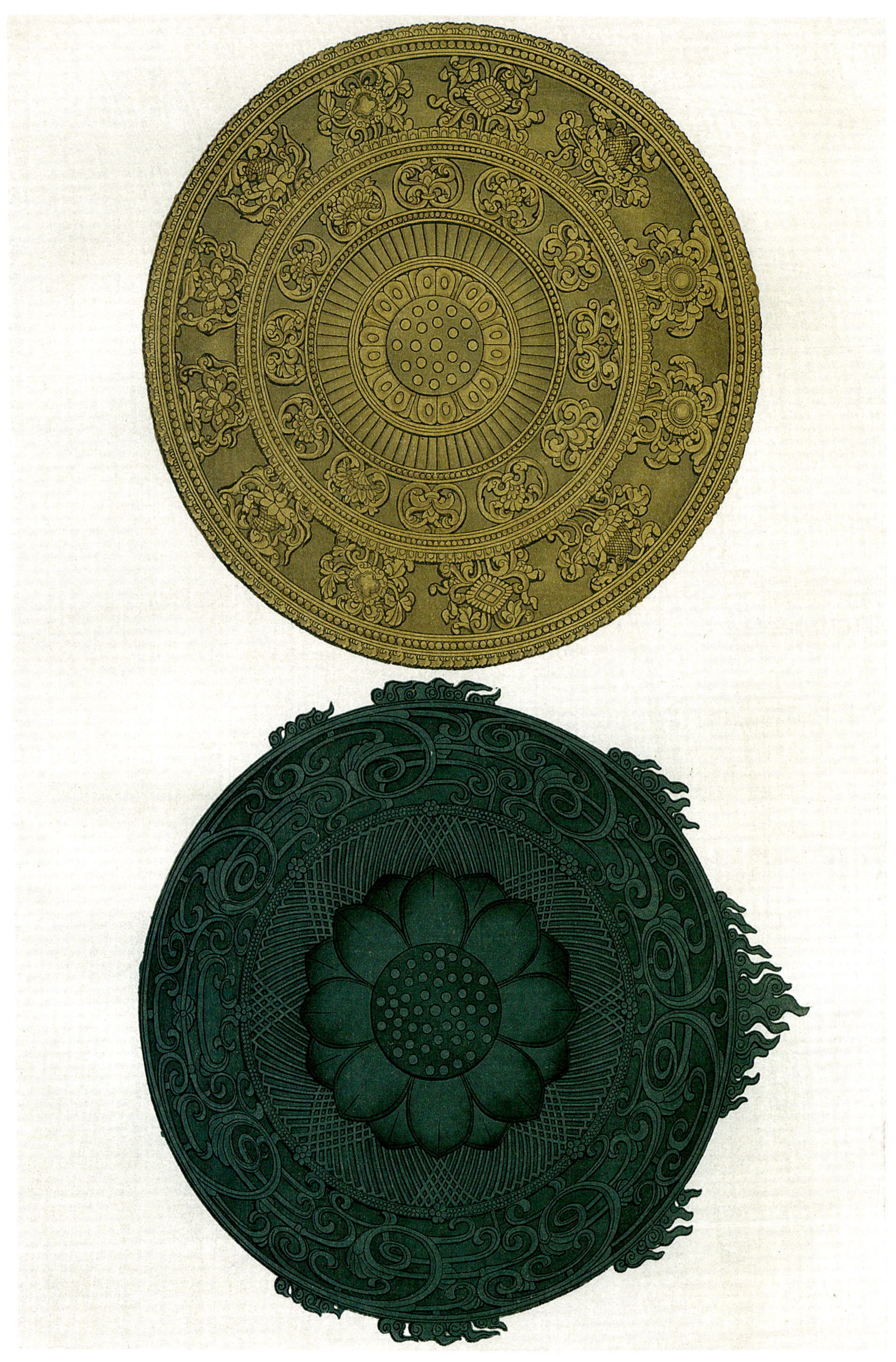

Plate 20

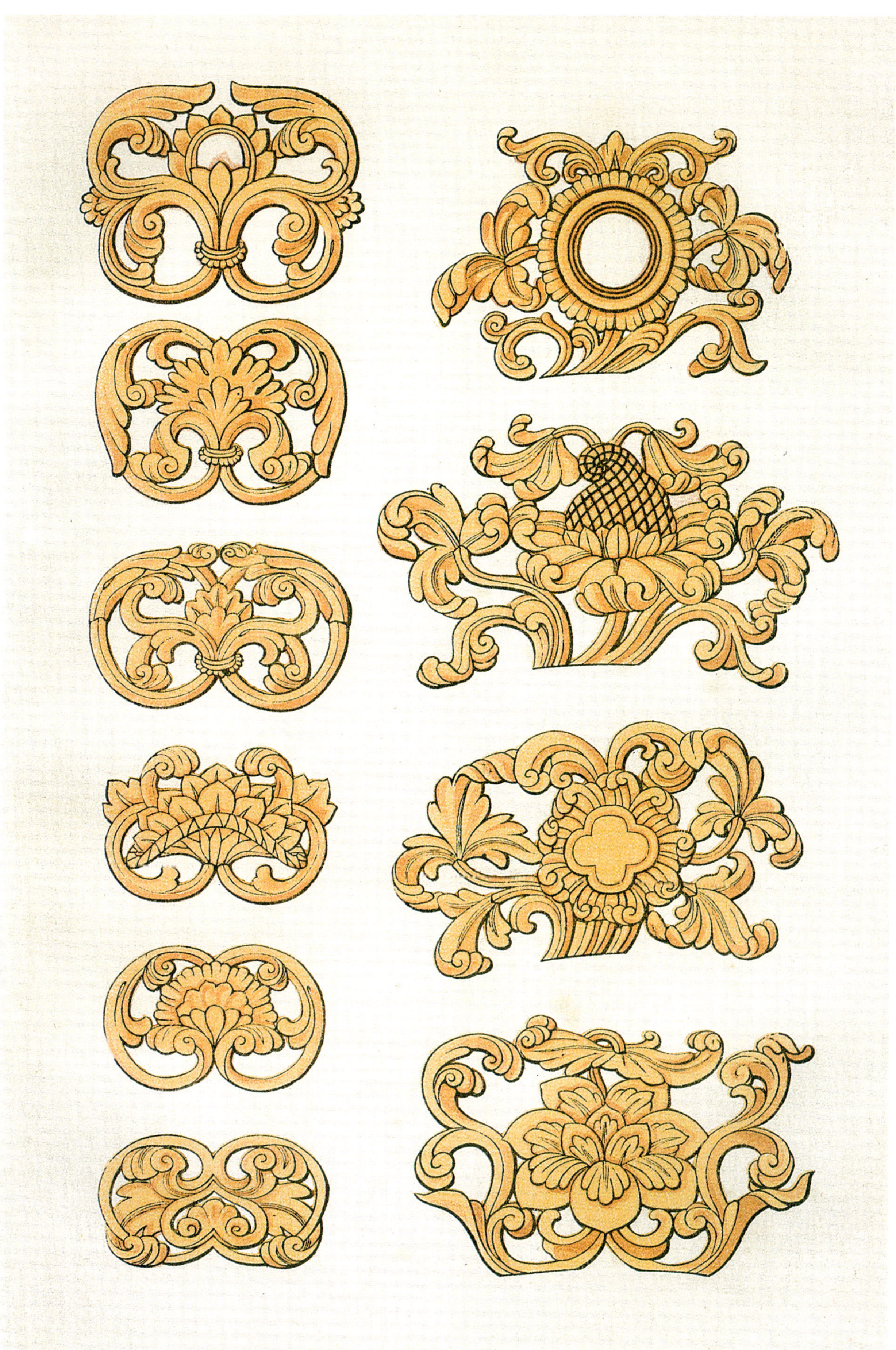

Plate 21

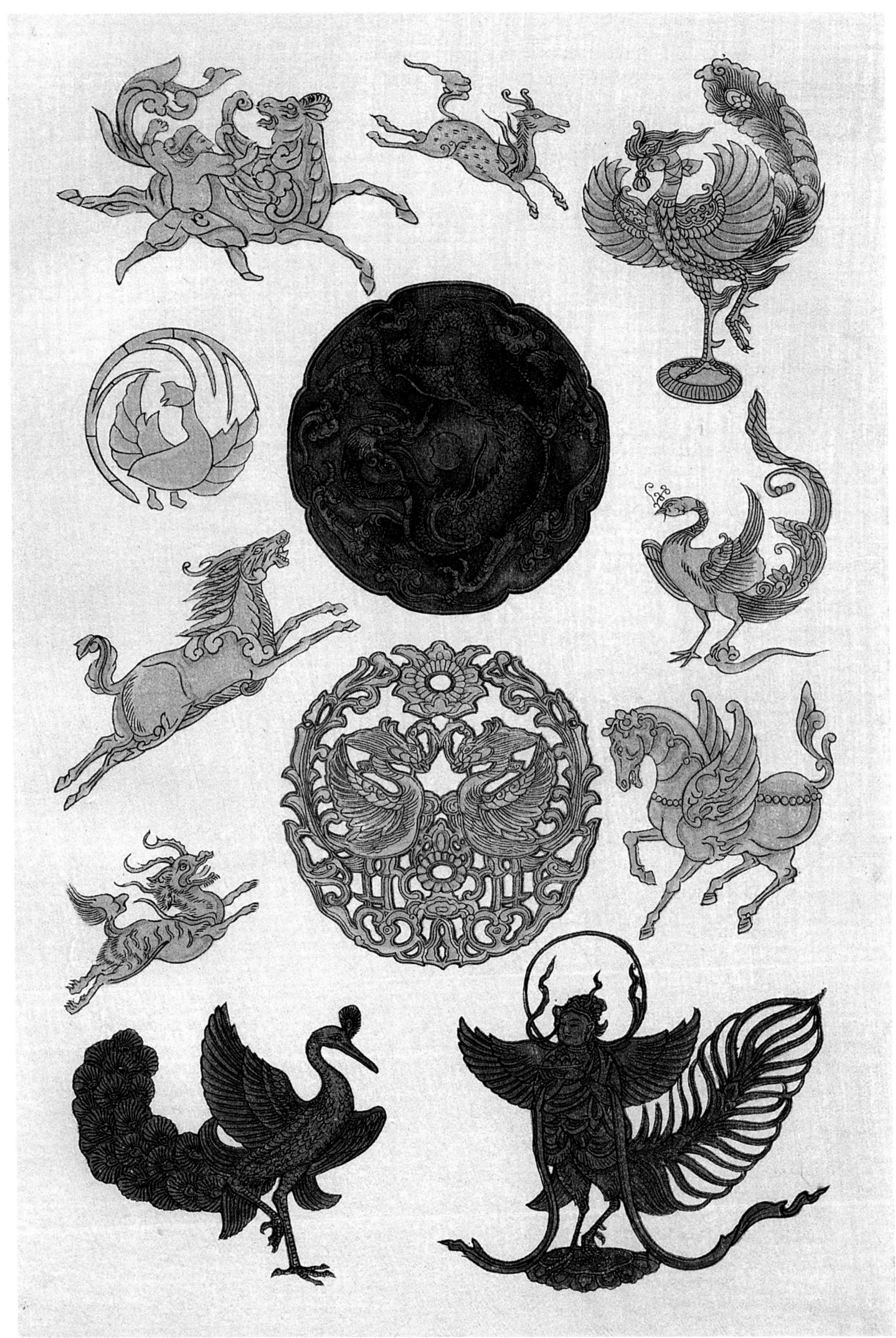

PLATE 22

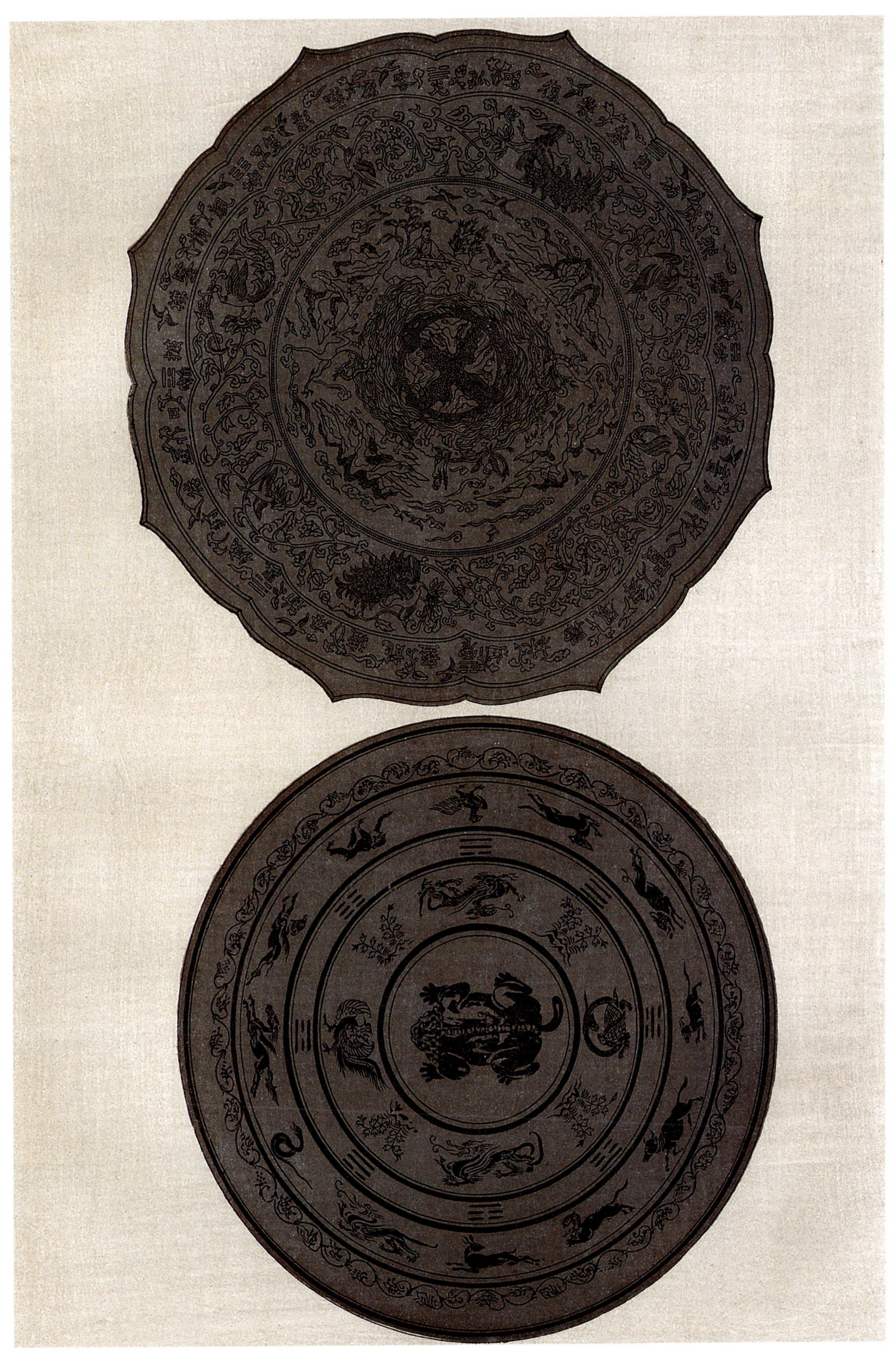

Plate 23

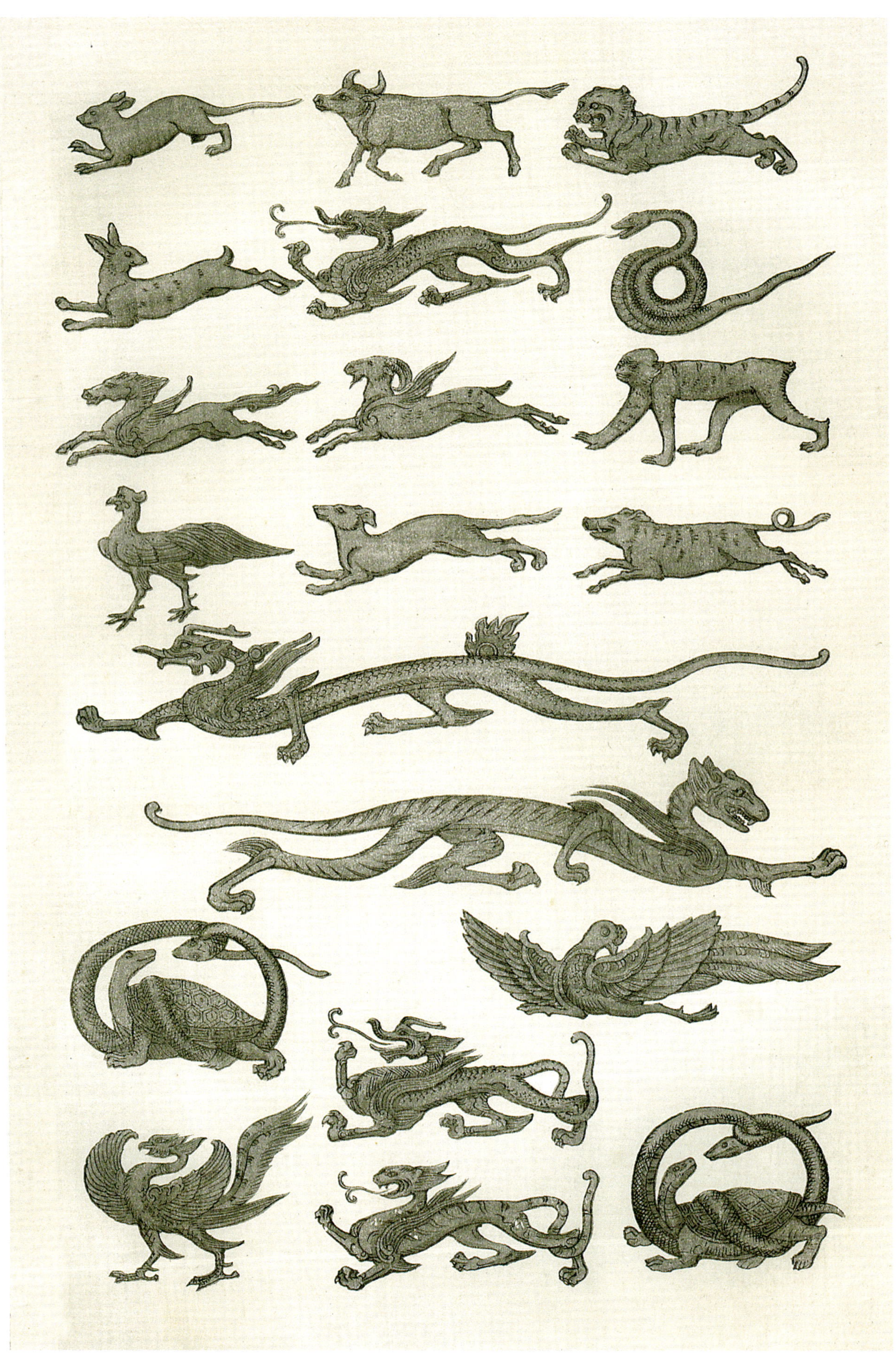

Plate 24

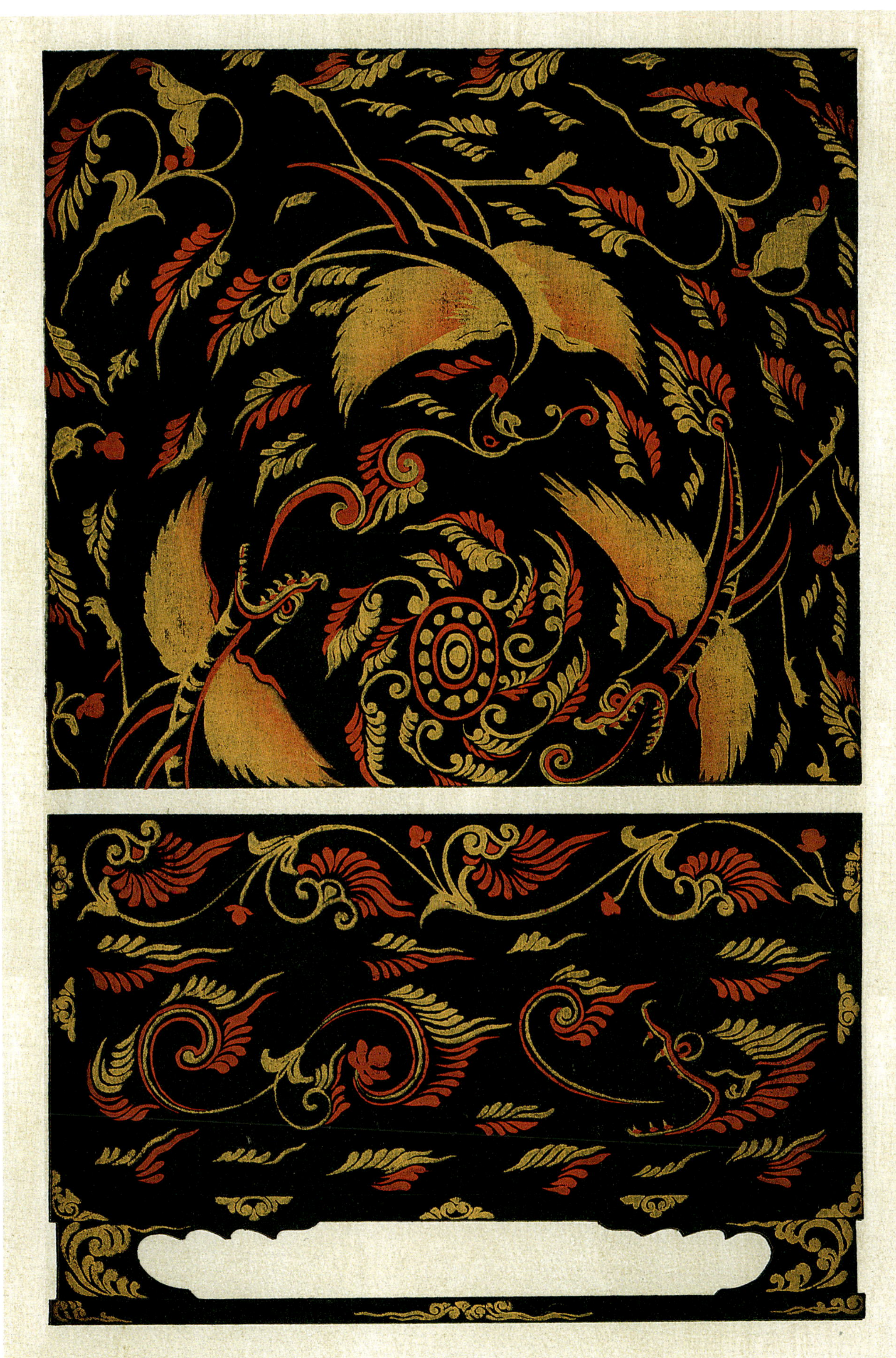

Plate 25

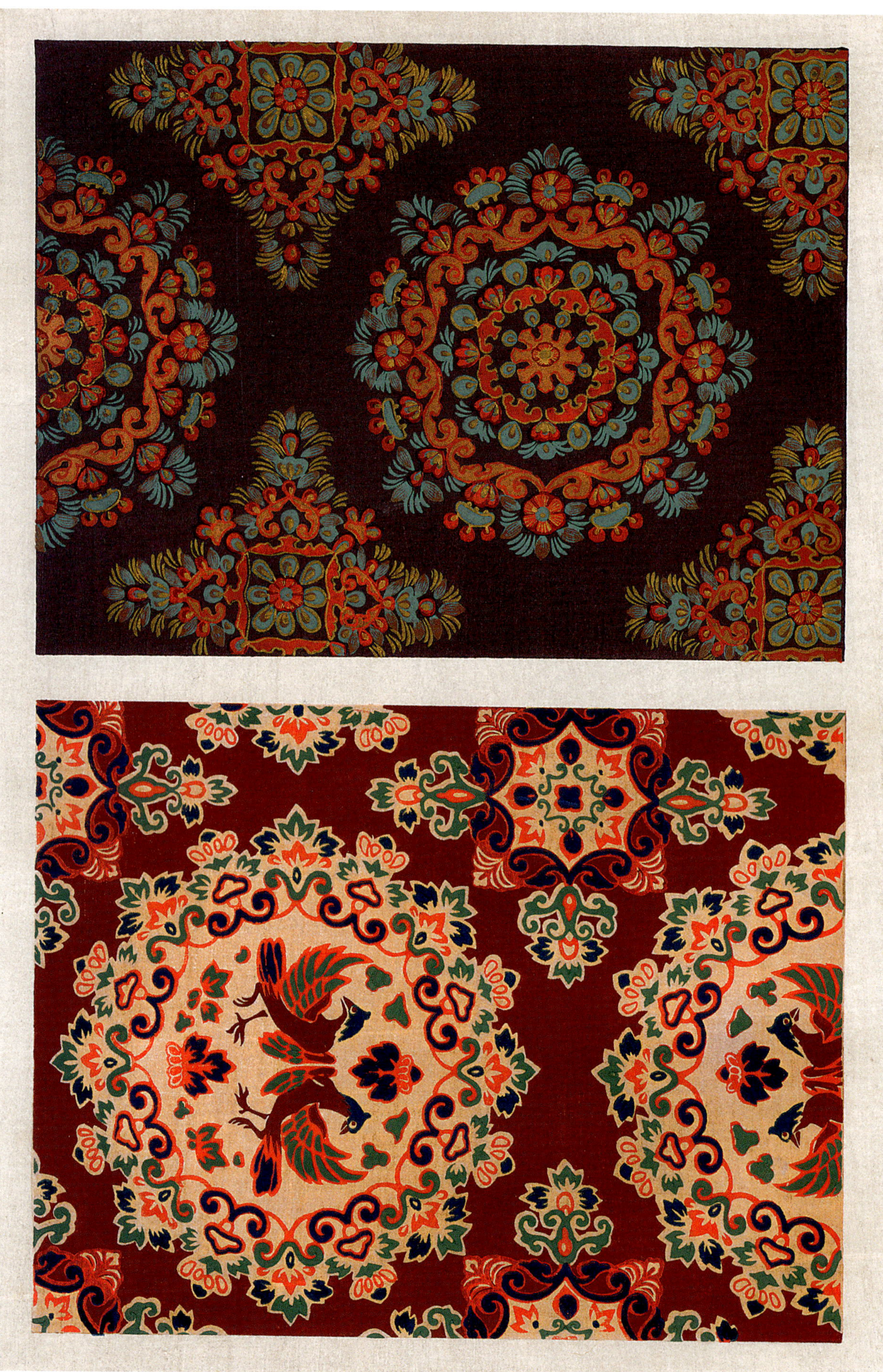

Plate 26

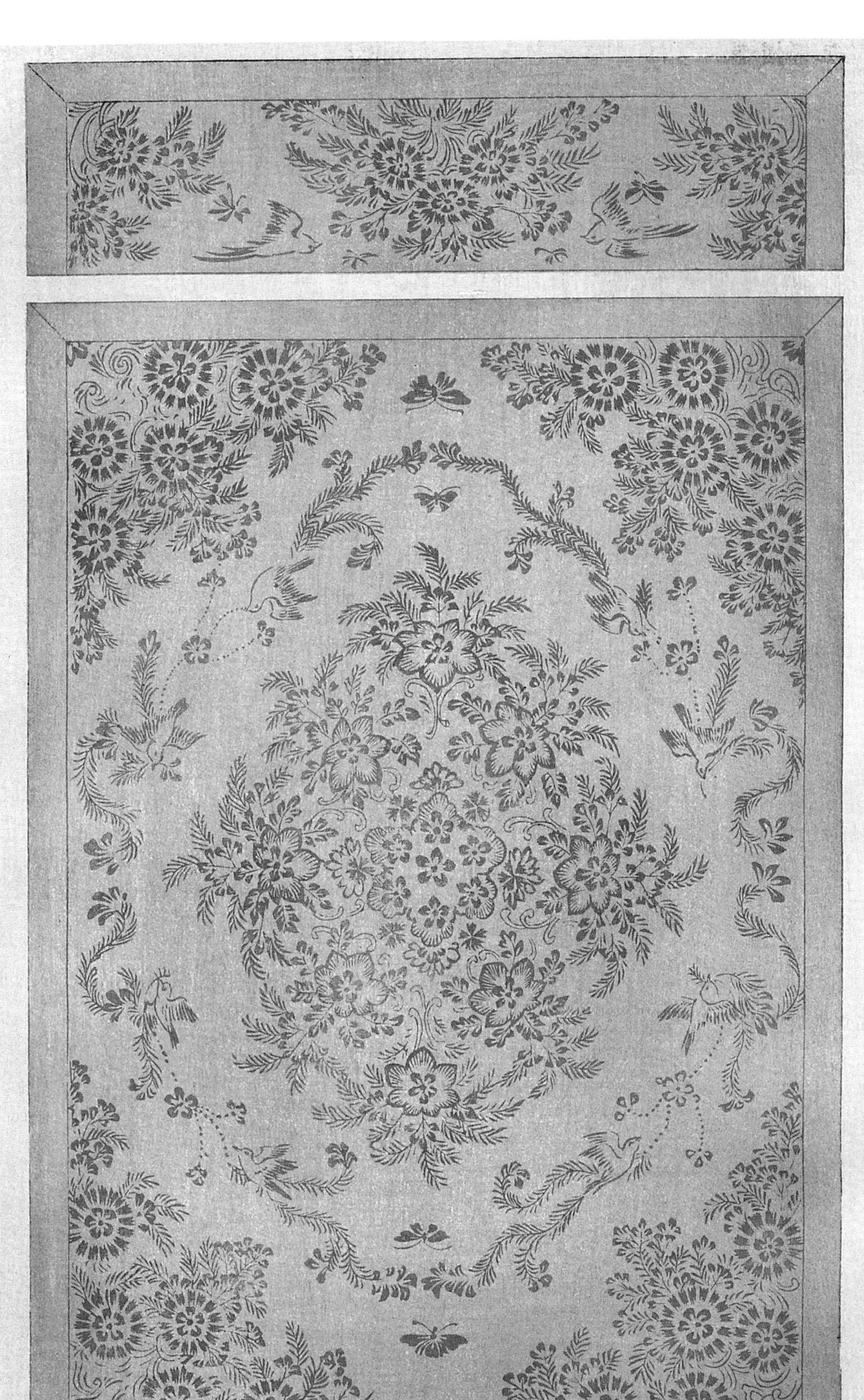

Plate 27

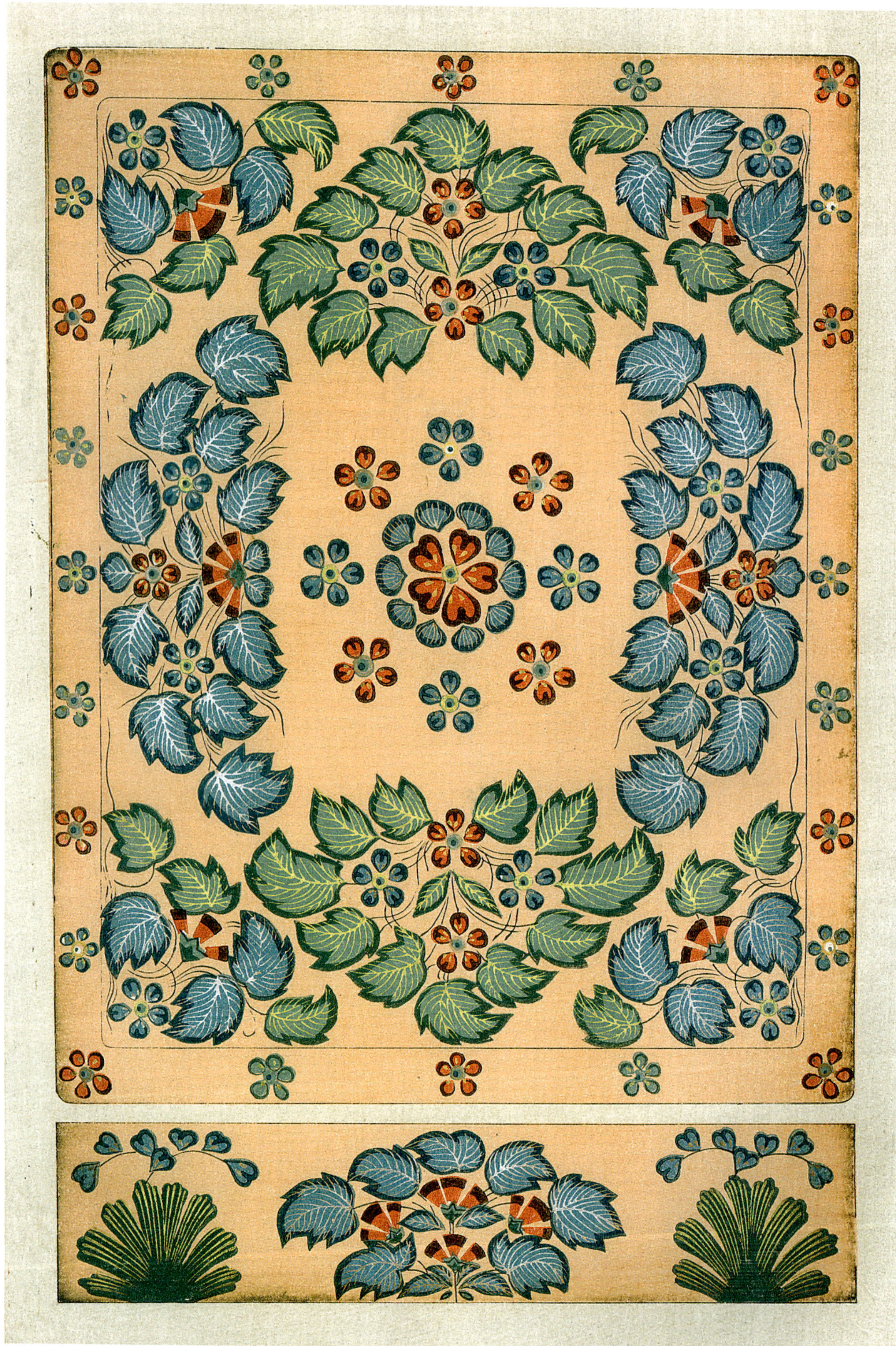

Plate 28

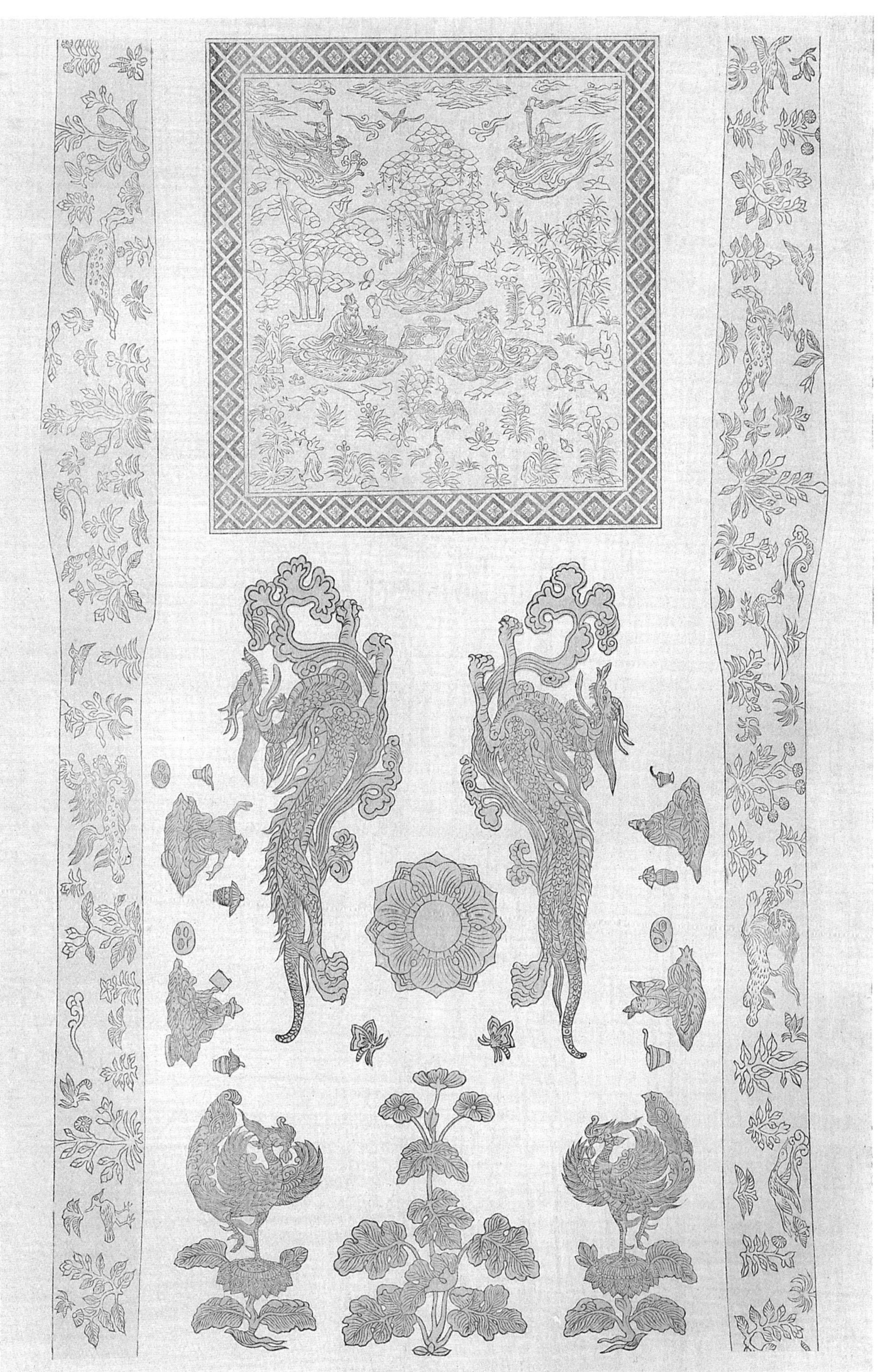

Plate 29

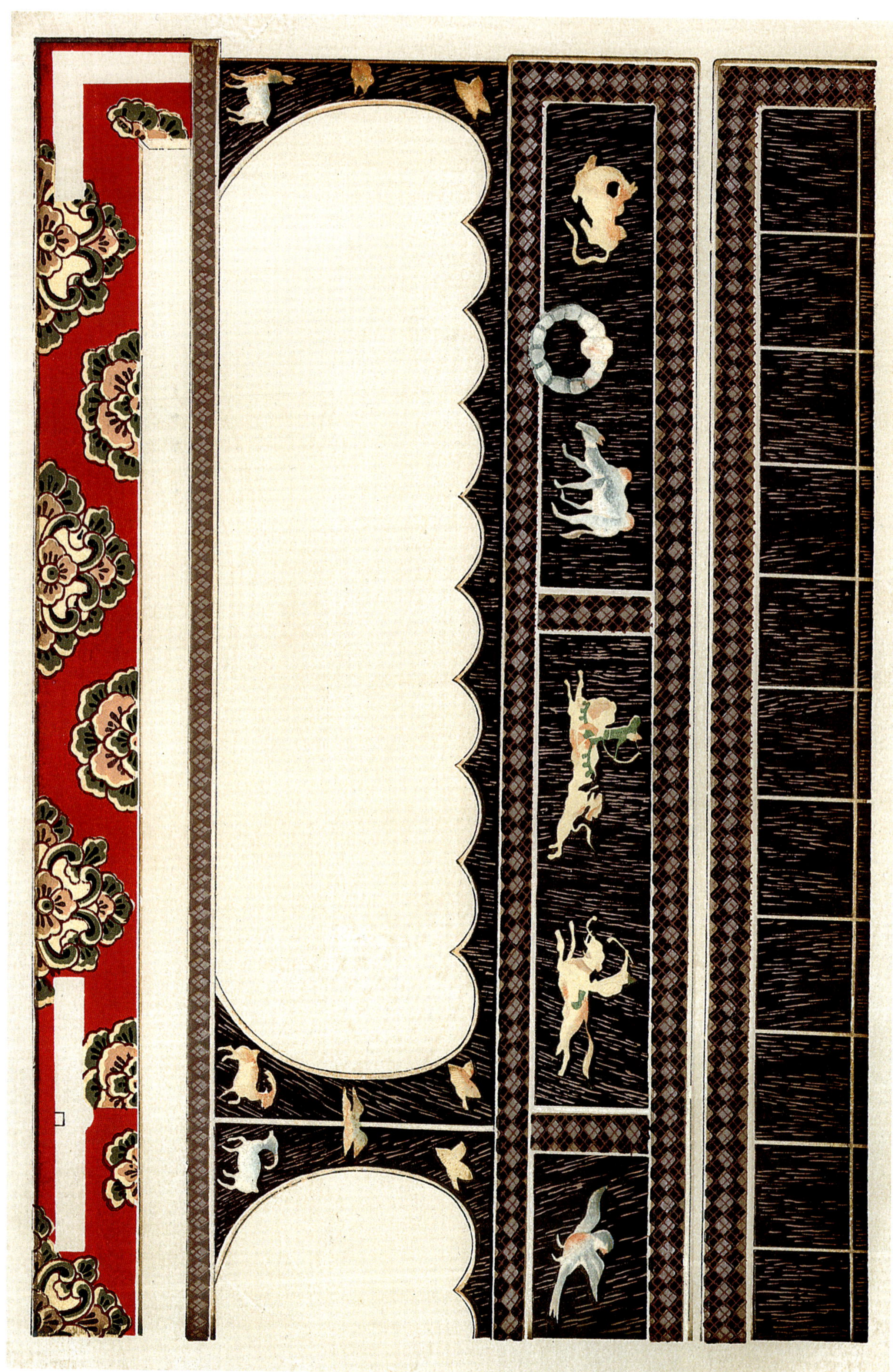

PLATE 30

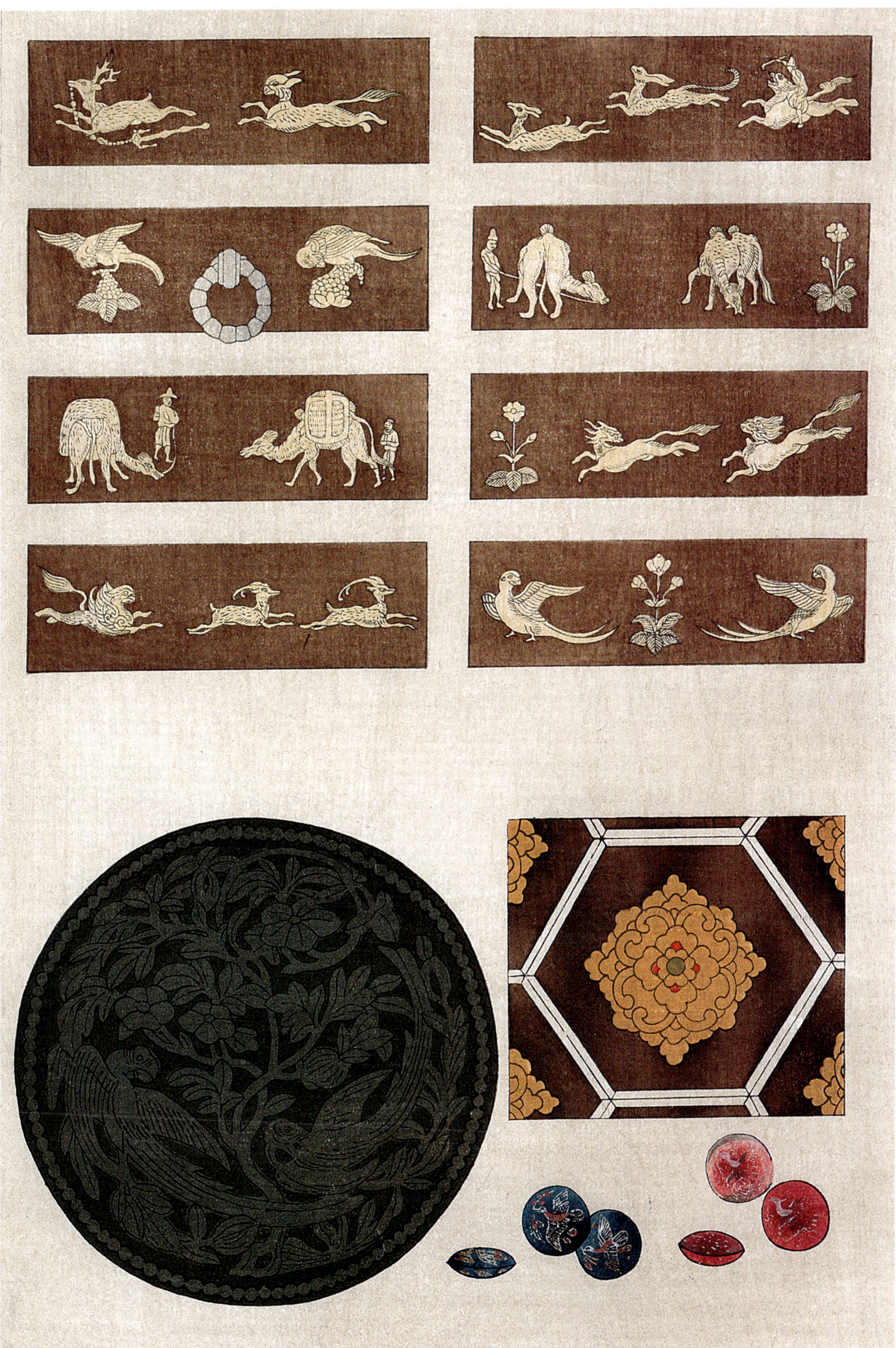

Plate 31

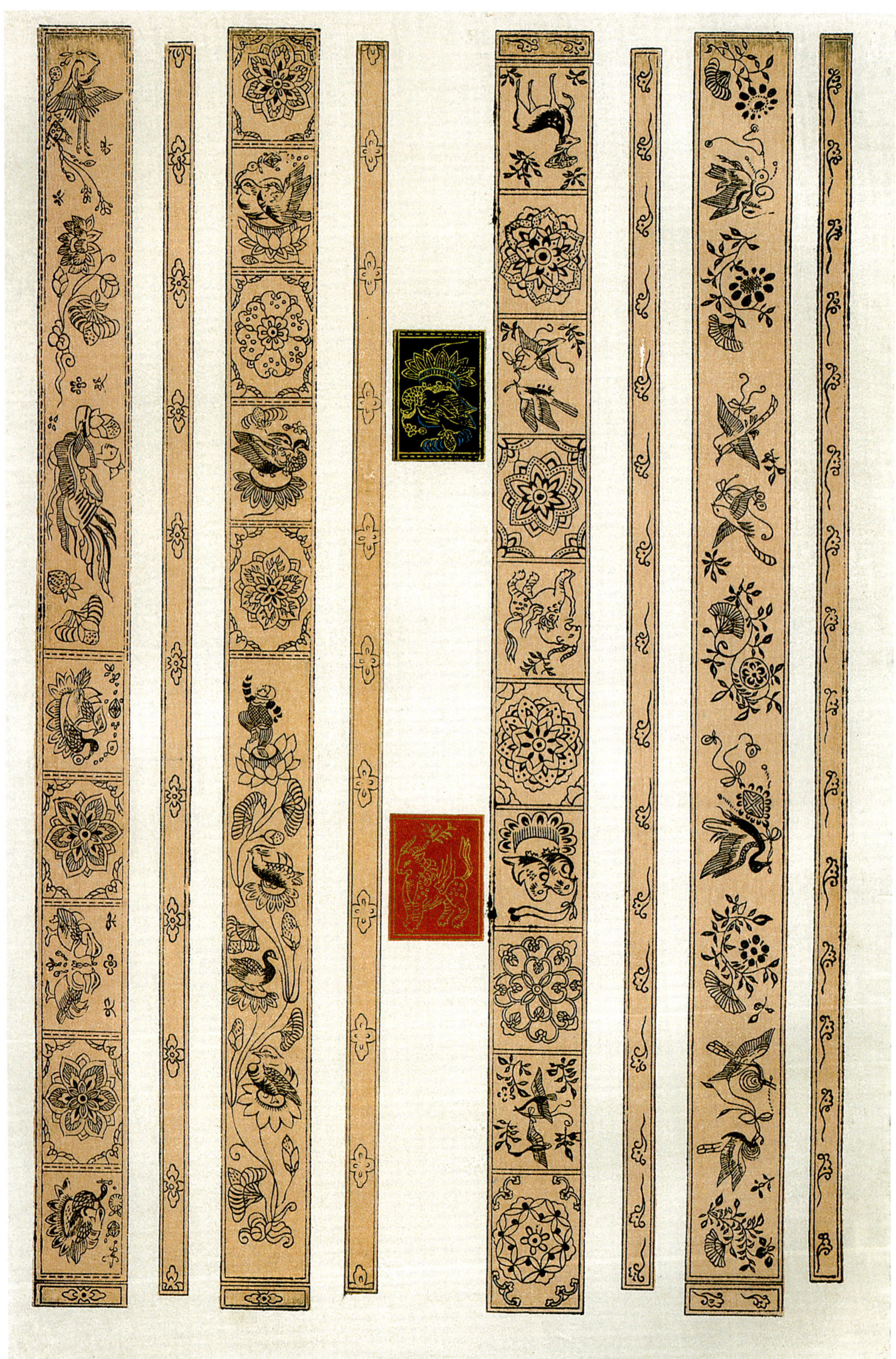

Plate 32

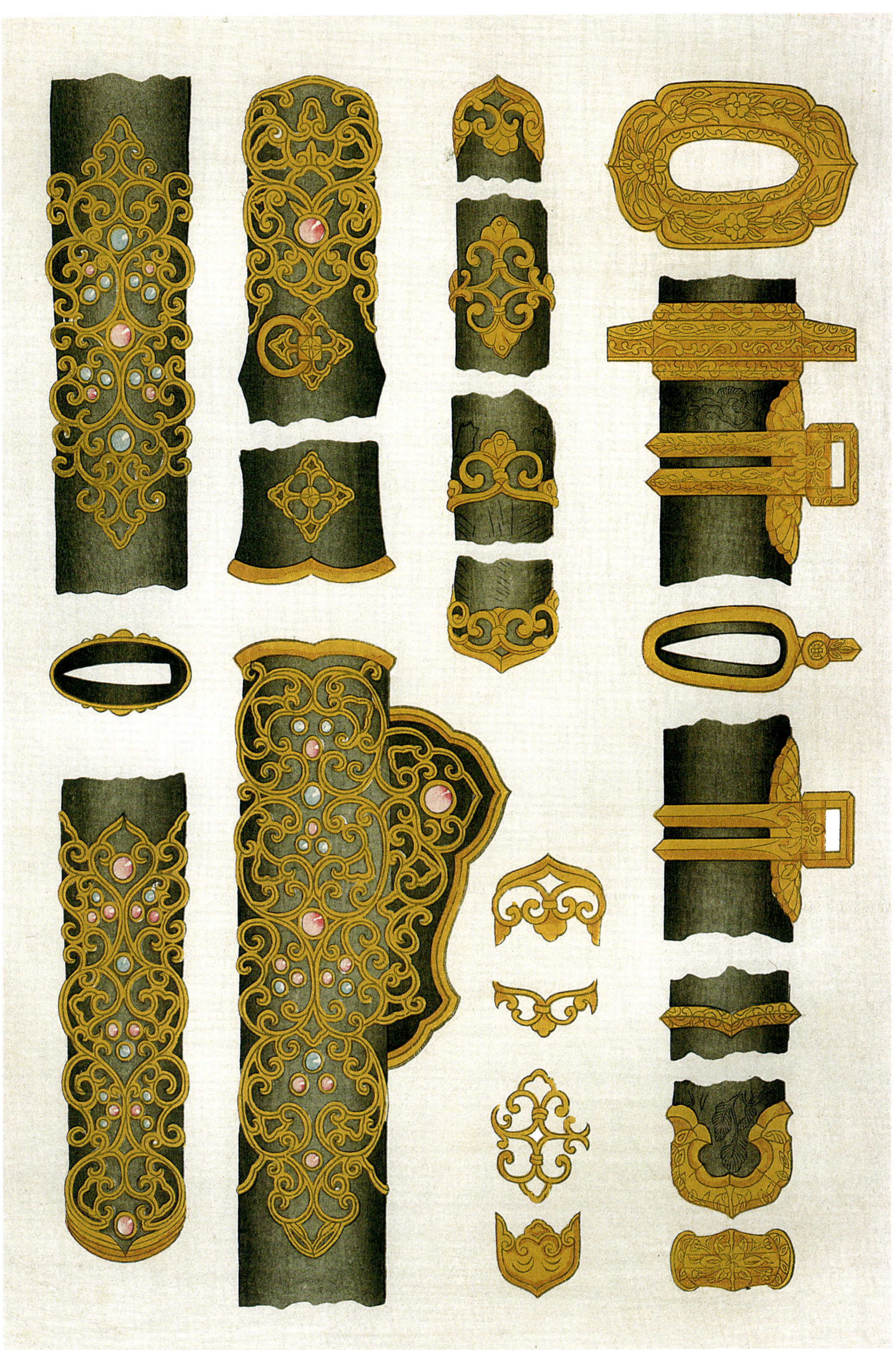

PLATE 33

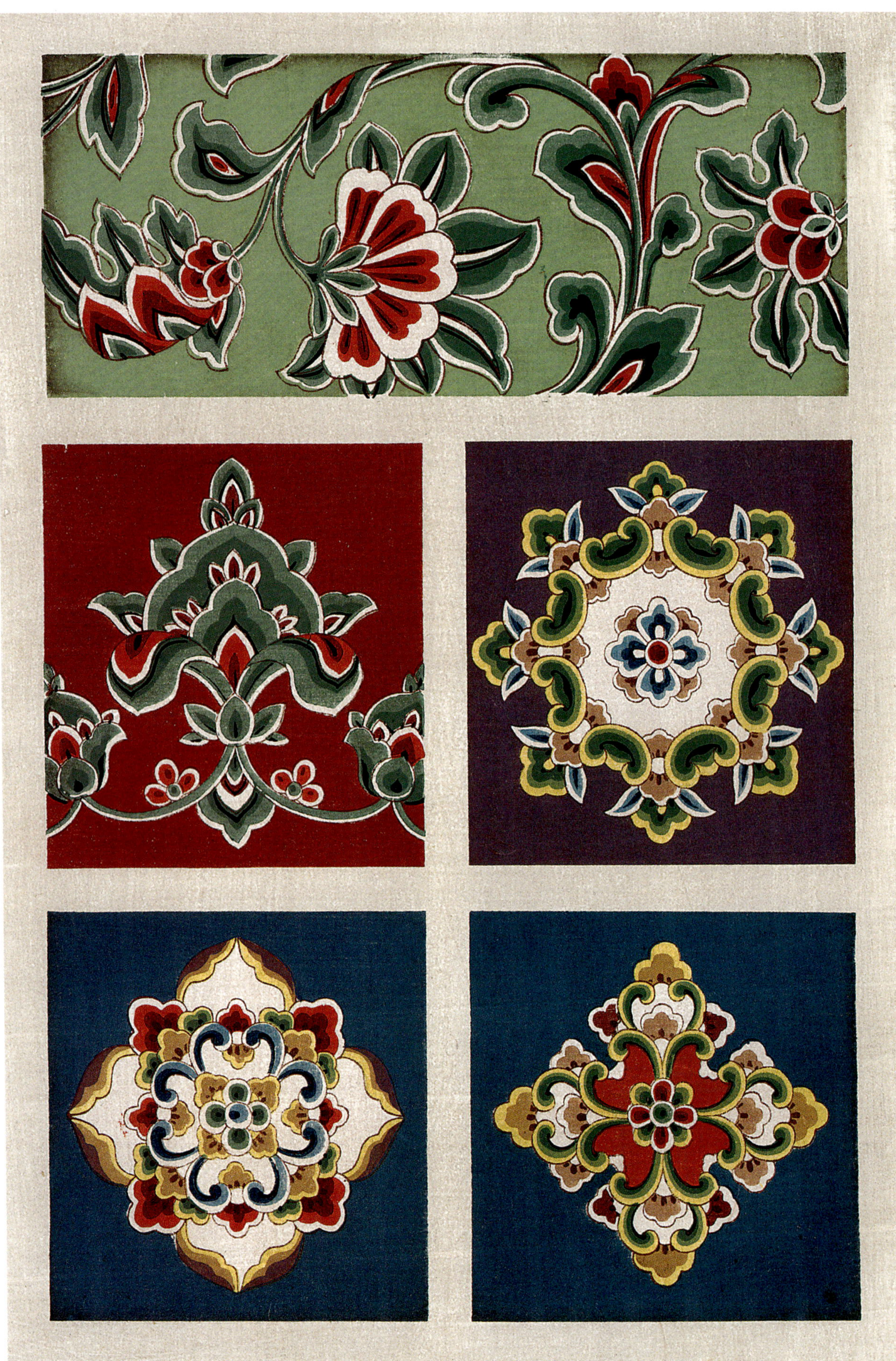

Plate 34

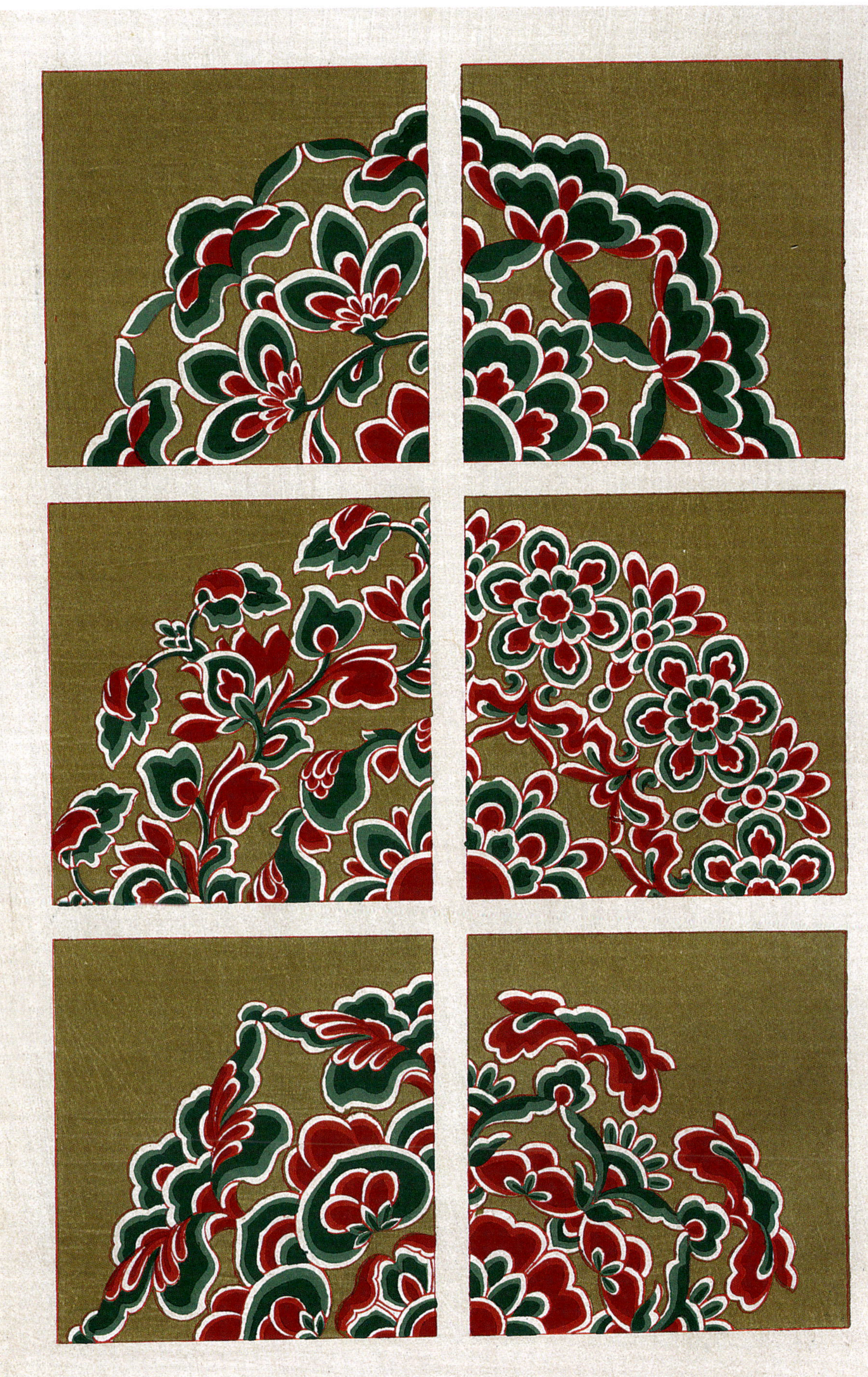

Plate 35

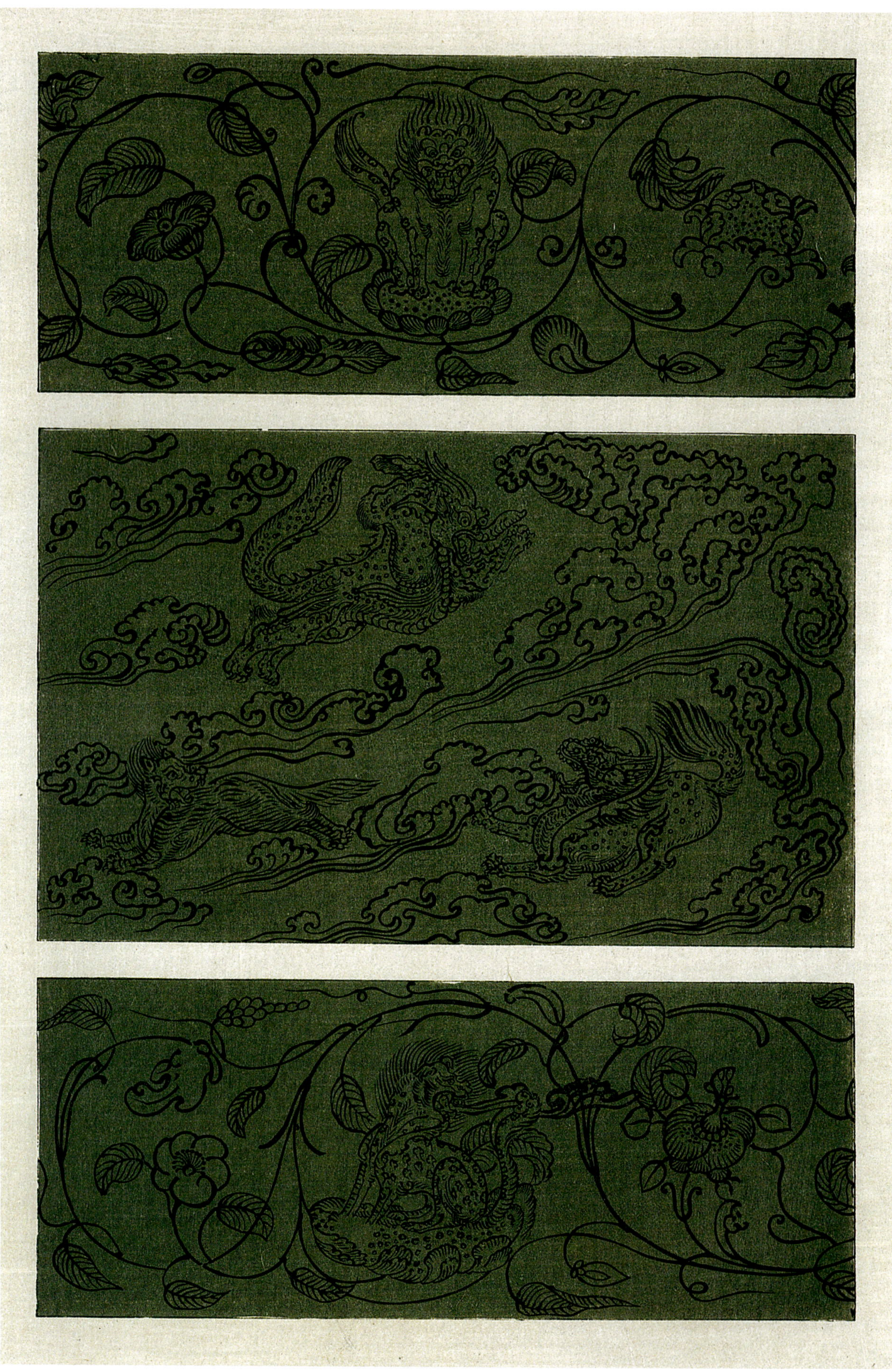

PLATE 36

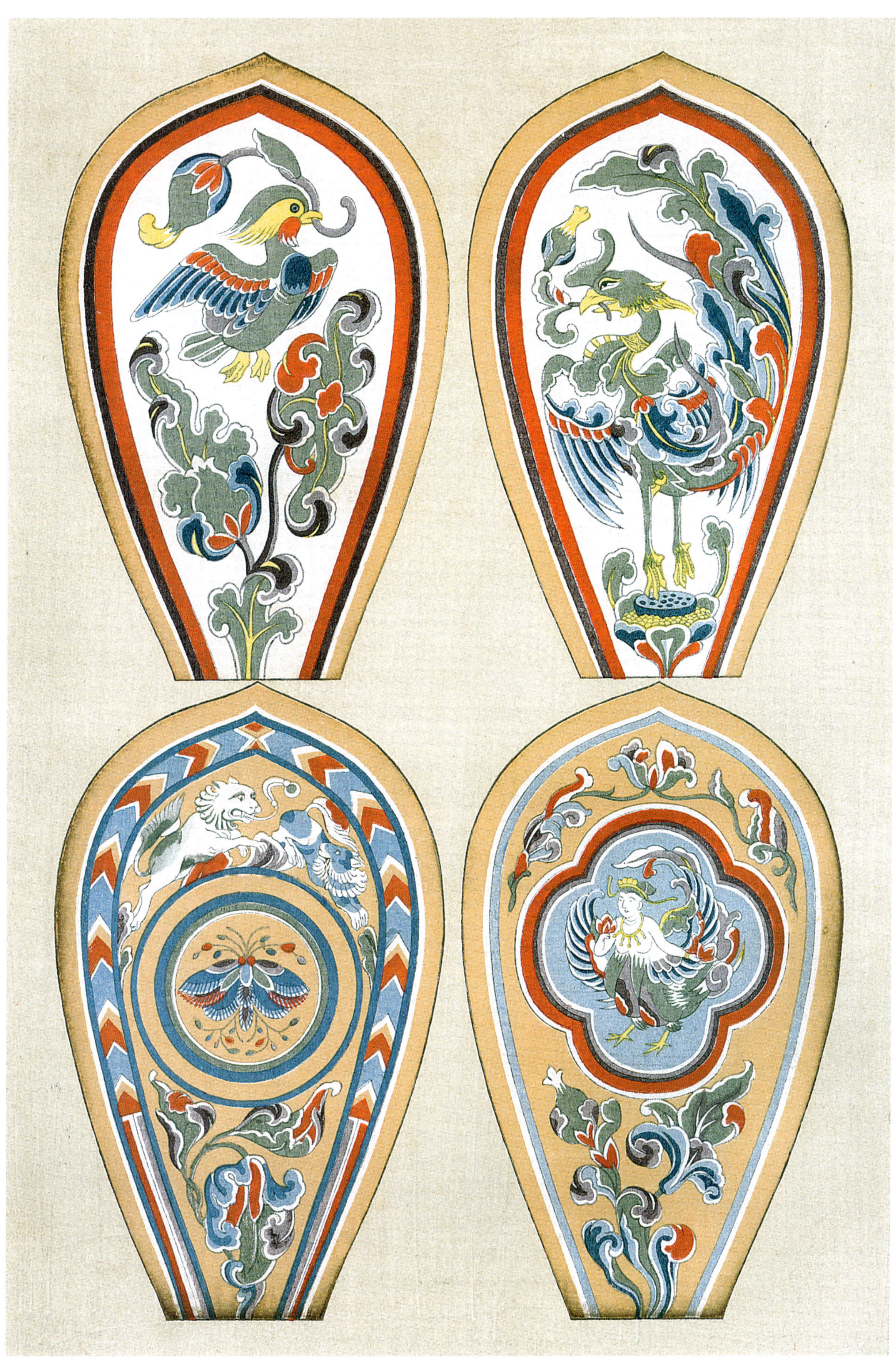

Plate 37

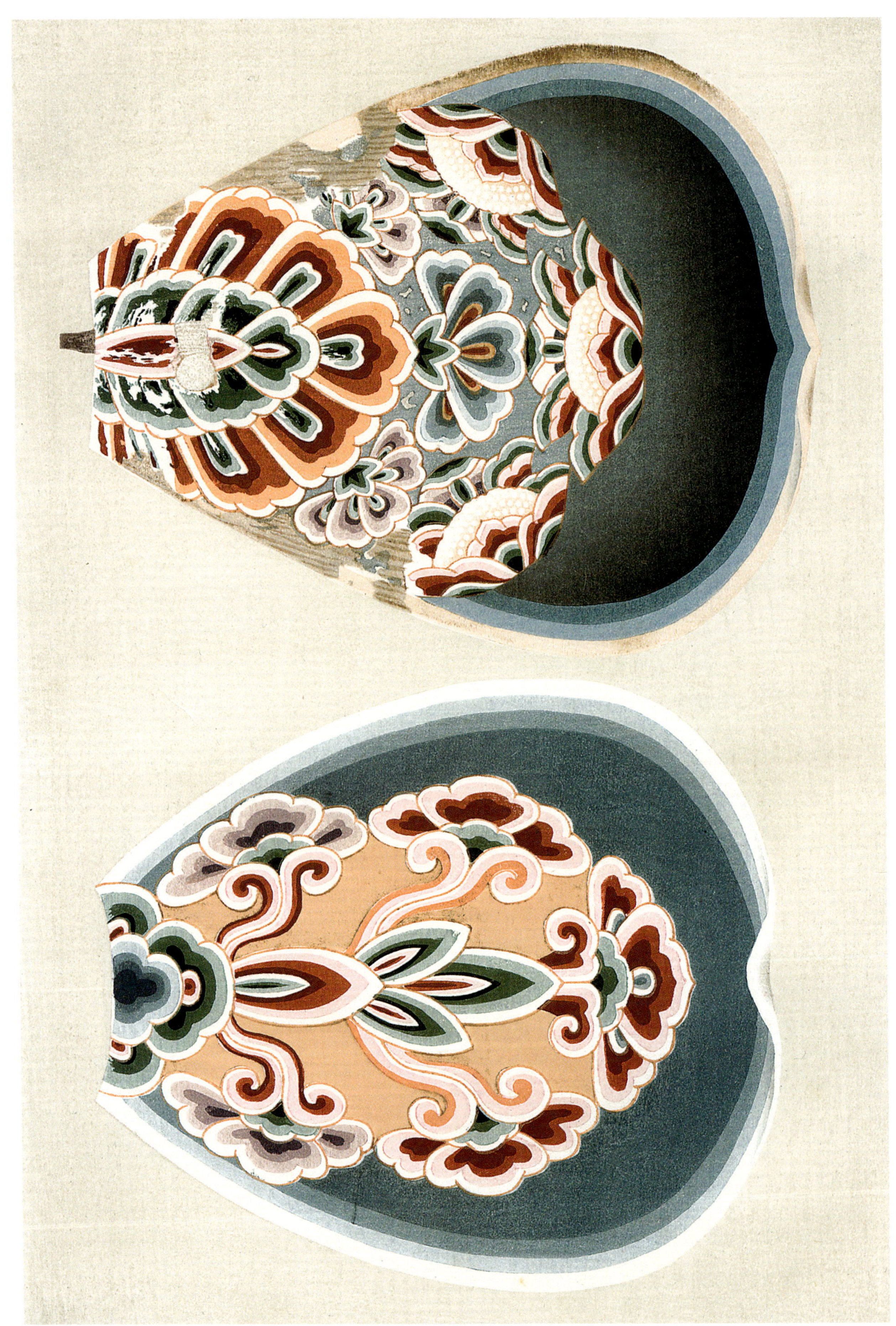

Plate 38

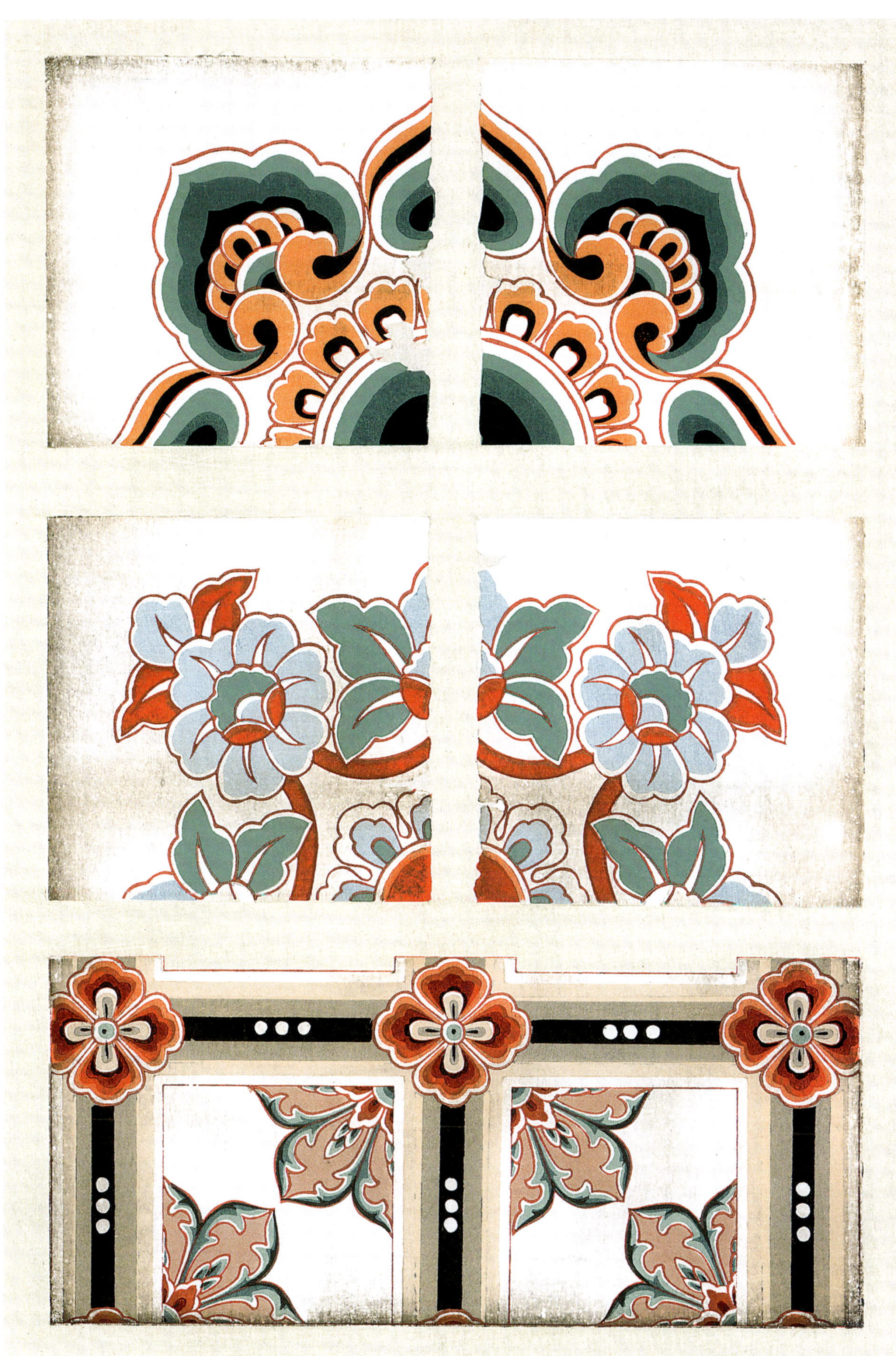

Plate 39

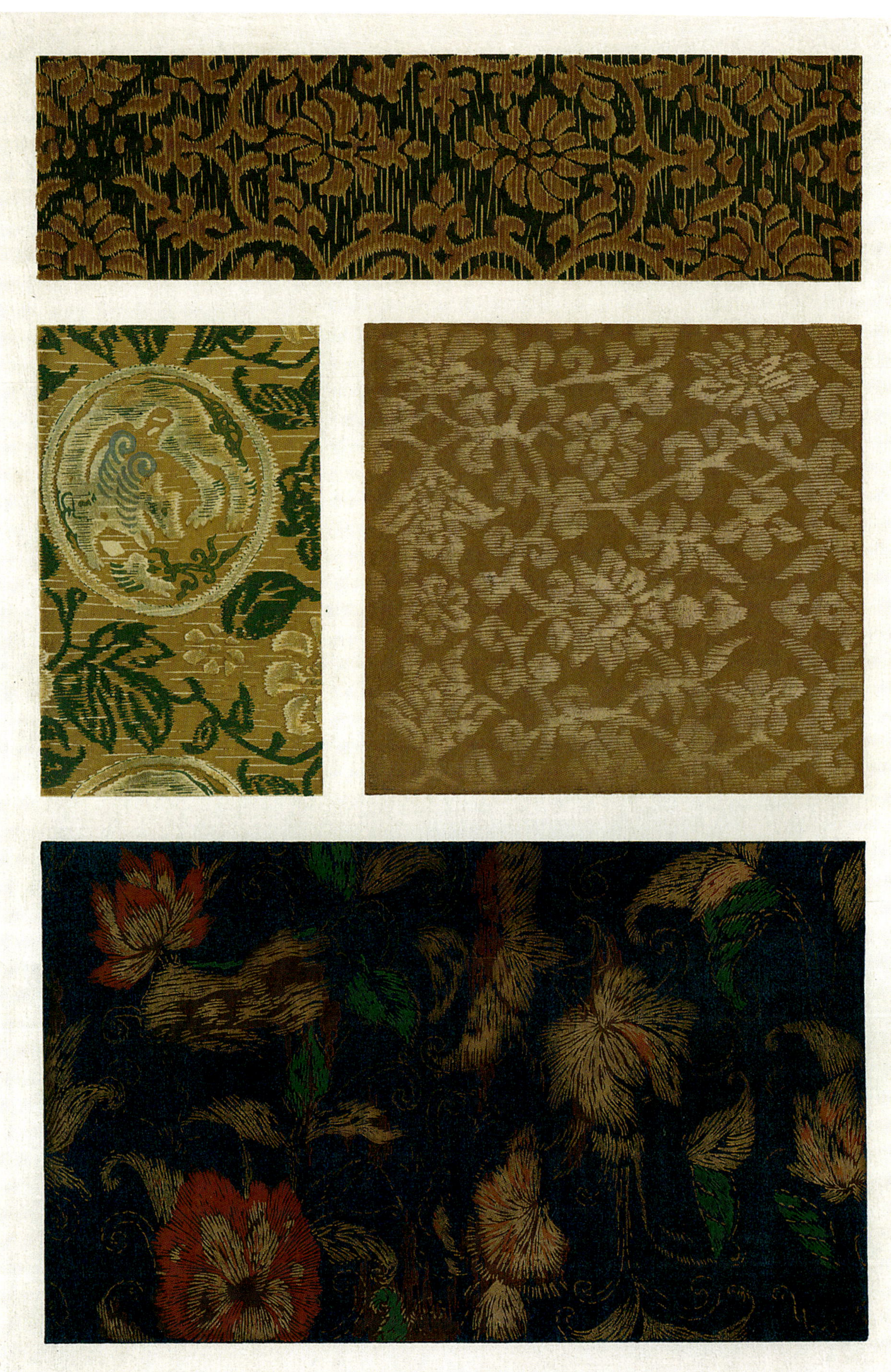

Plate 40

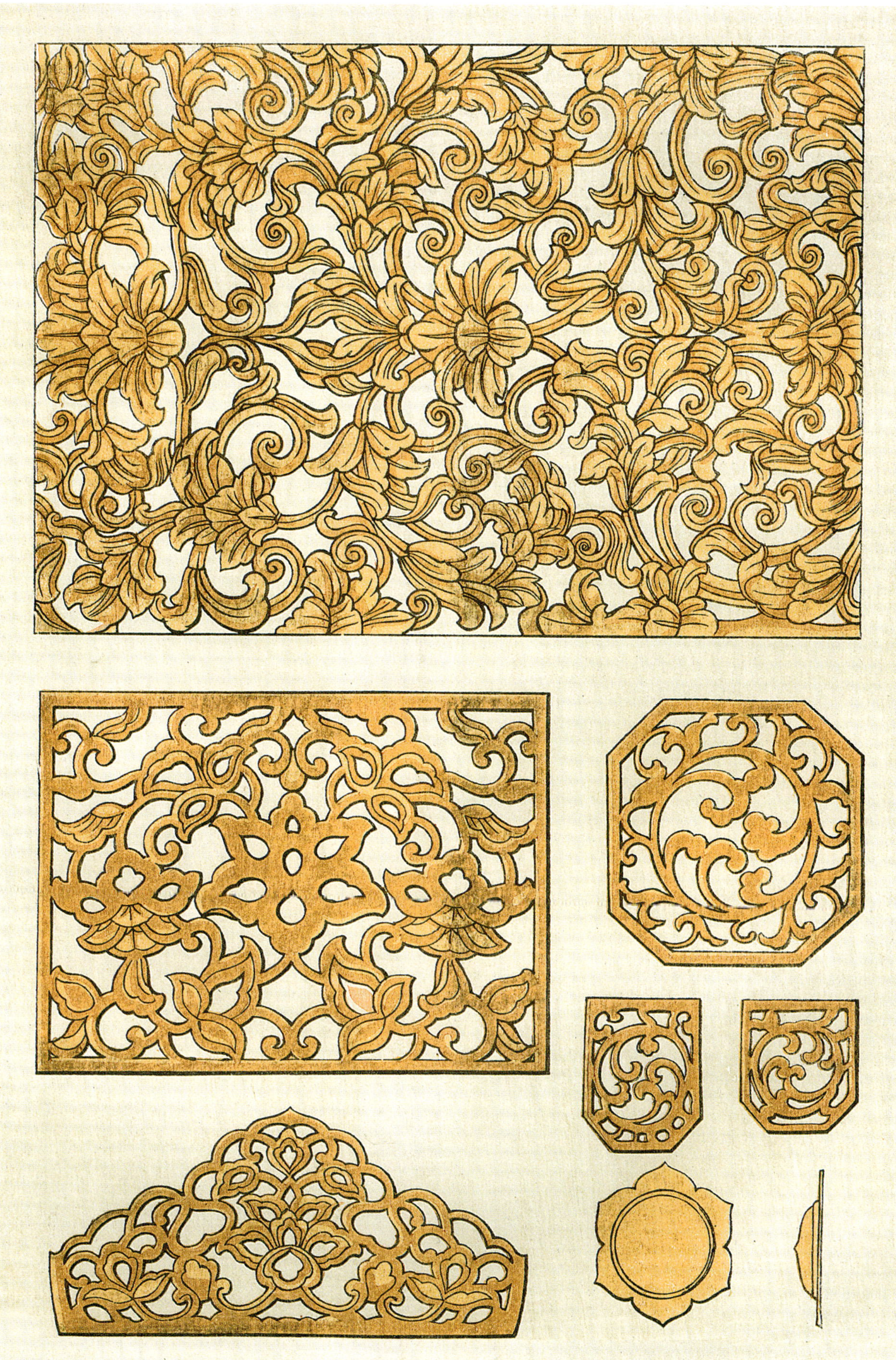

Plate 41

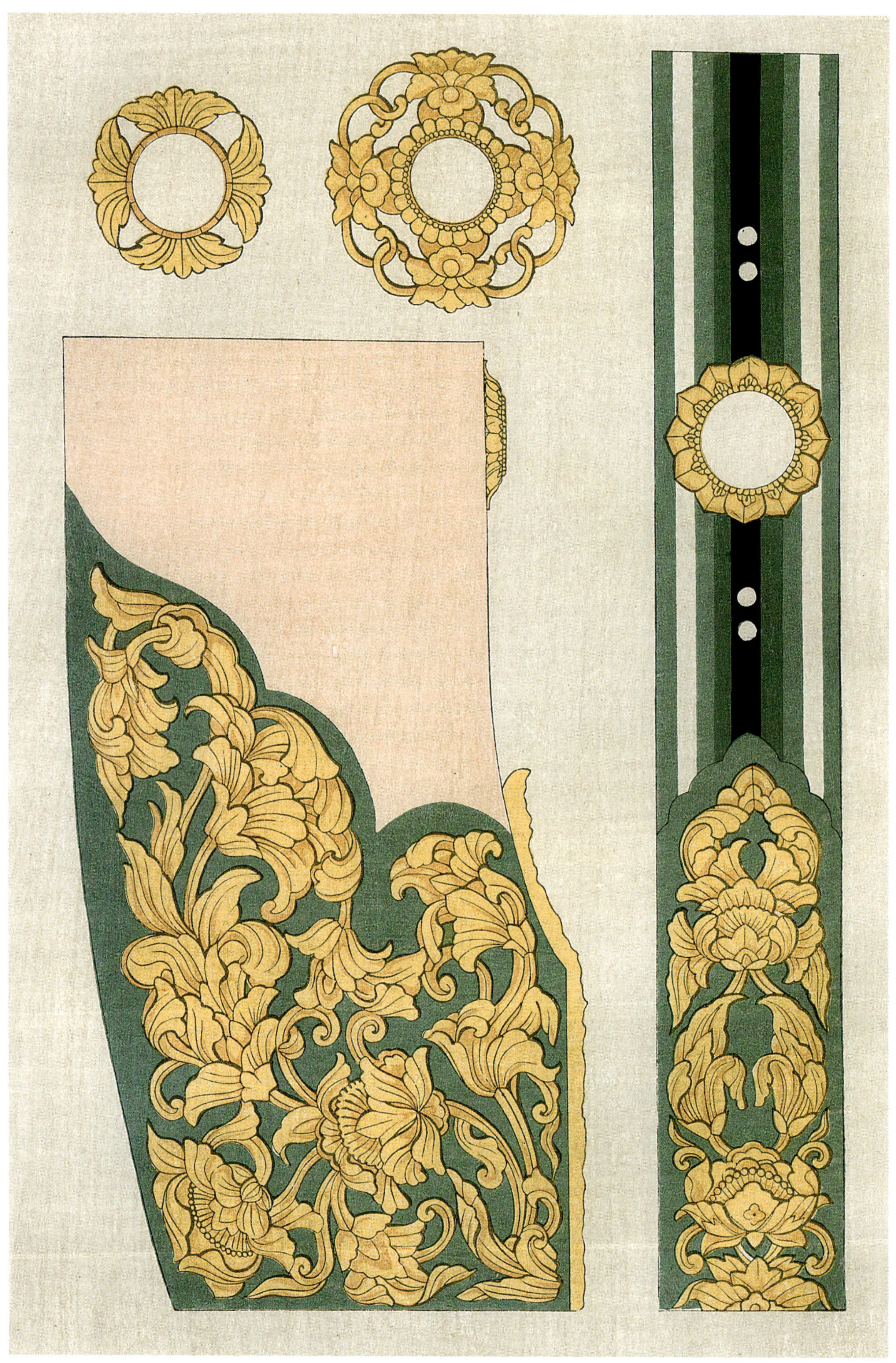

Plate 42

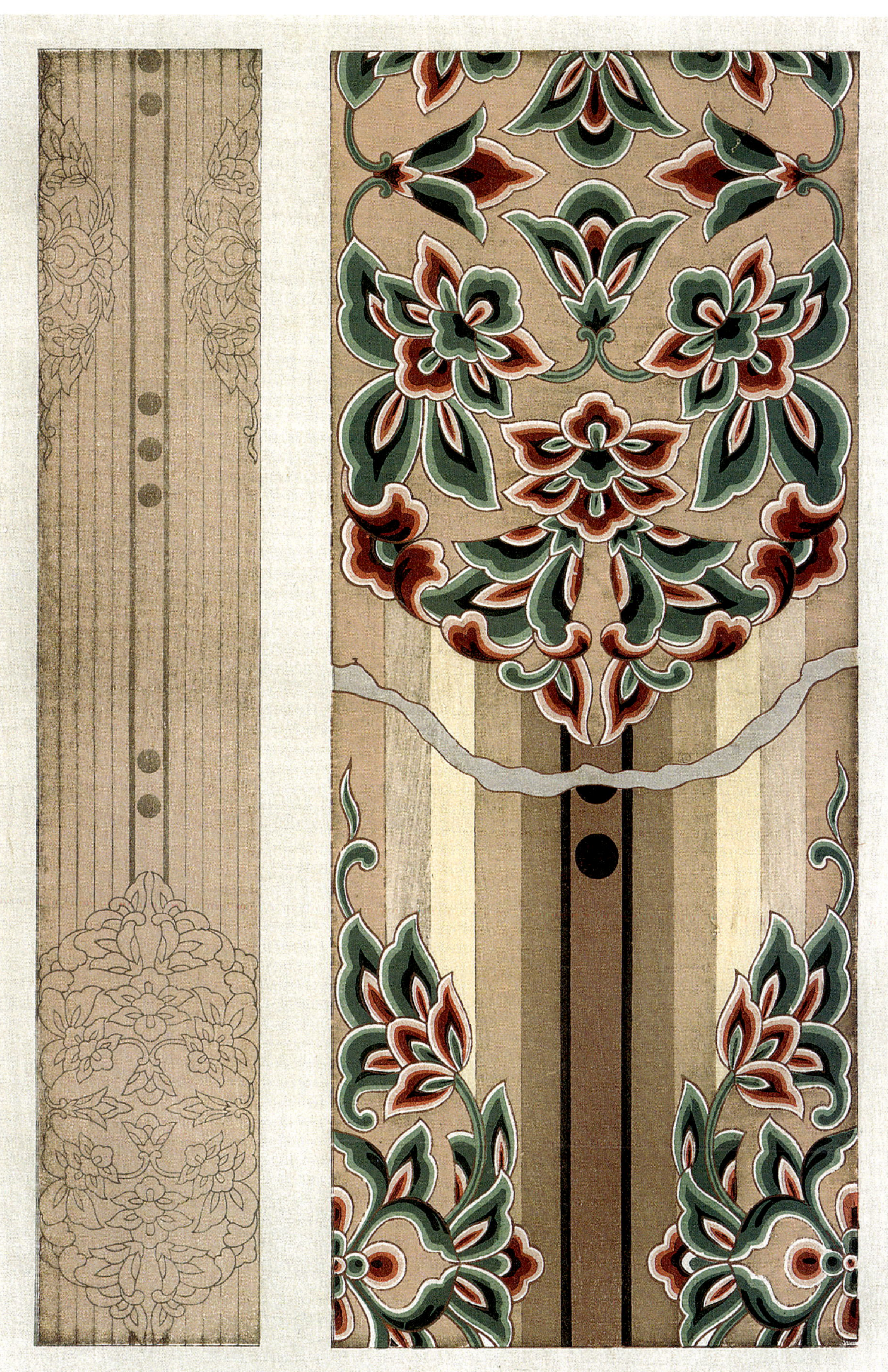

Plate 43

PLATE 44

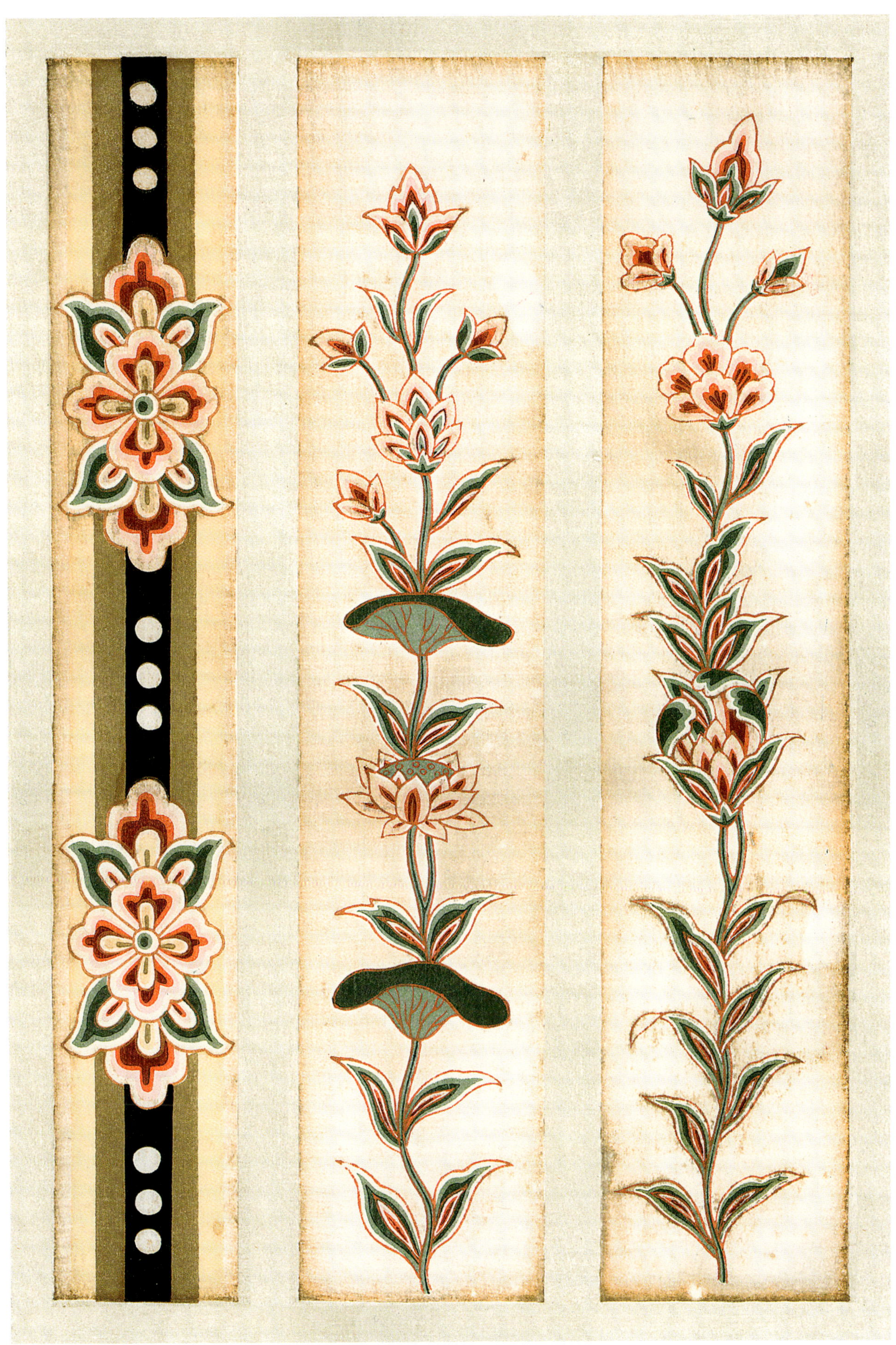

Plate 45

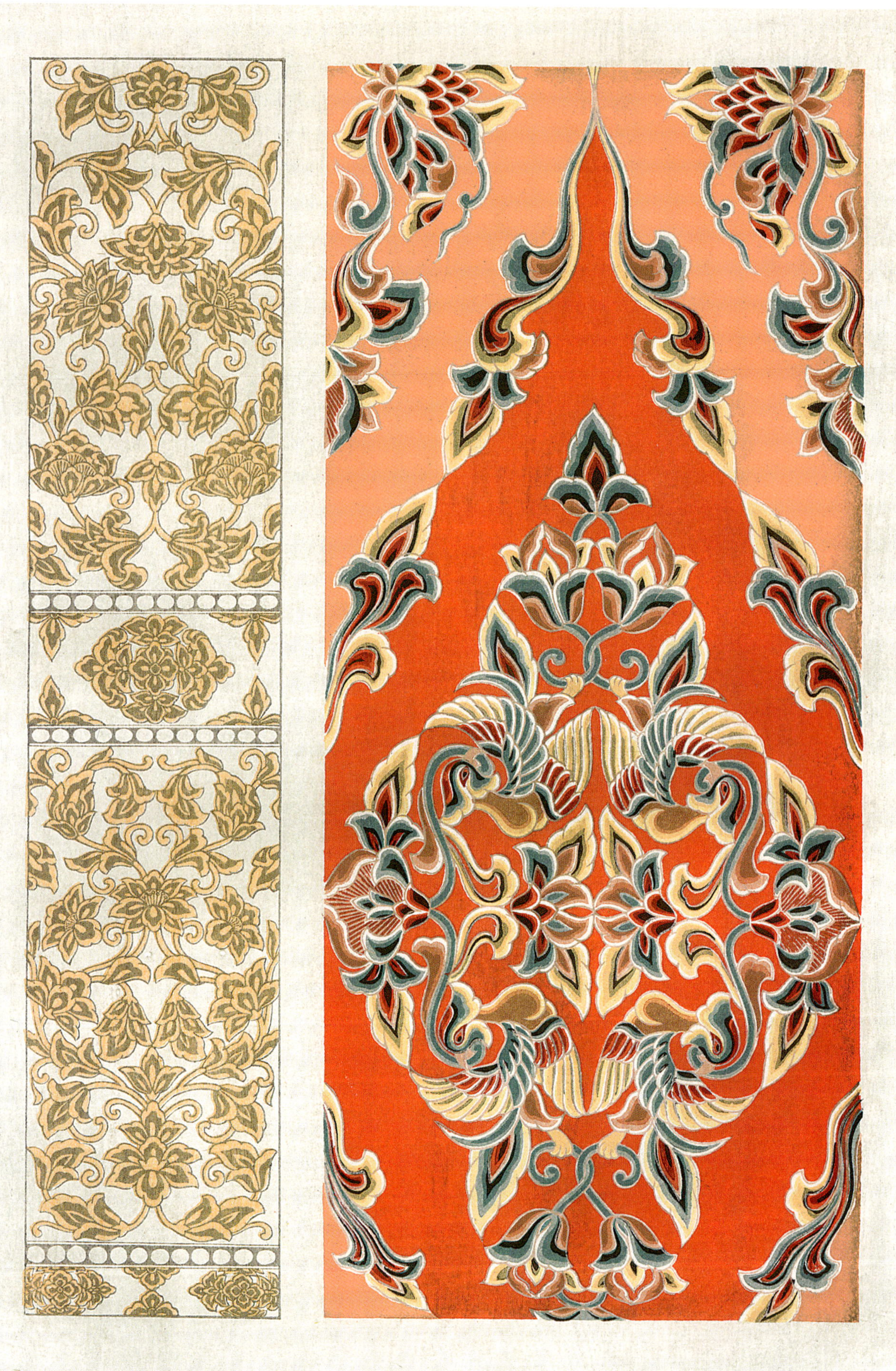

Plate 46

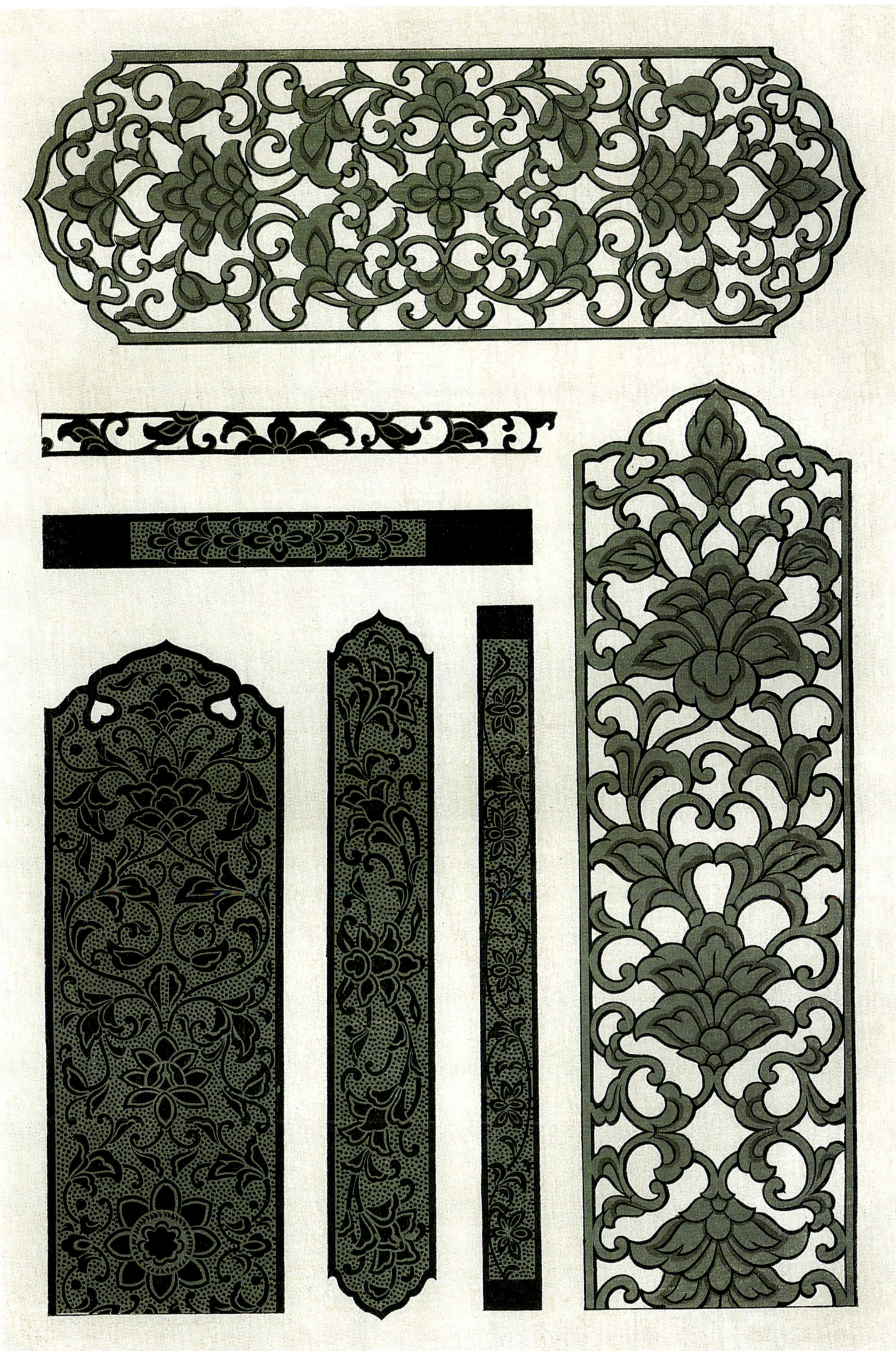

Plate 47

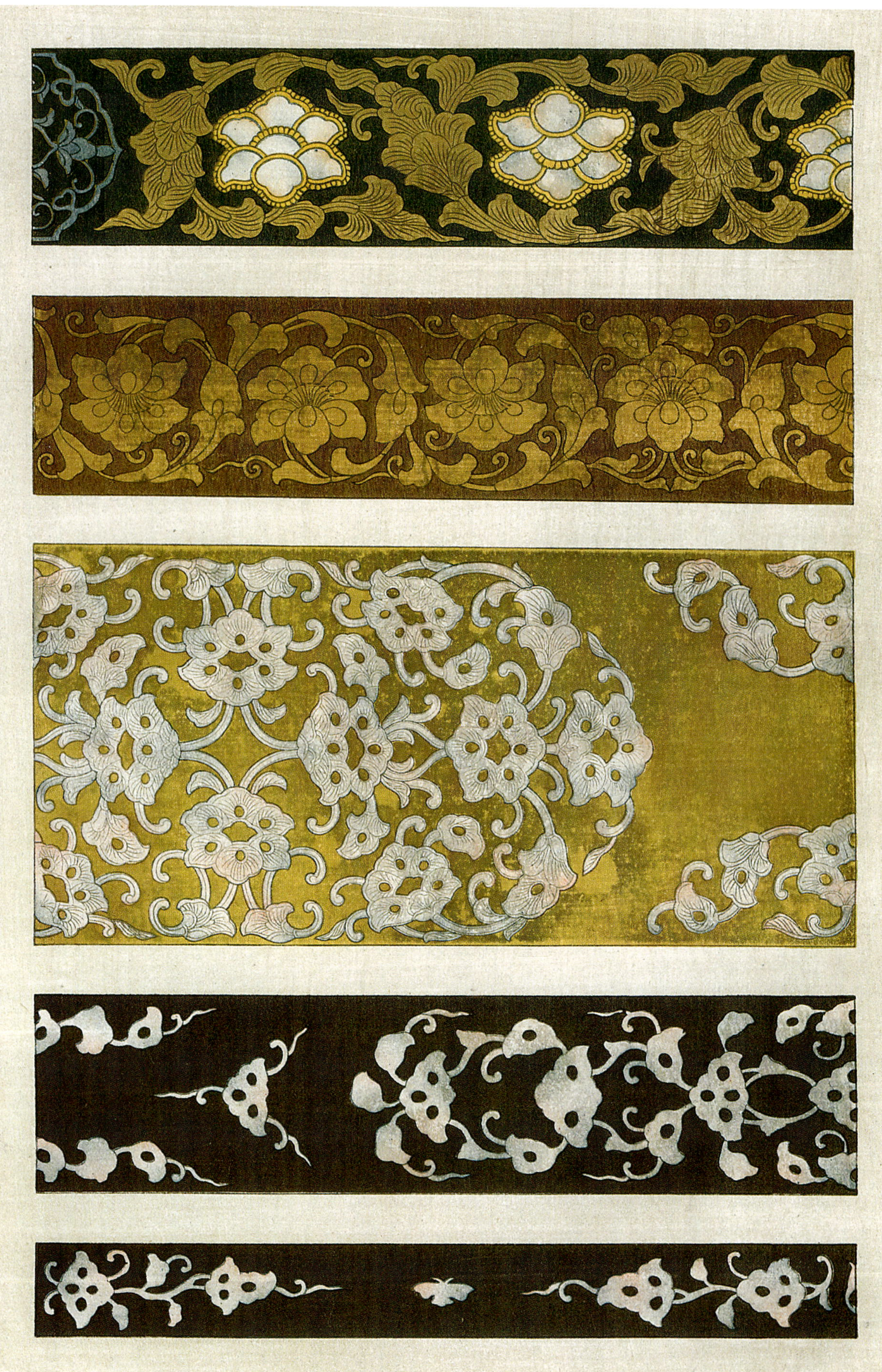

Plate 48

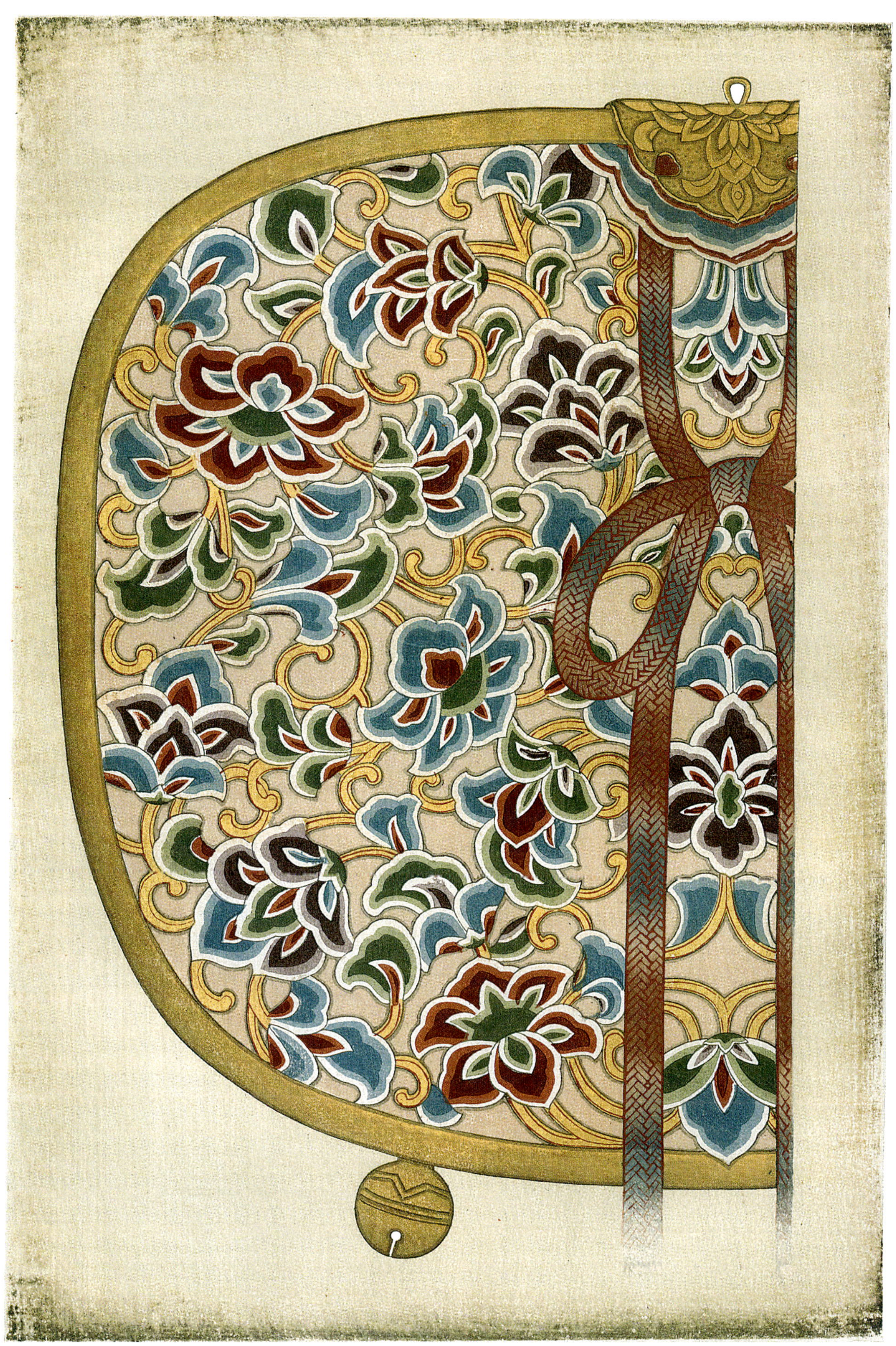

Plate 49

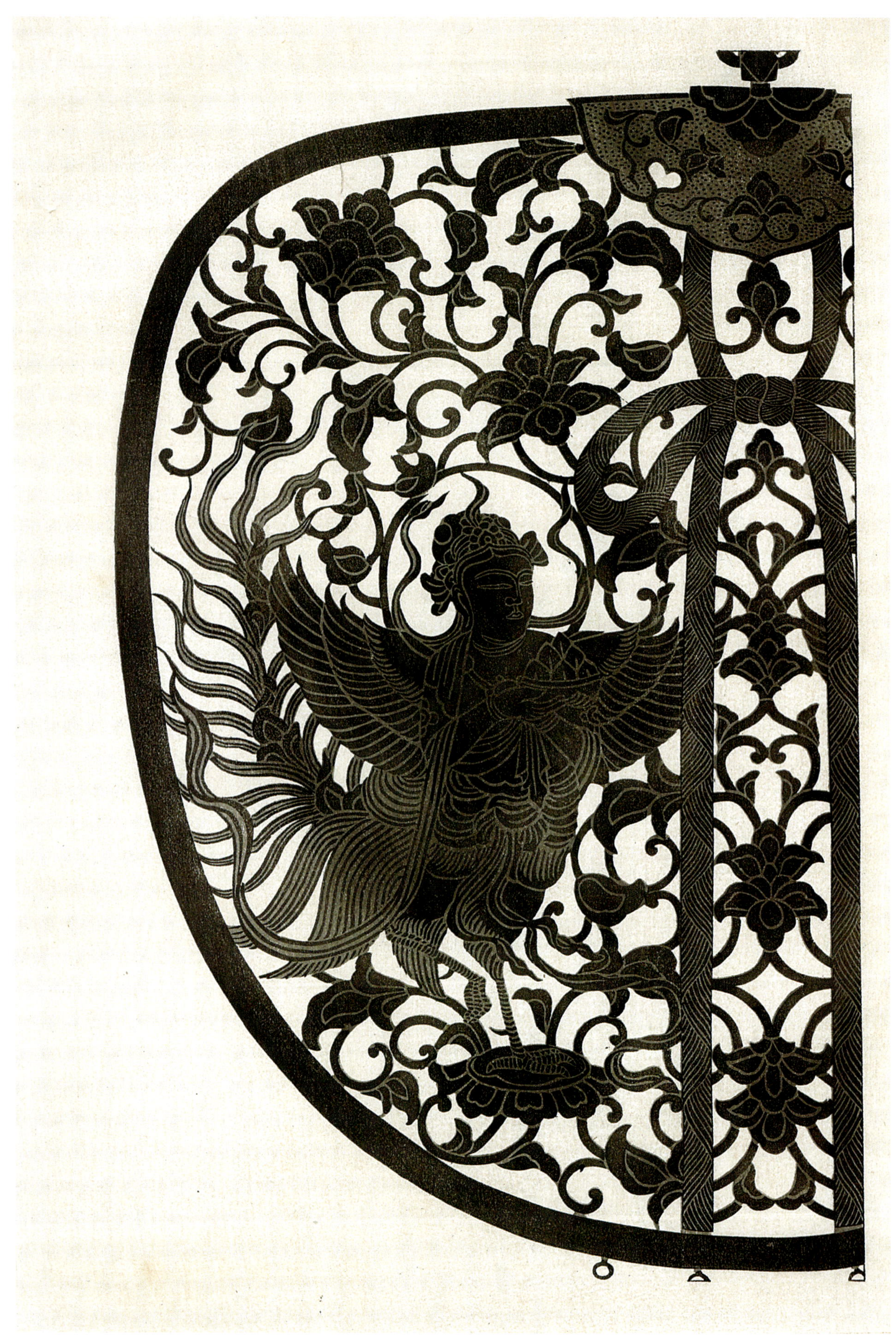

Plate 50

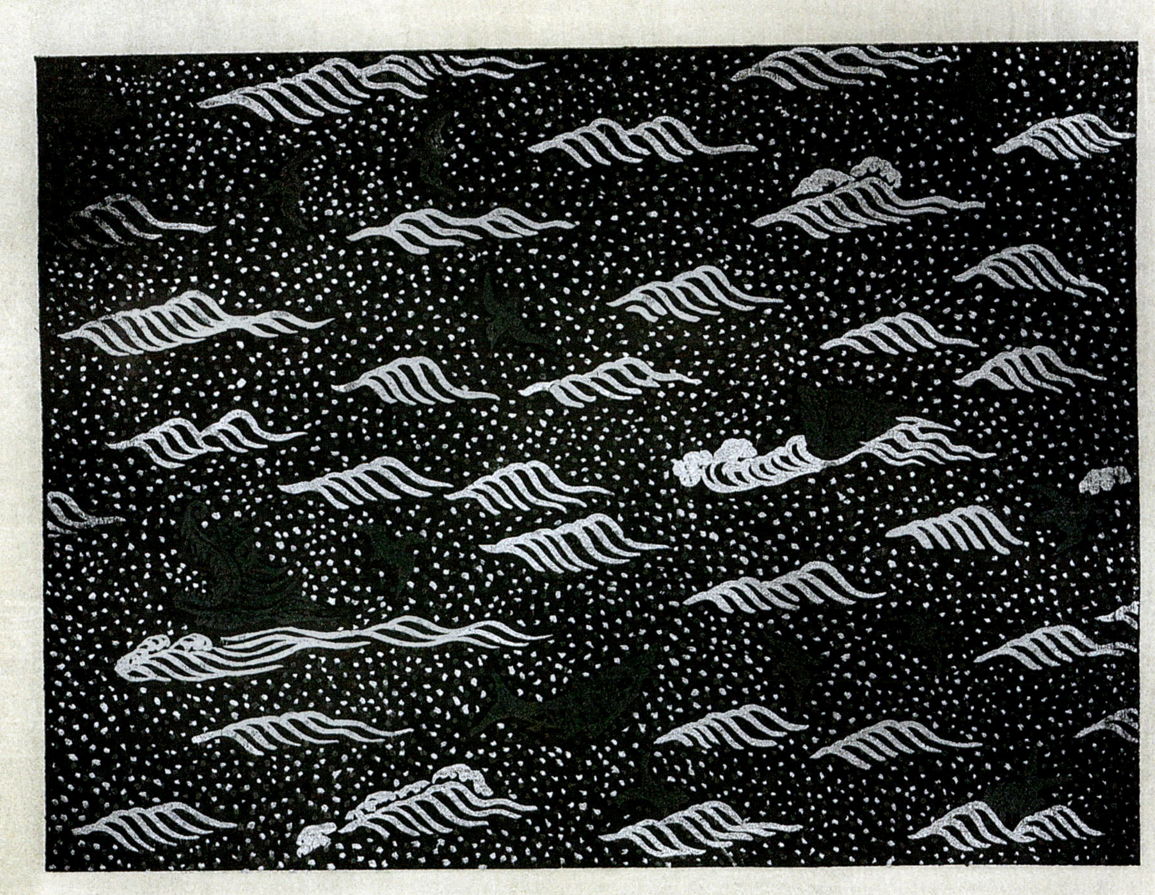

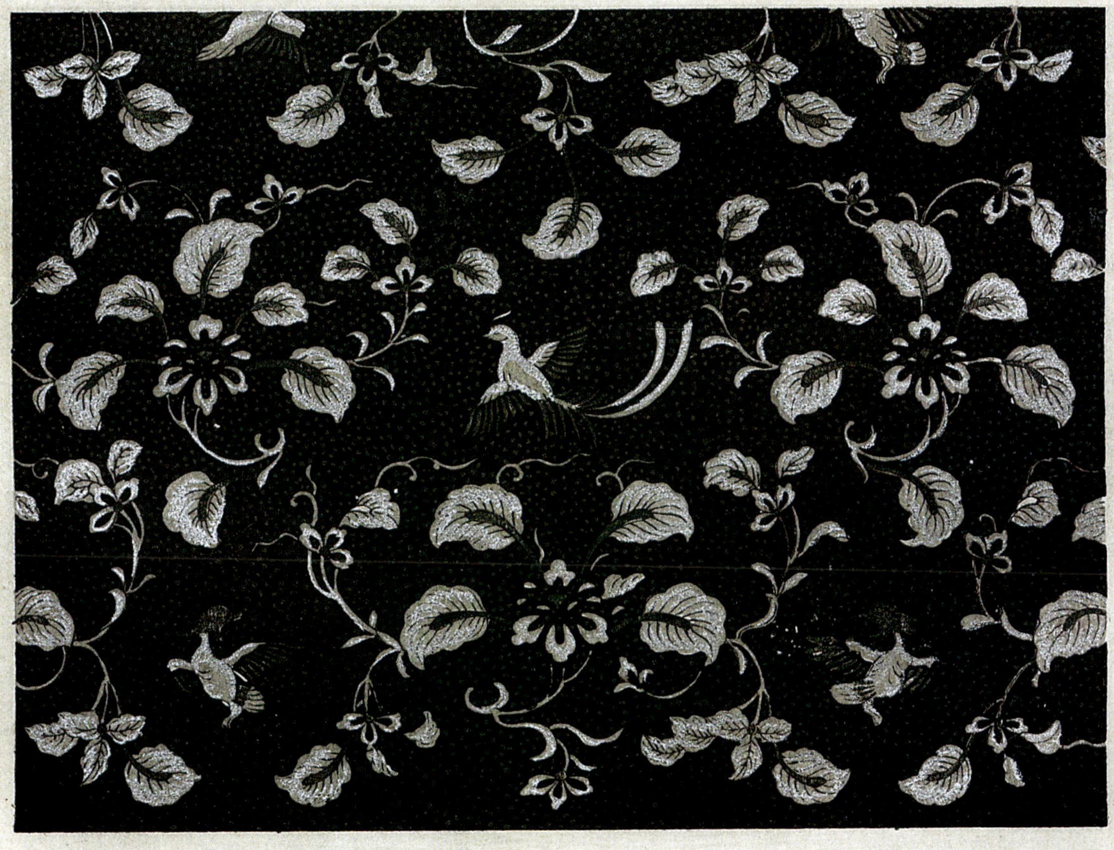

Plate 51

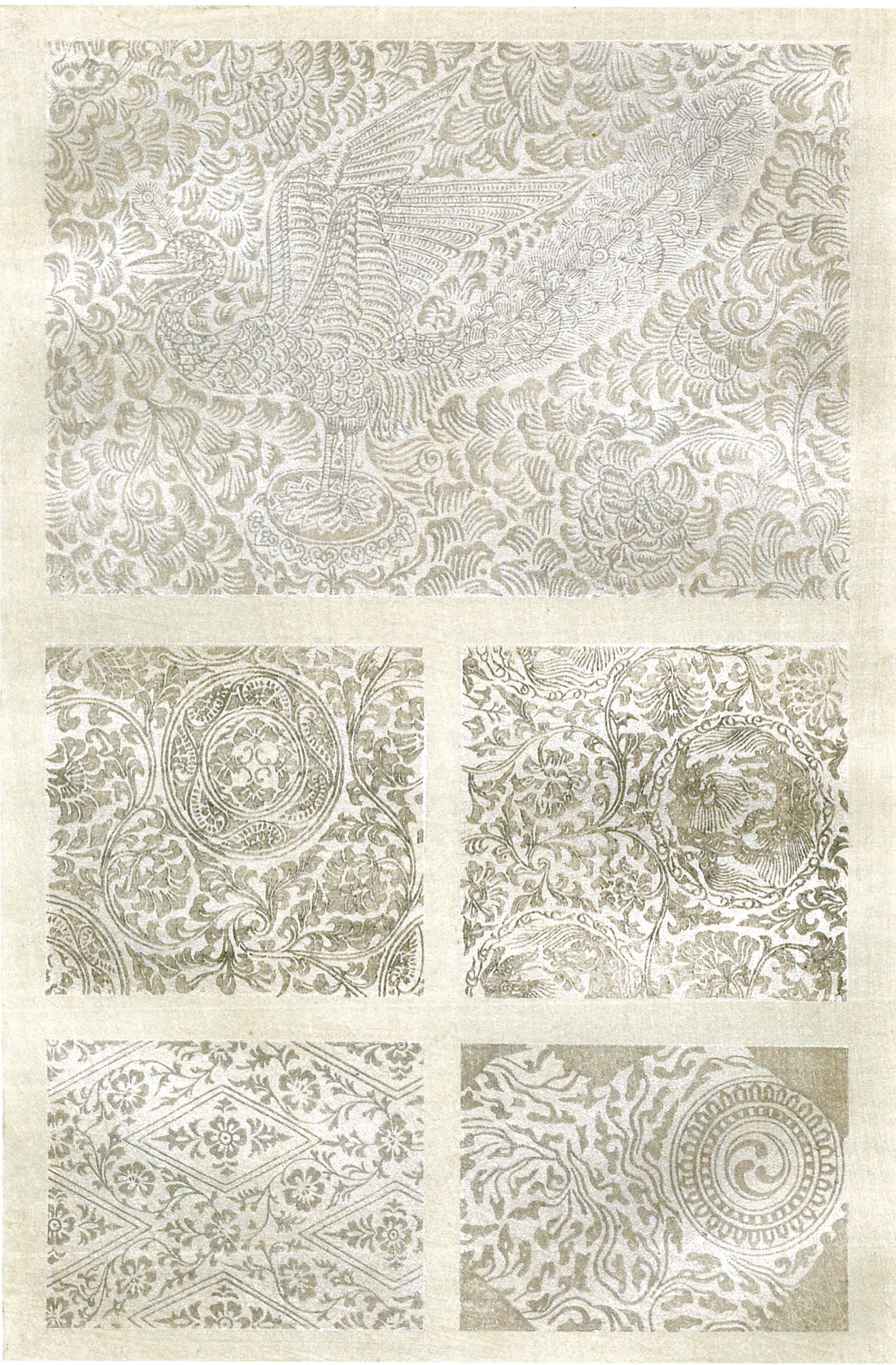

Plate 52

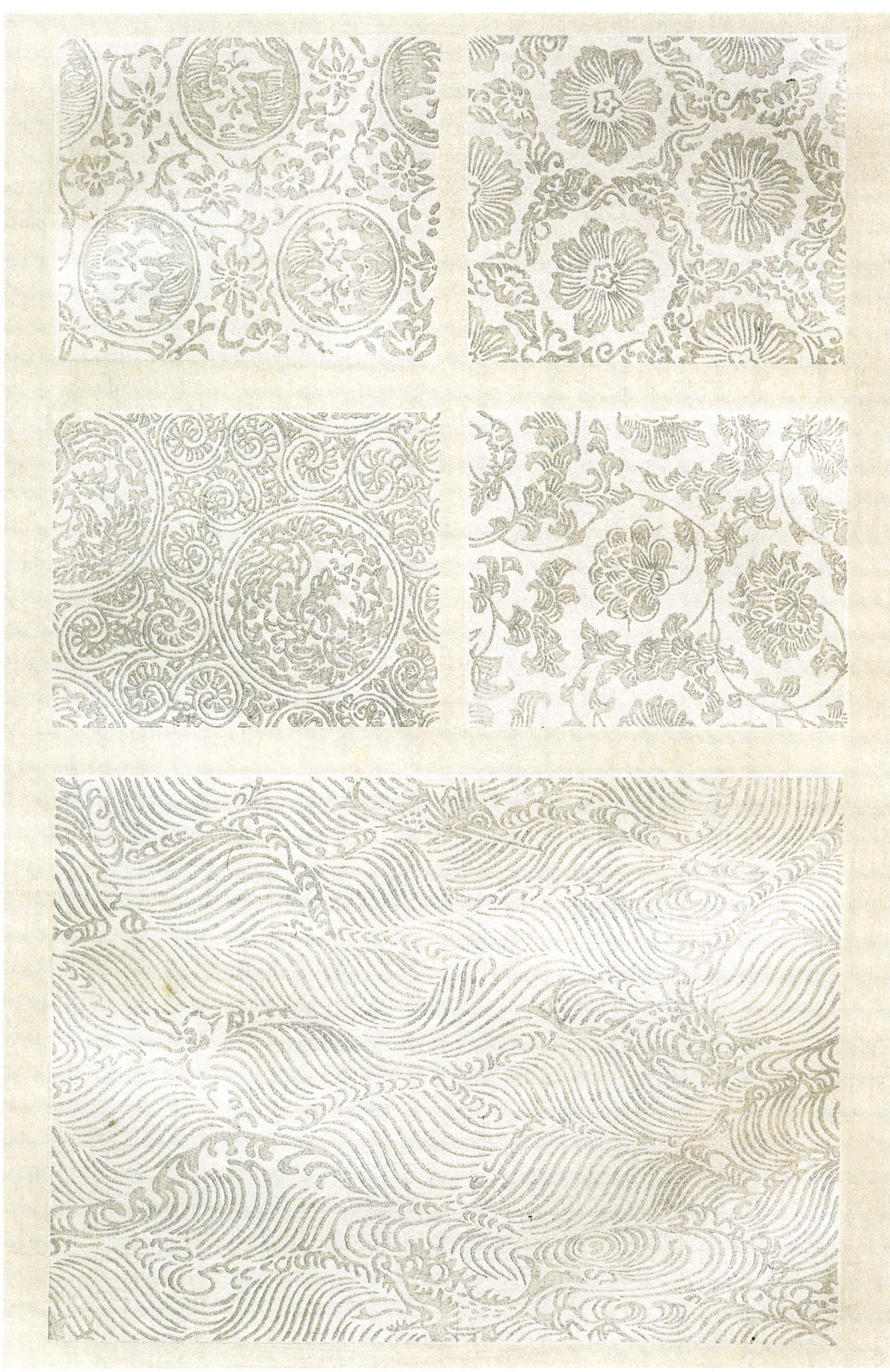

Plate 53

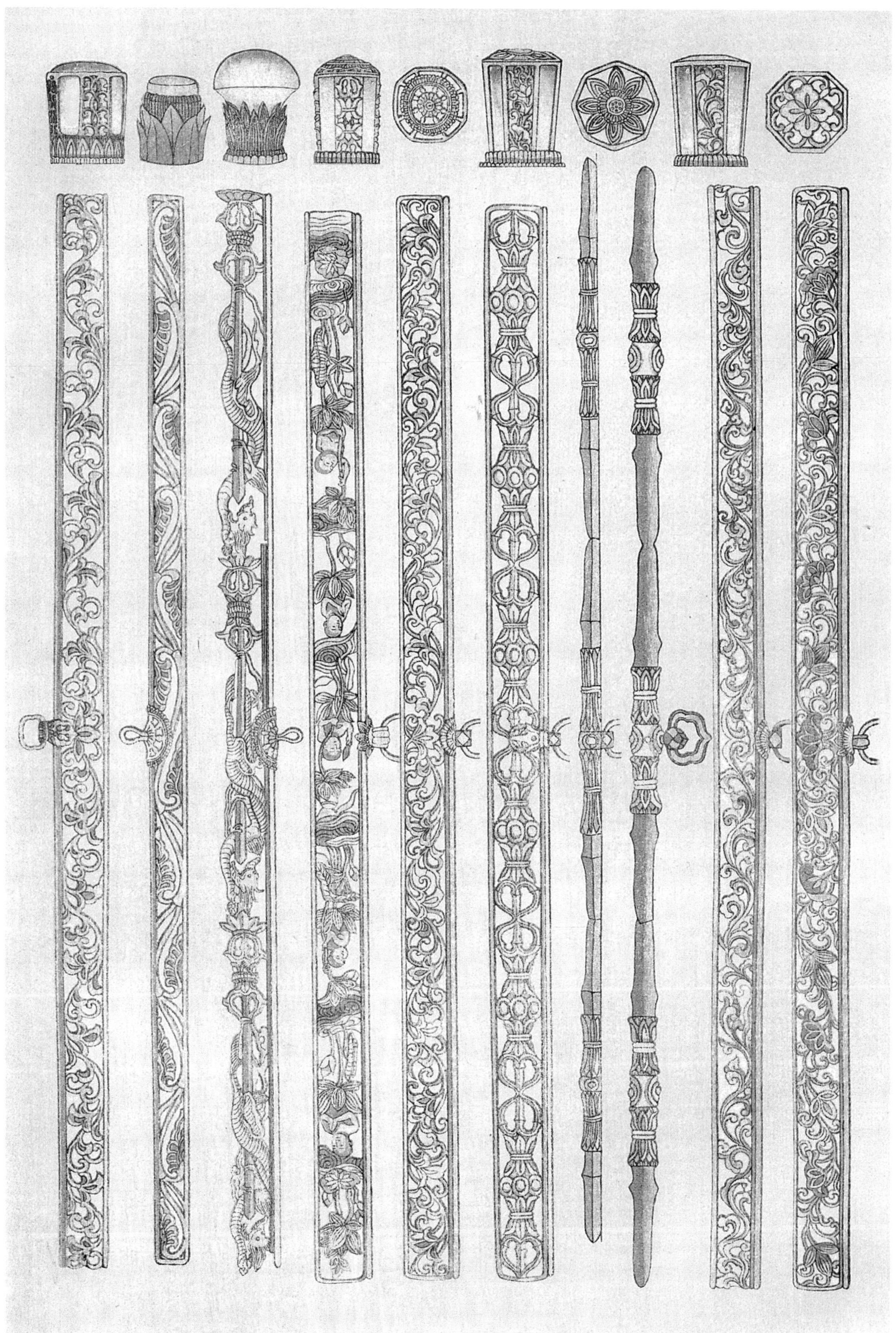

Plate 54

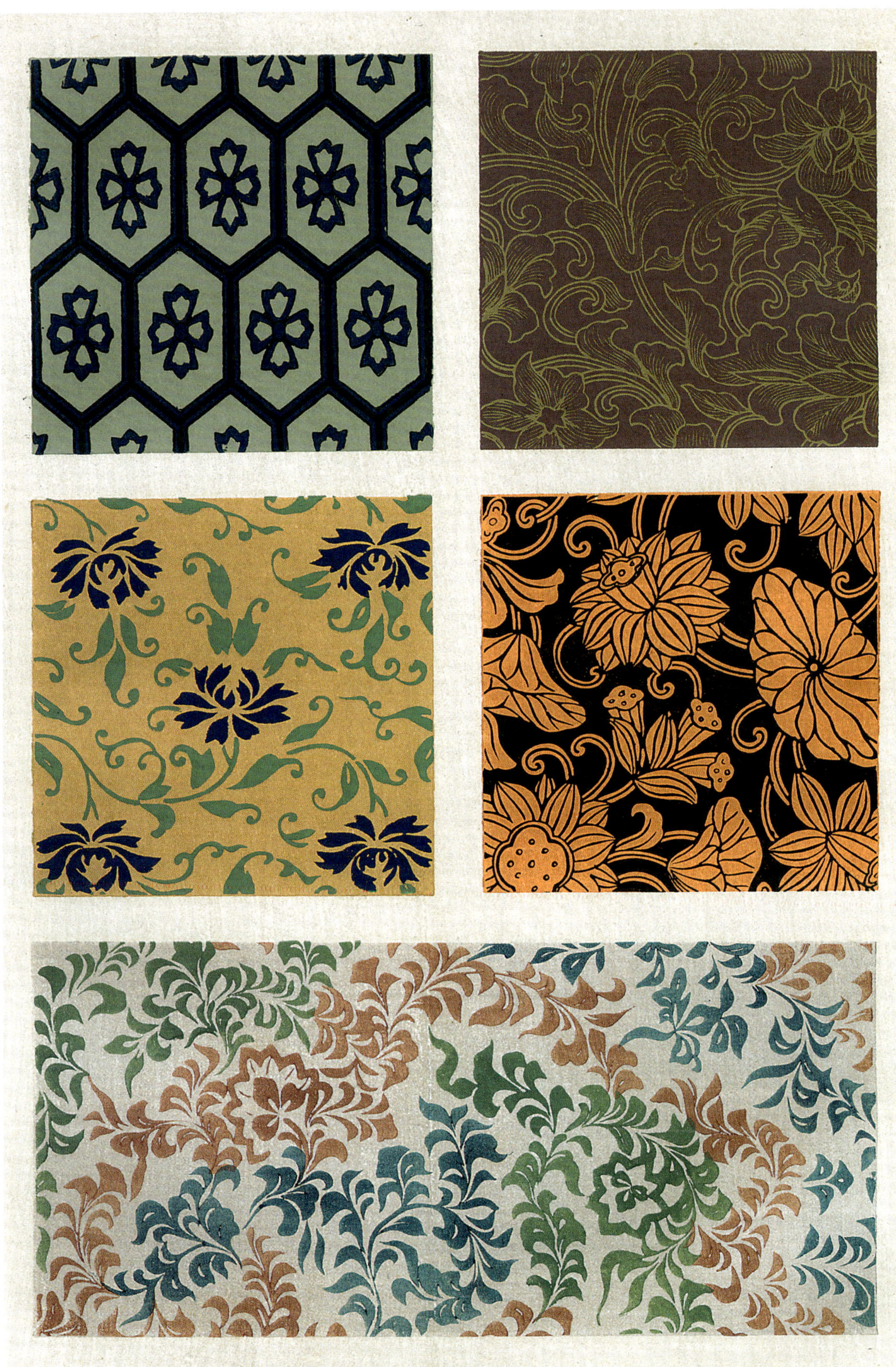

Plate 55

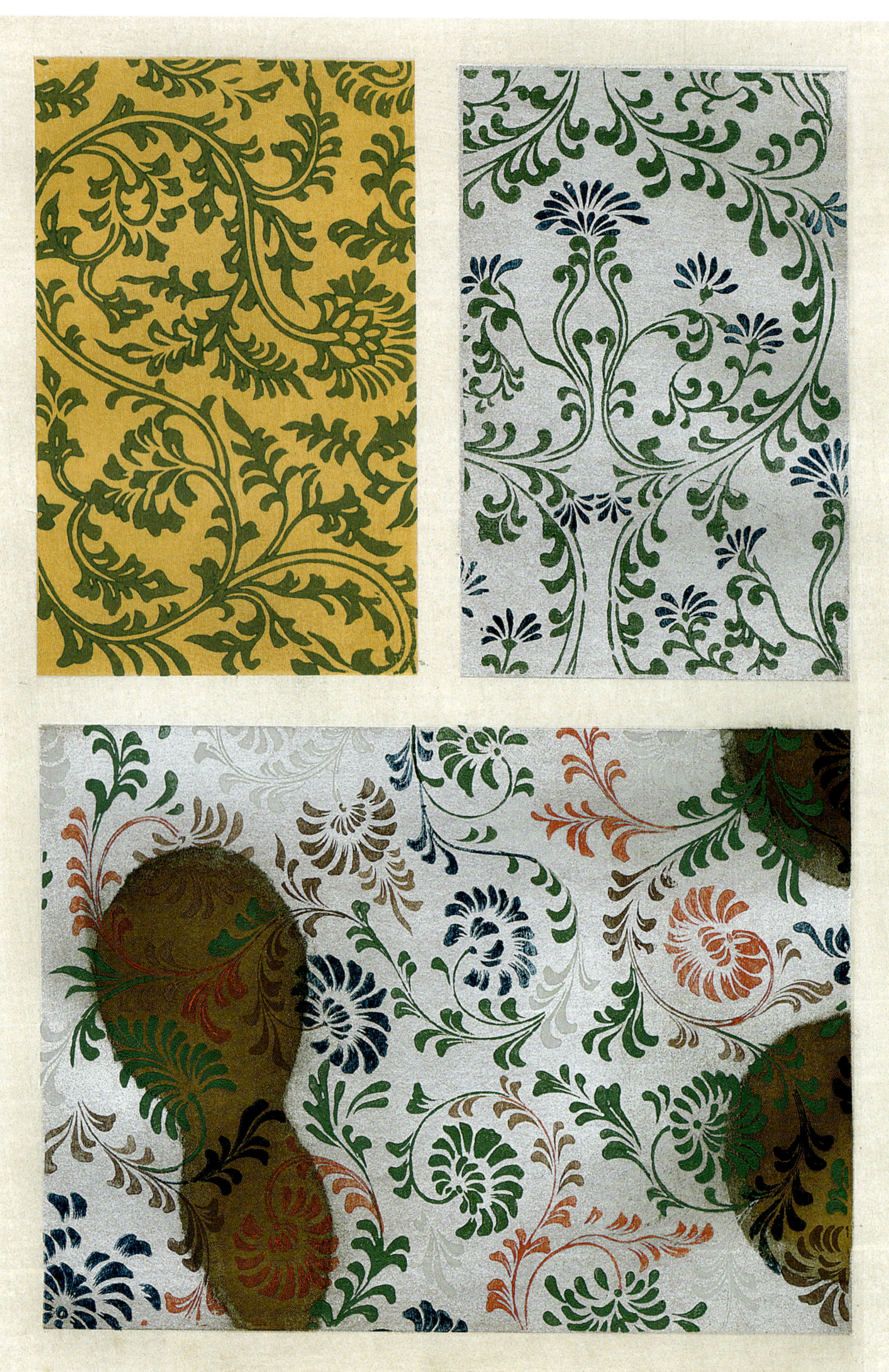

Plate 56

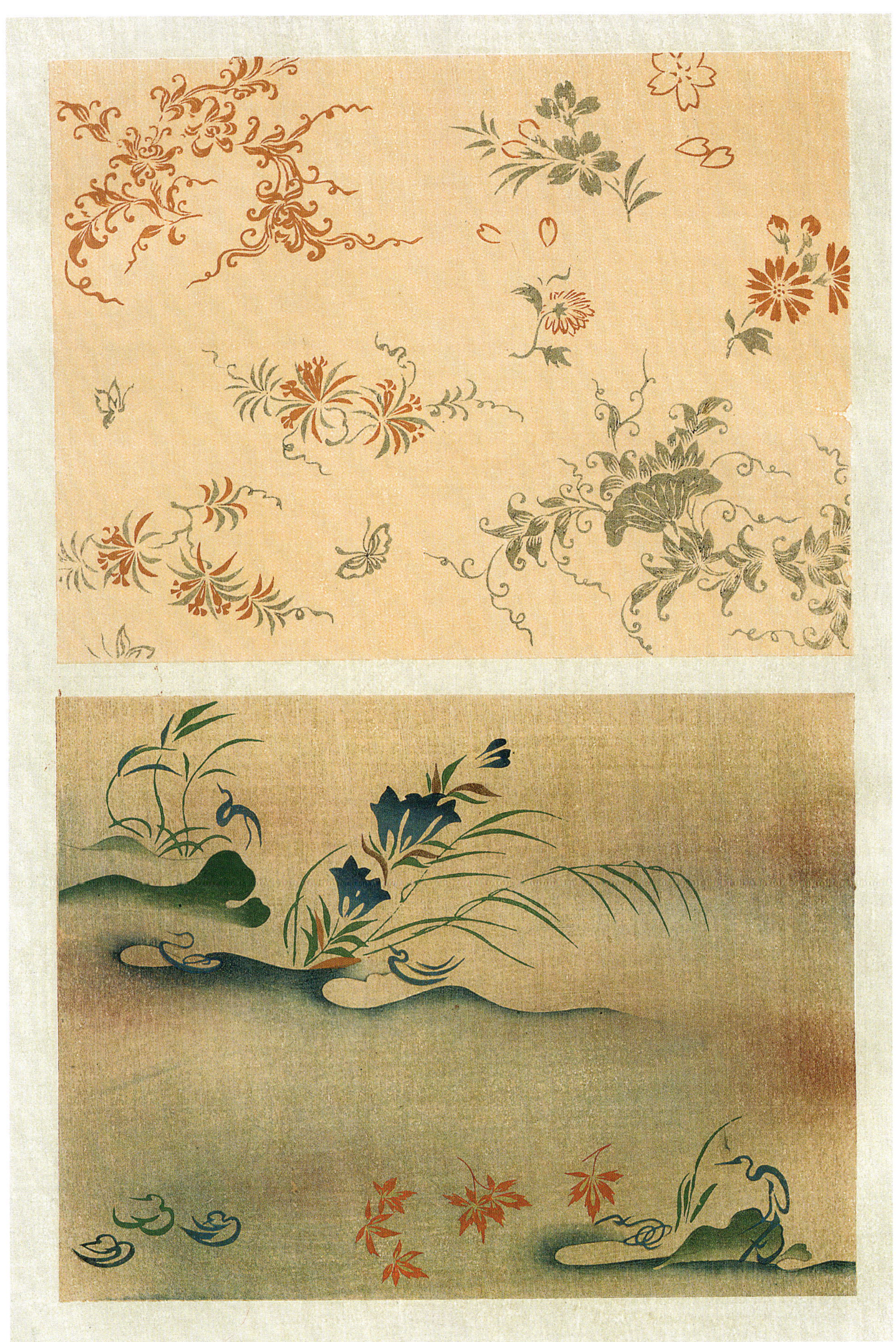

Plate 57

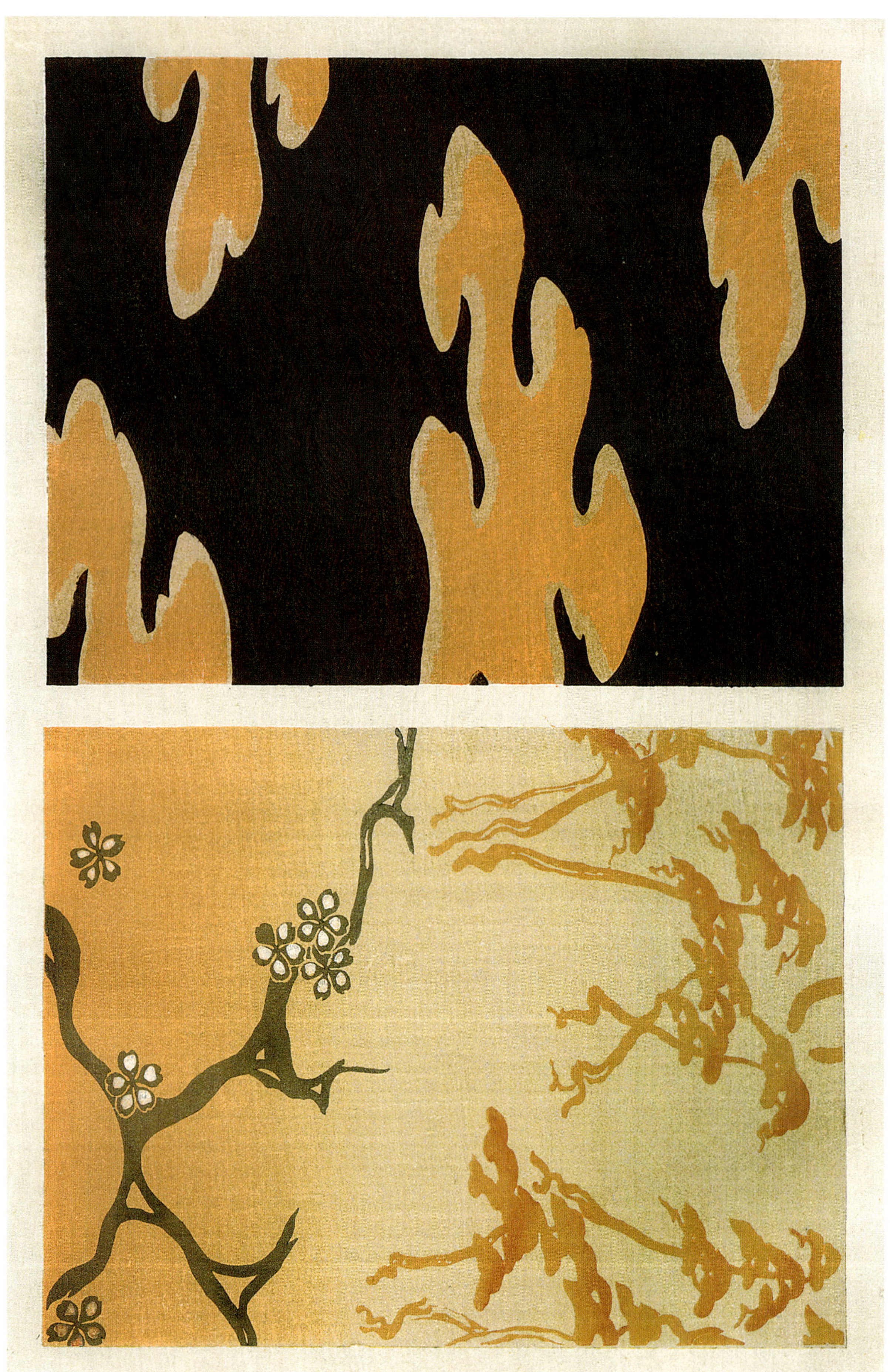

PLATE 58

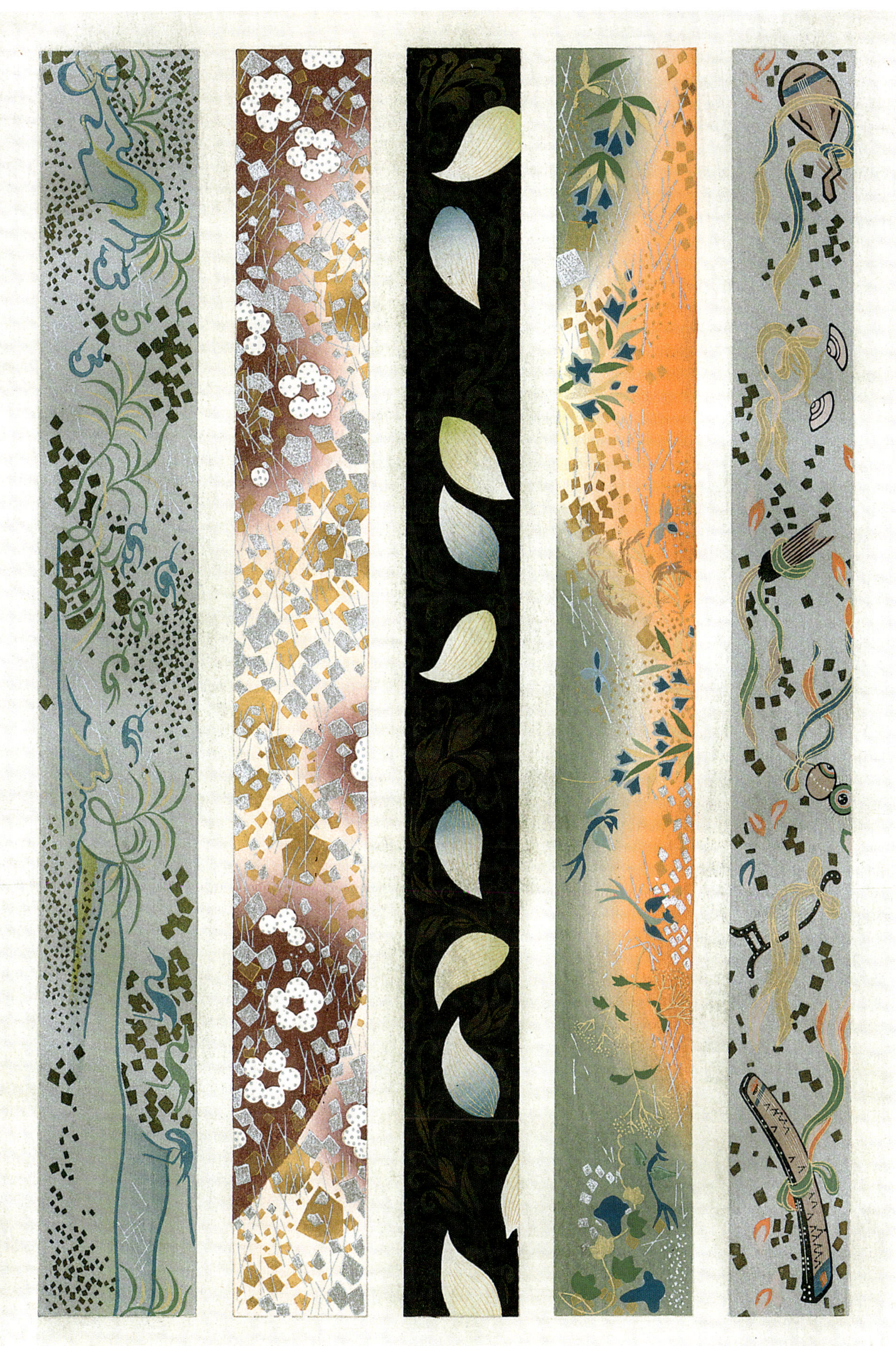

PLATE 59

Plate 60

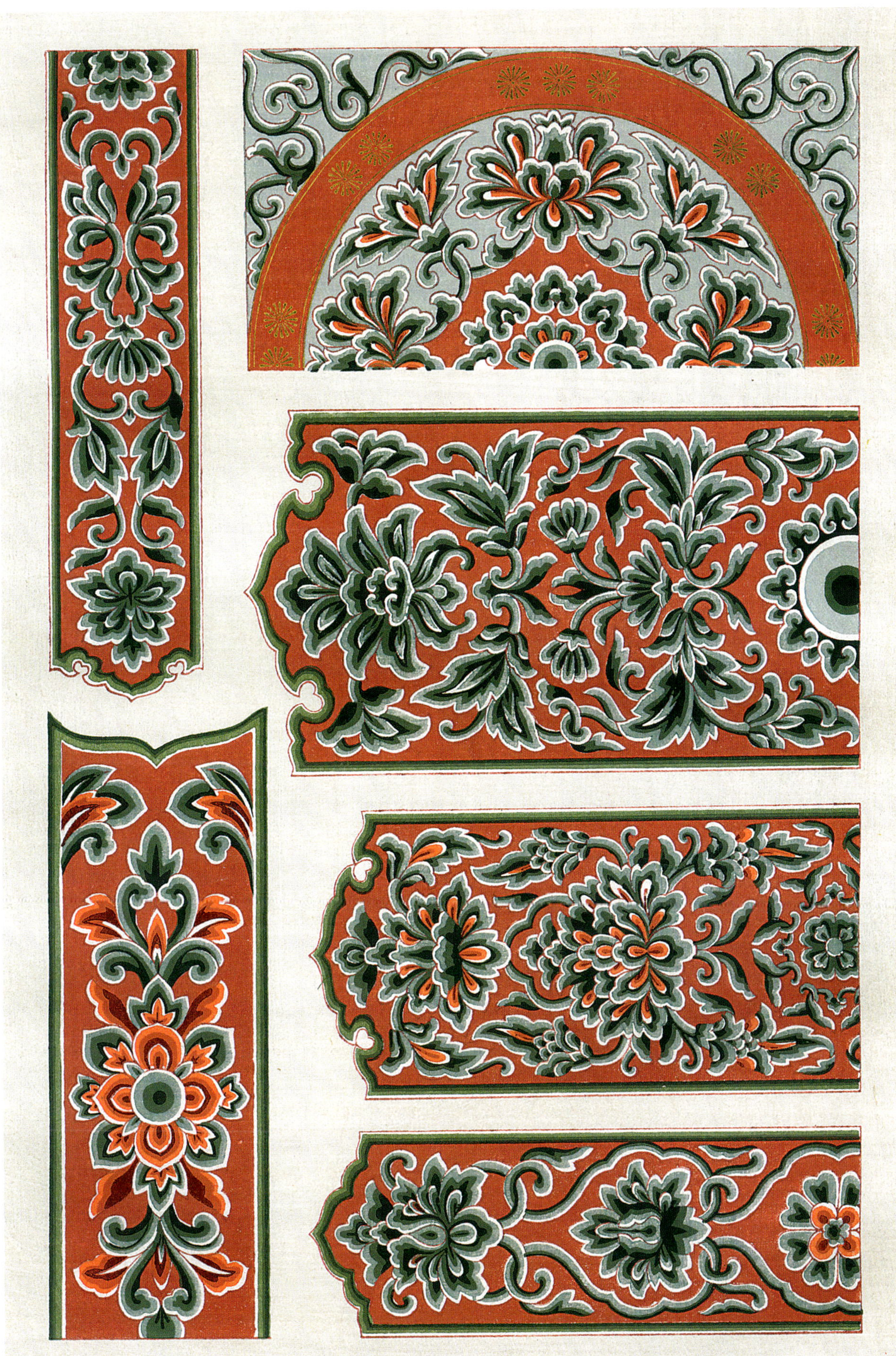

PLATE 61

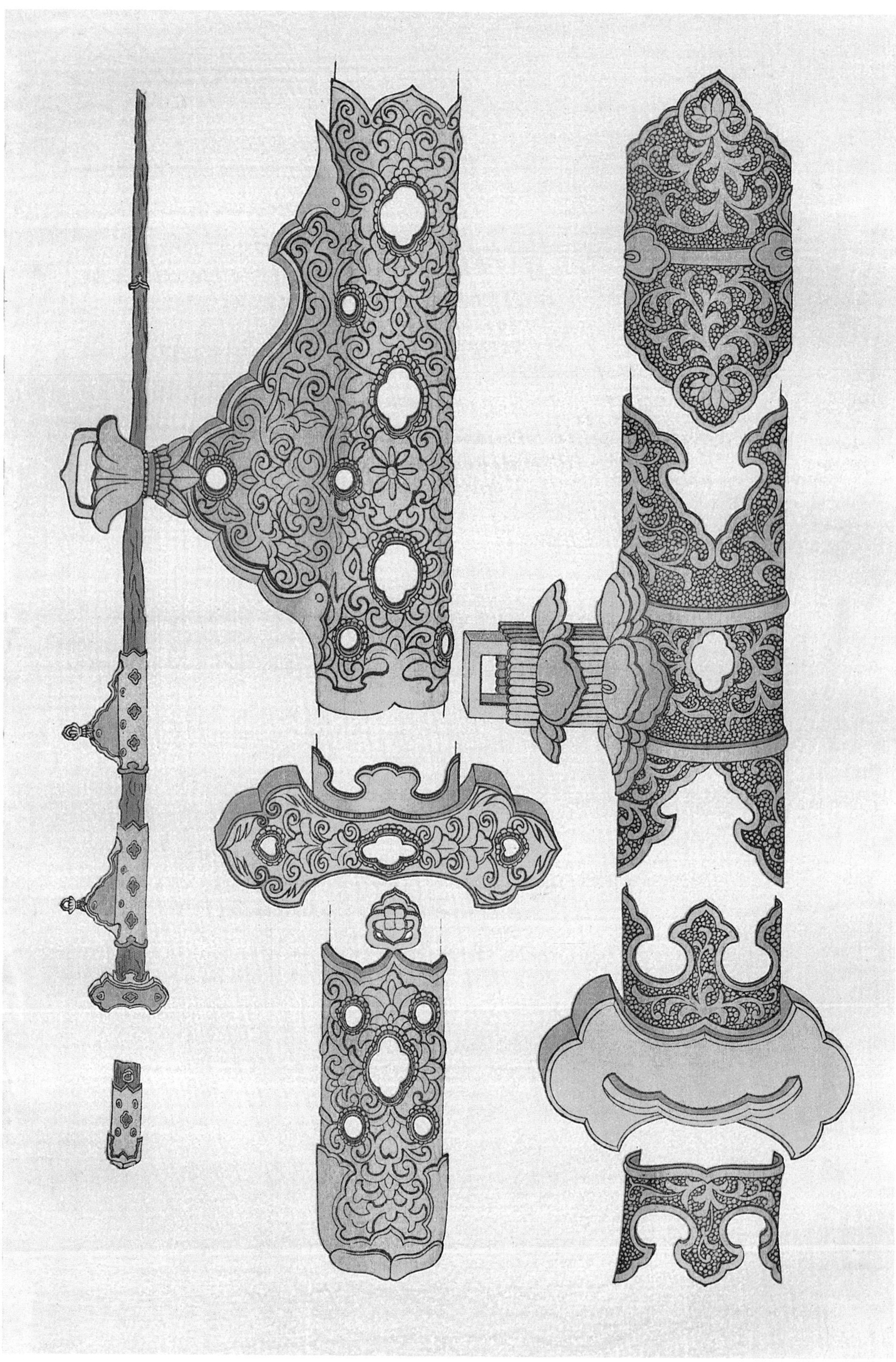

Plate 62

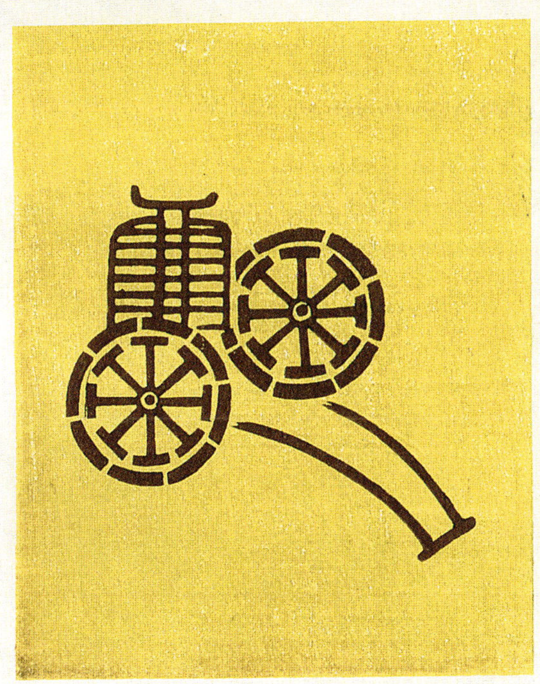

Plate 63

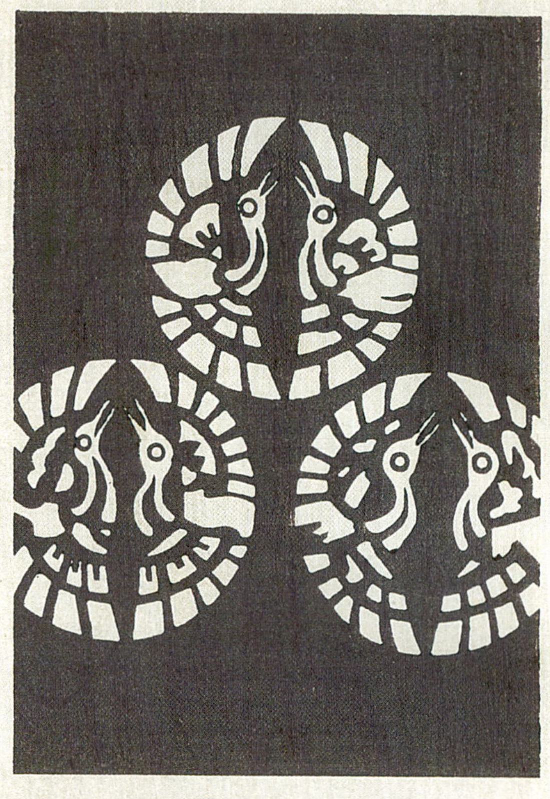
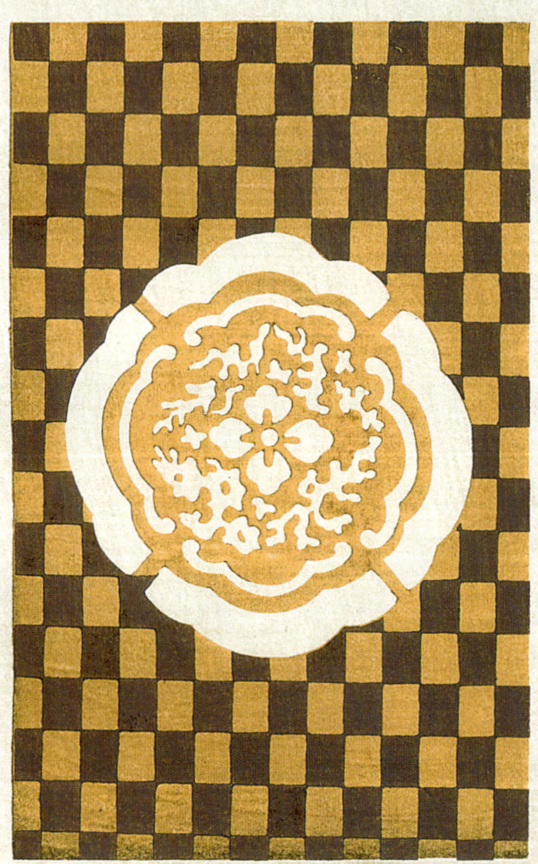
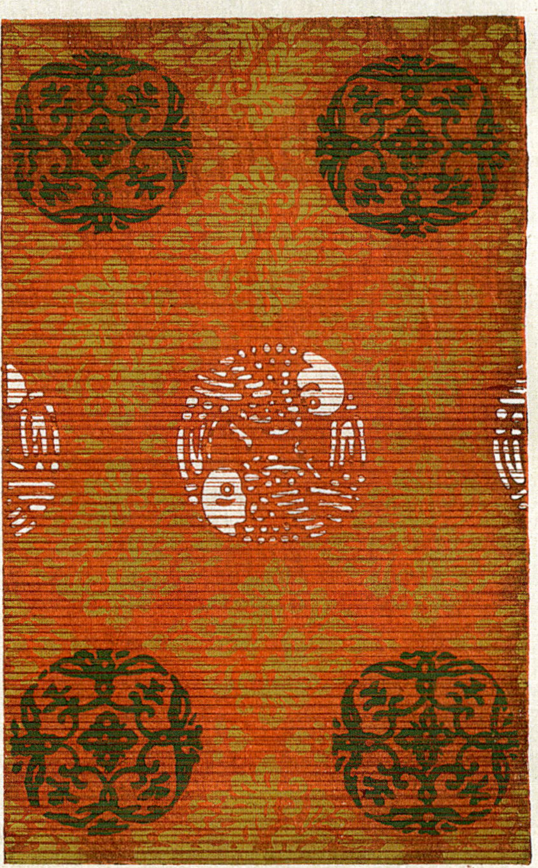

Plate 64

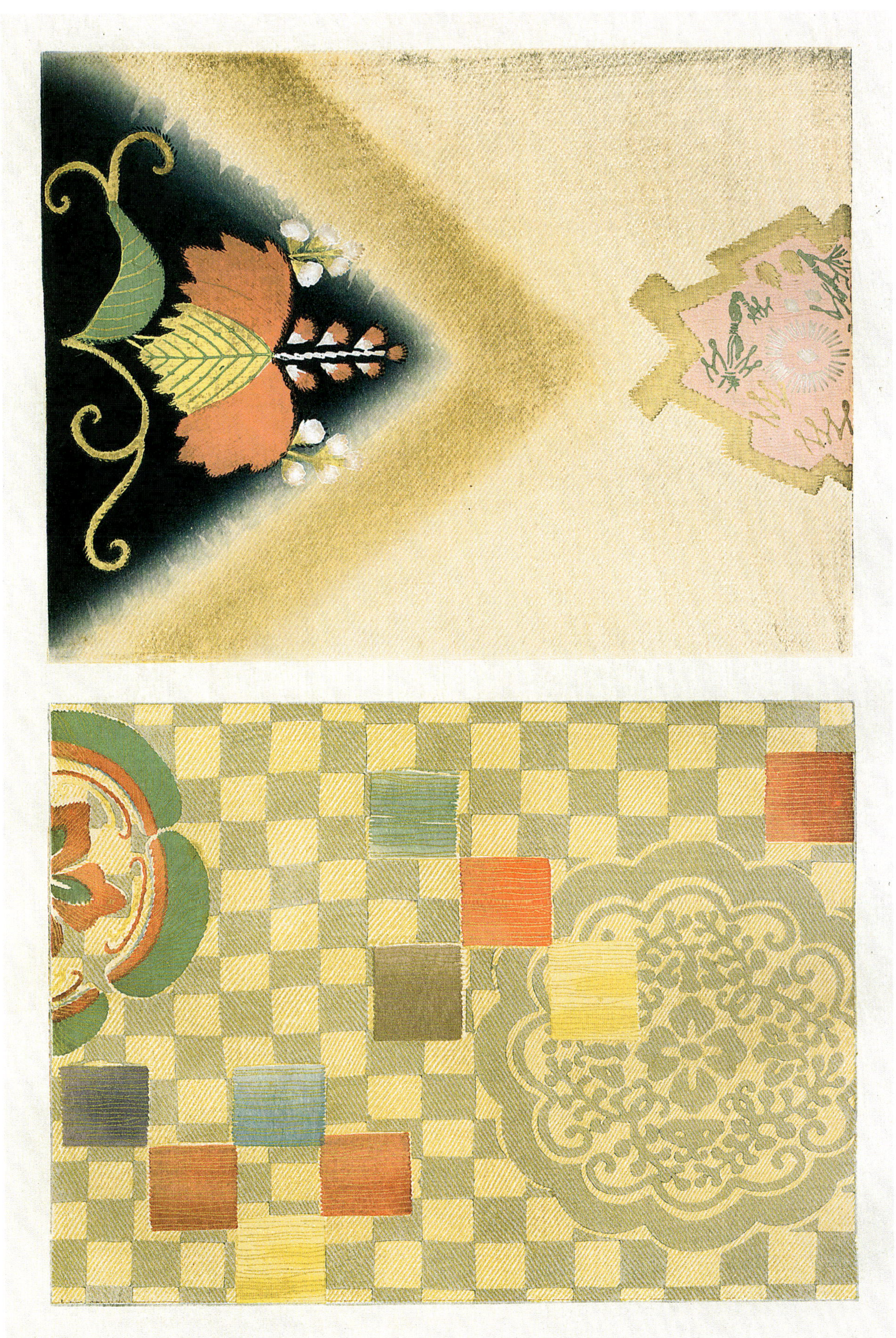

PLATE 65

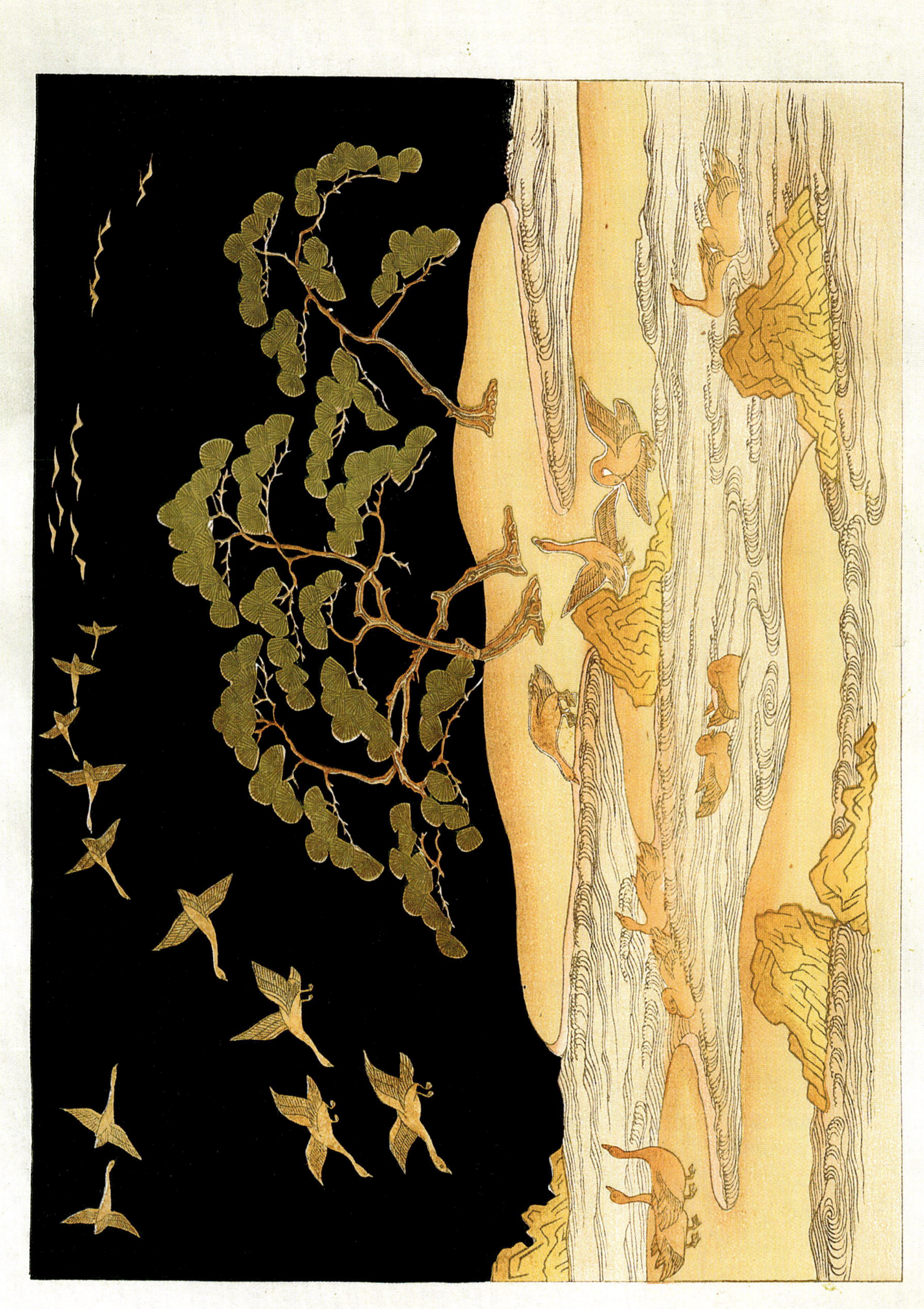

PLATE 66

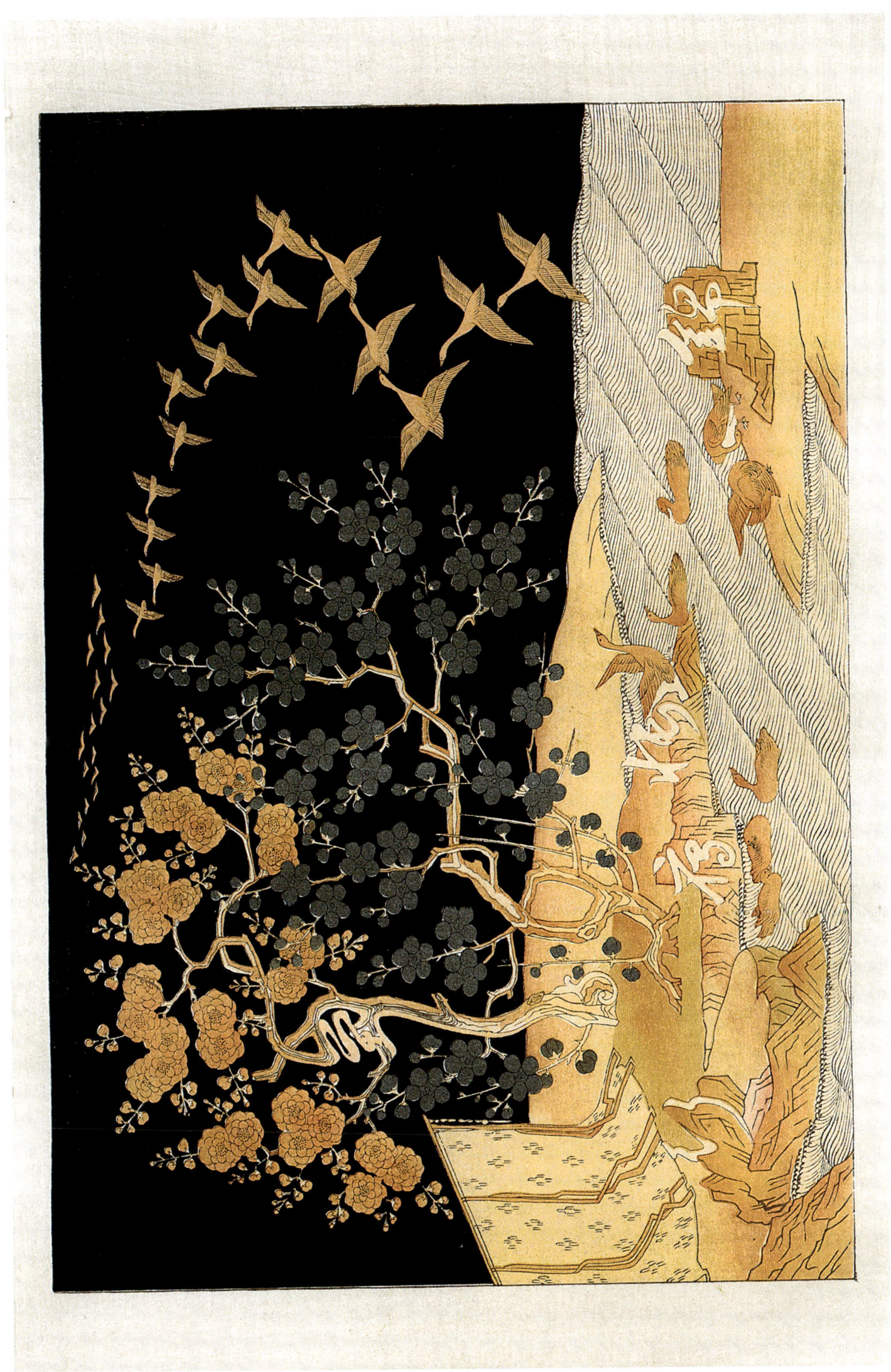

PLATE 67

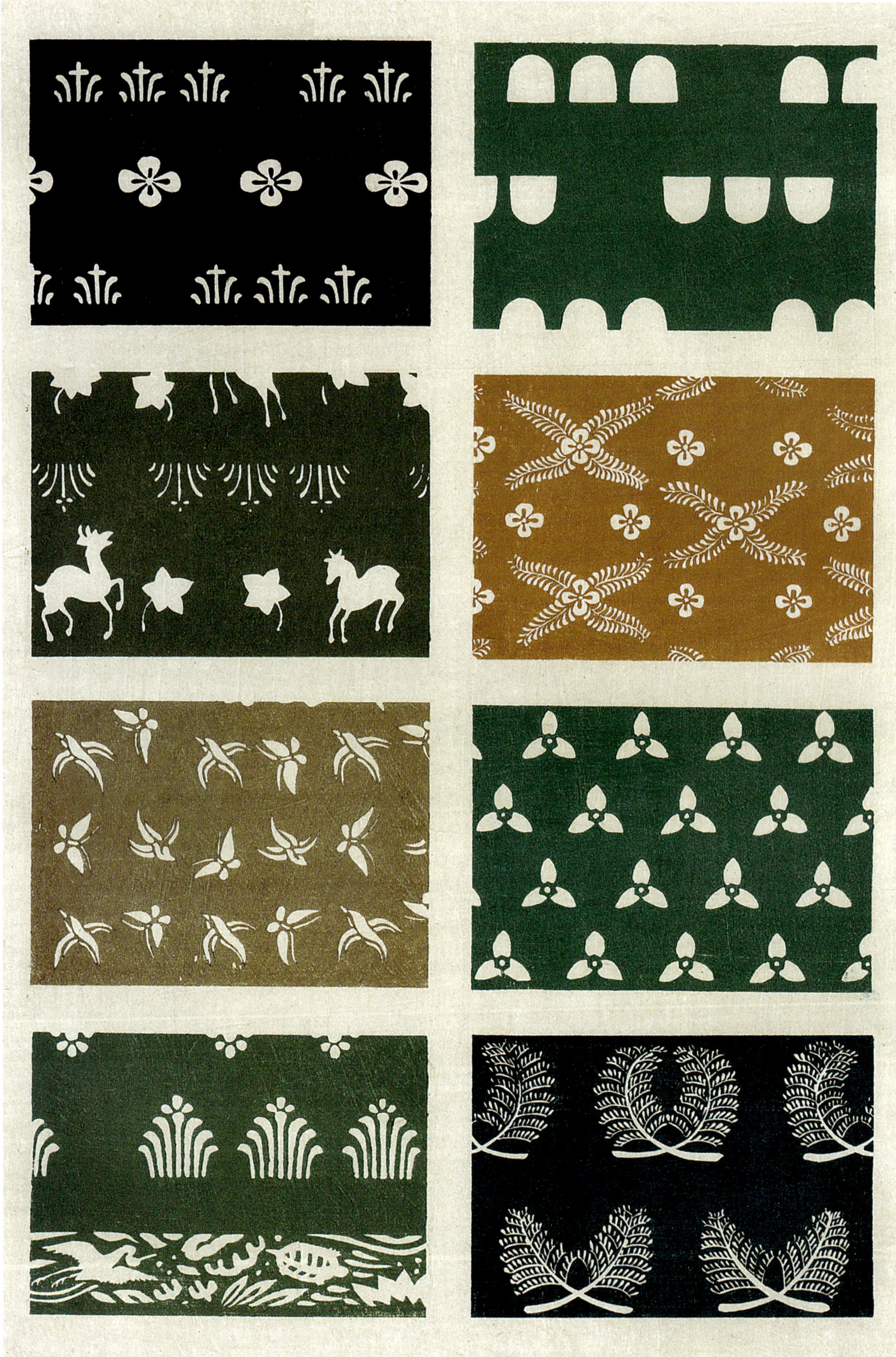

Plate 68

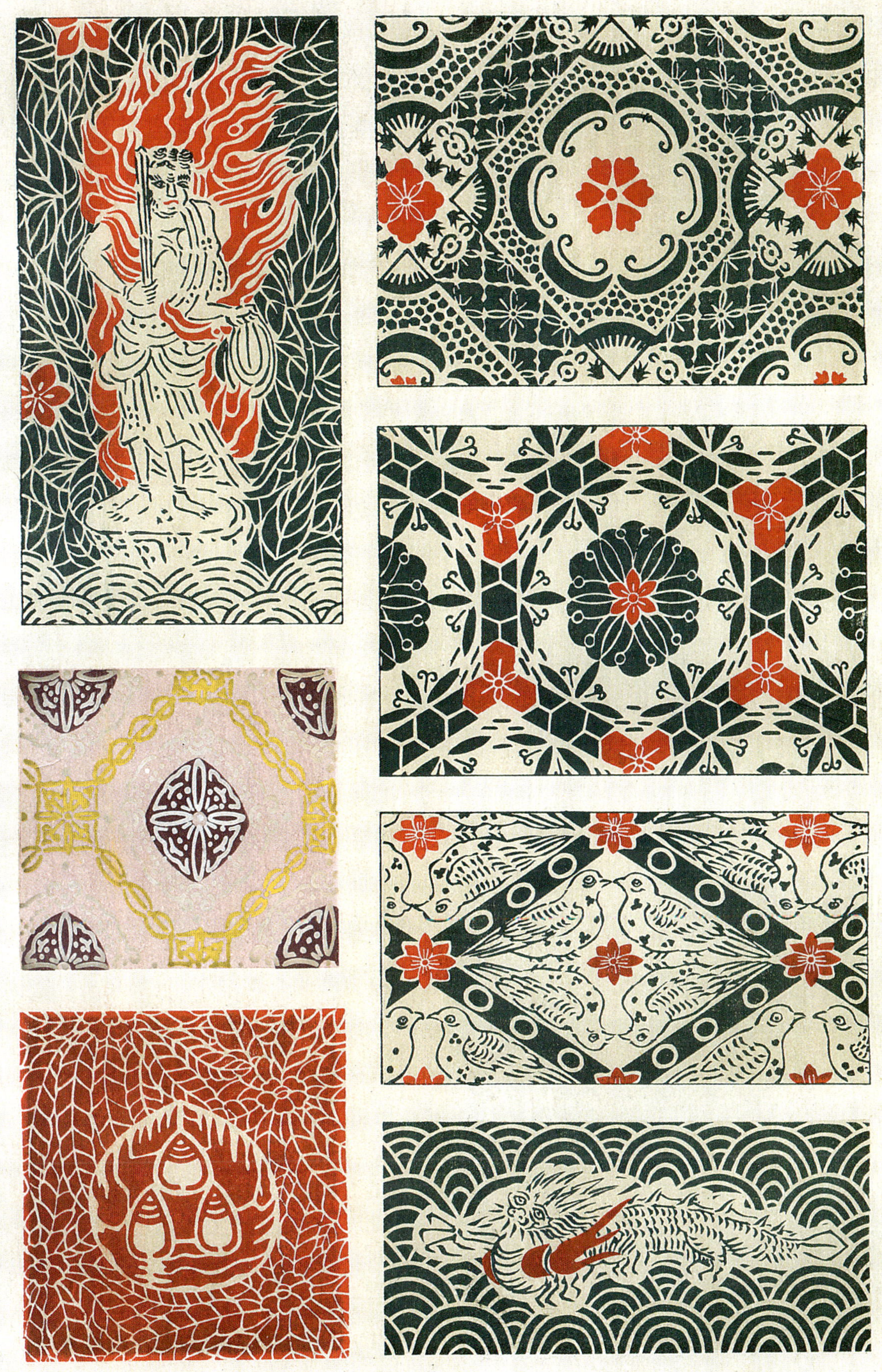

Plate 69

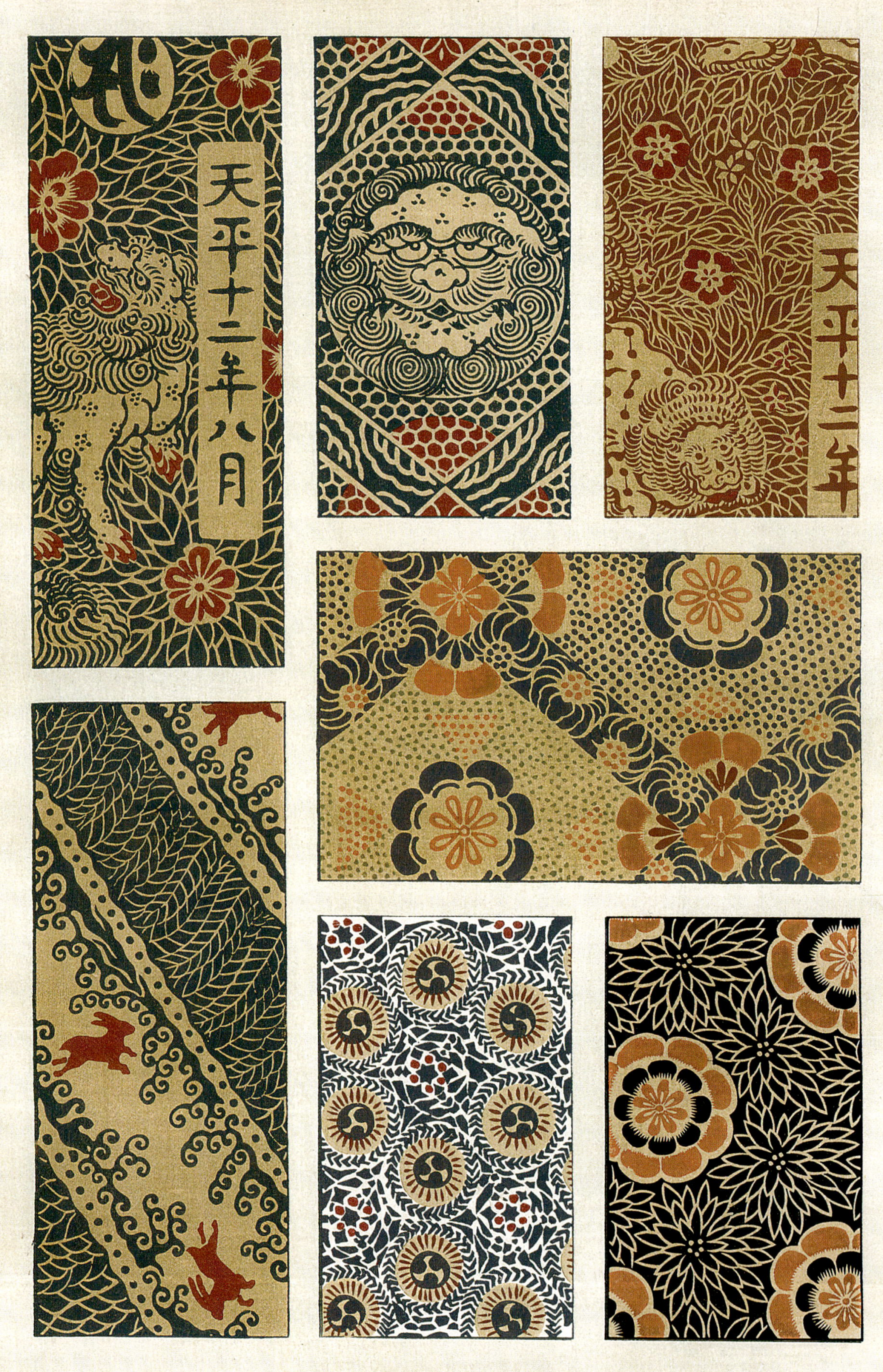

Plate 70

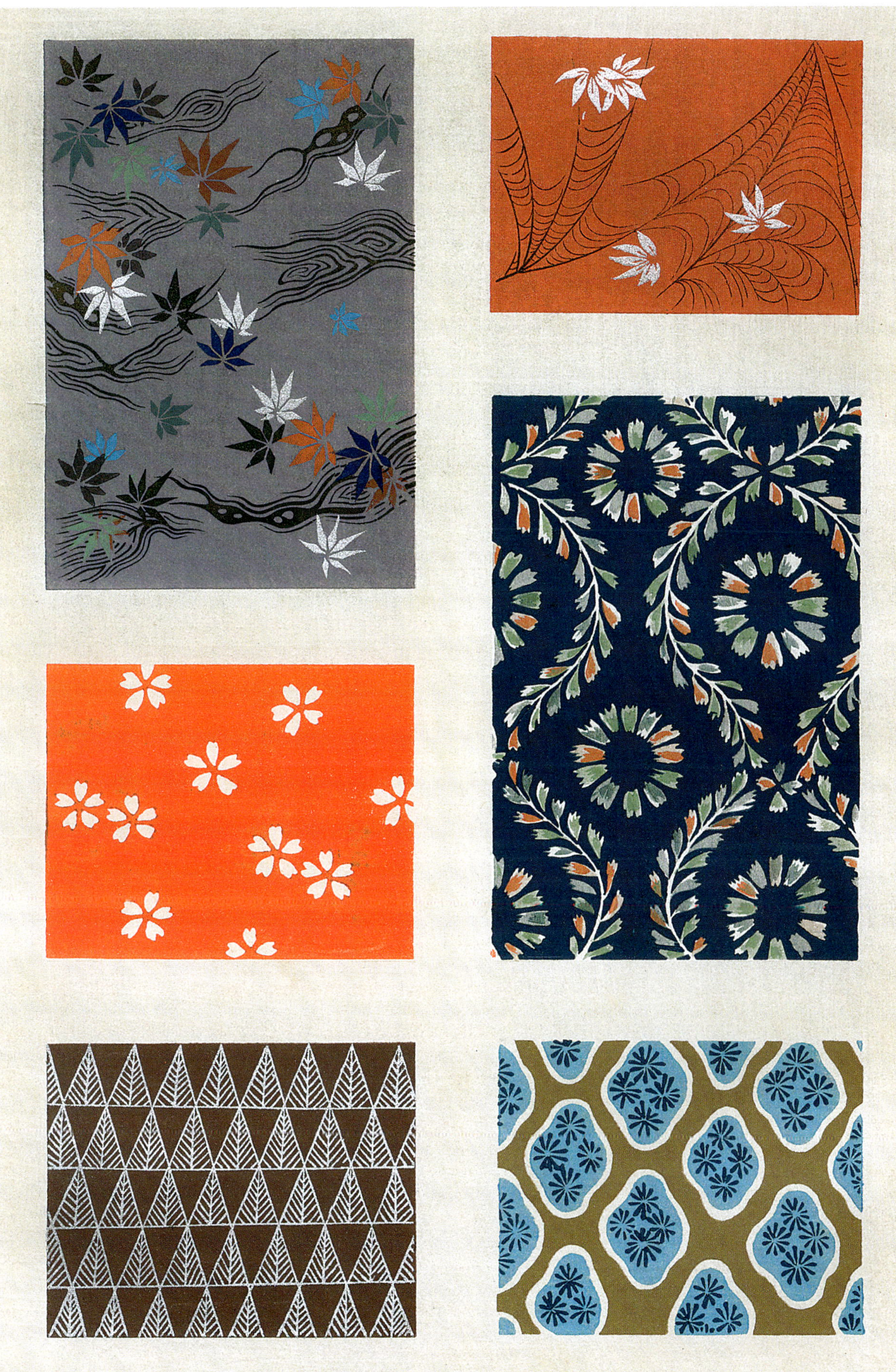

PLATE 71

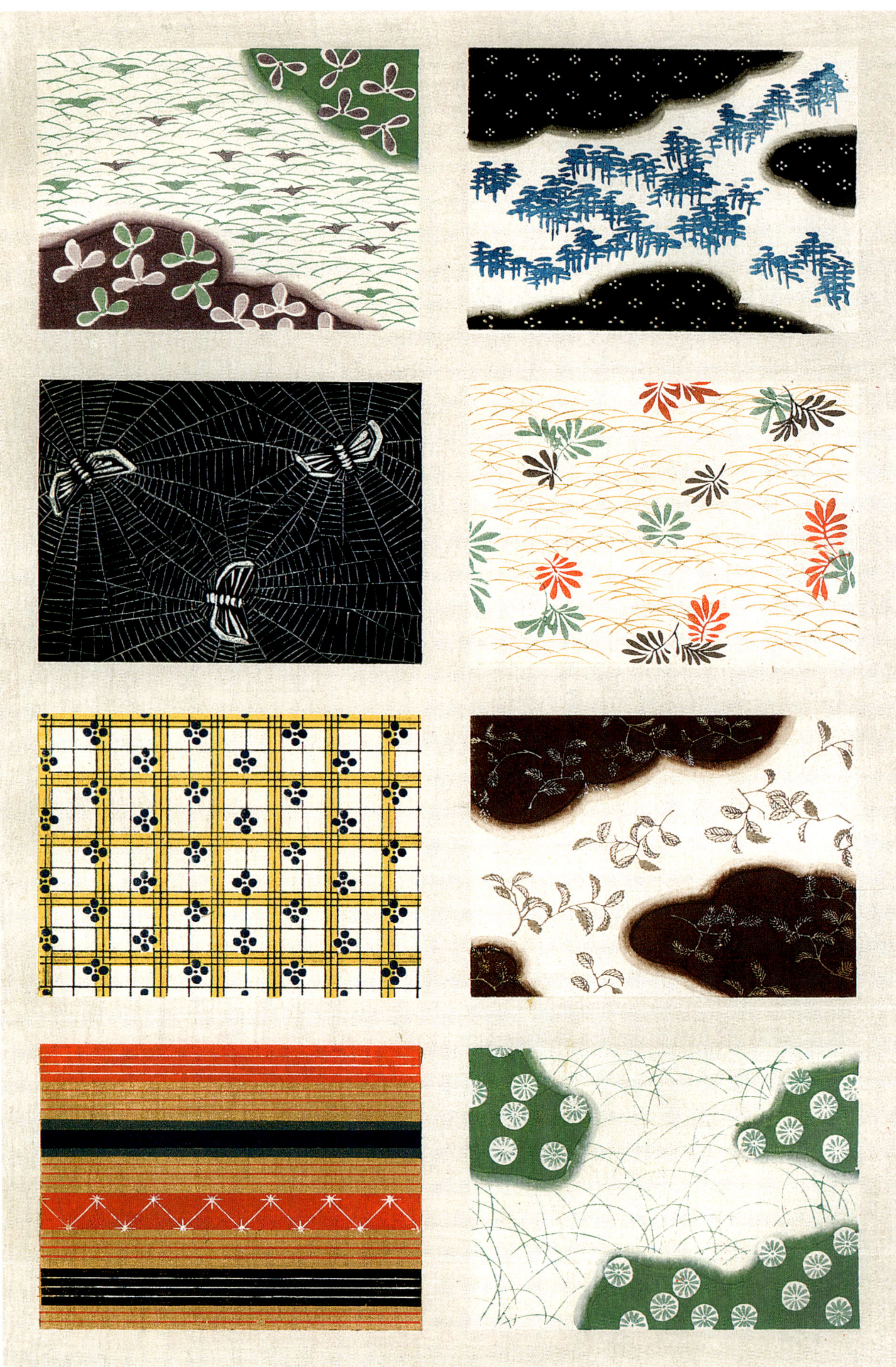

Plate 72

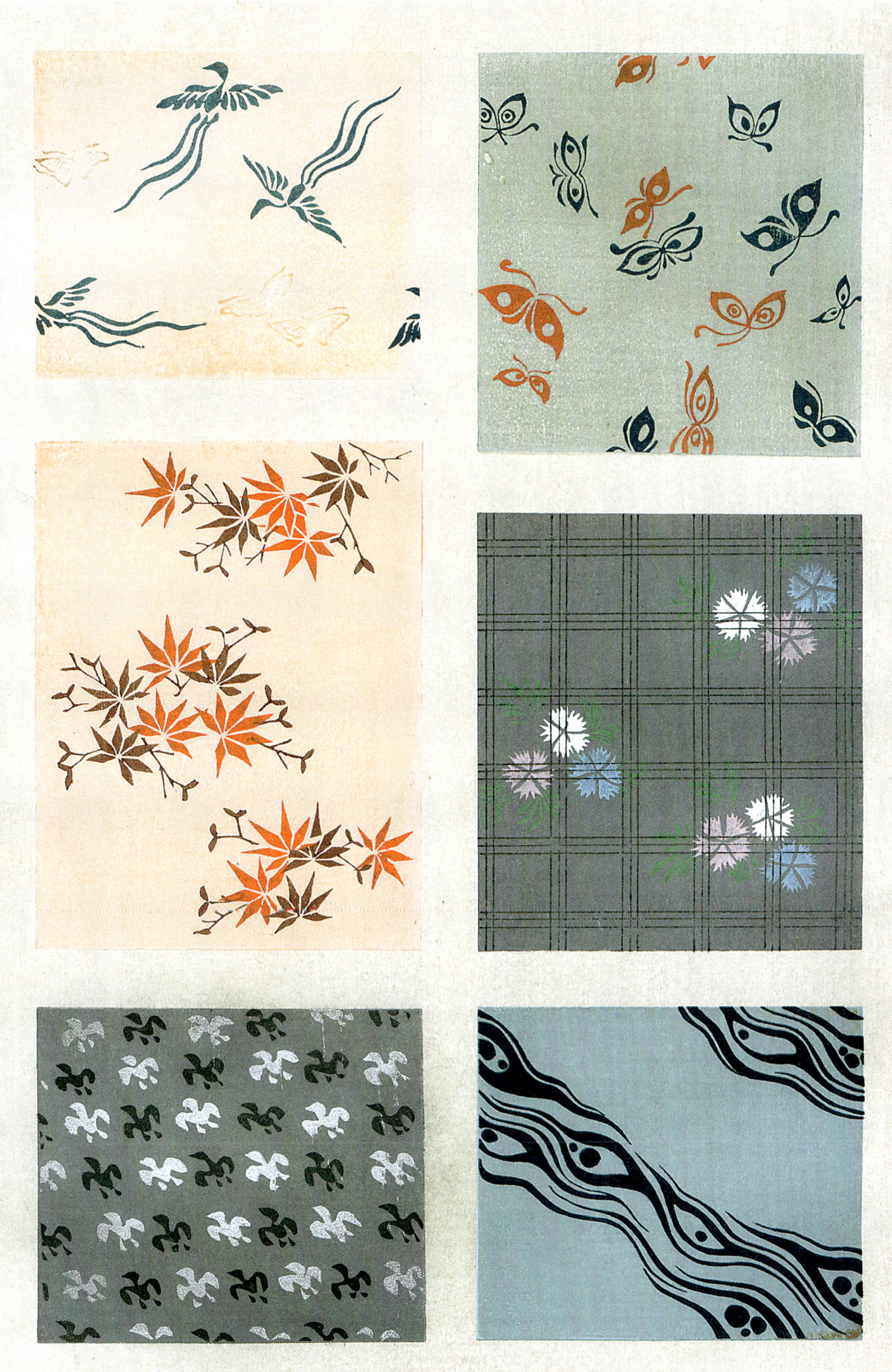

Plate 73

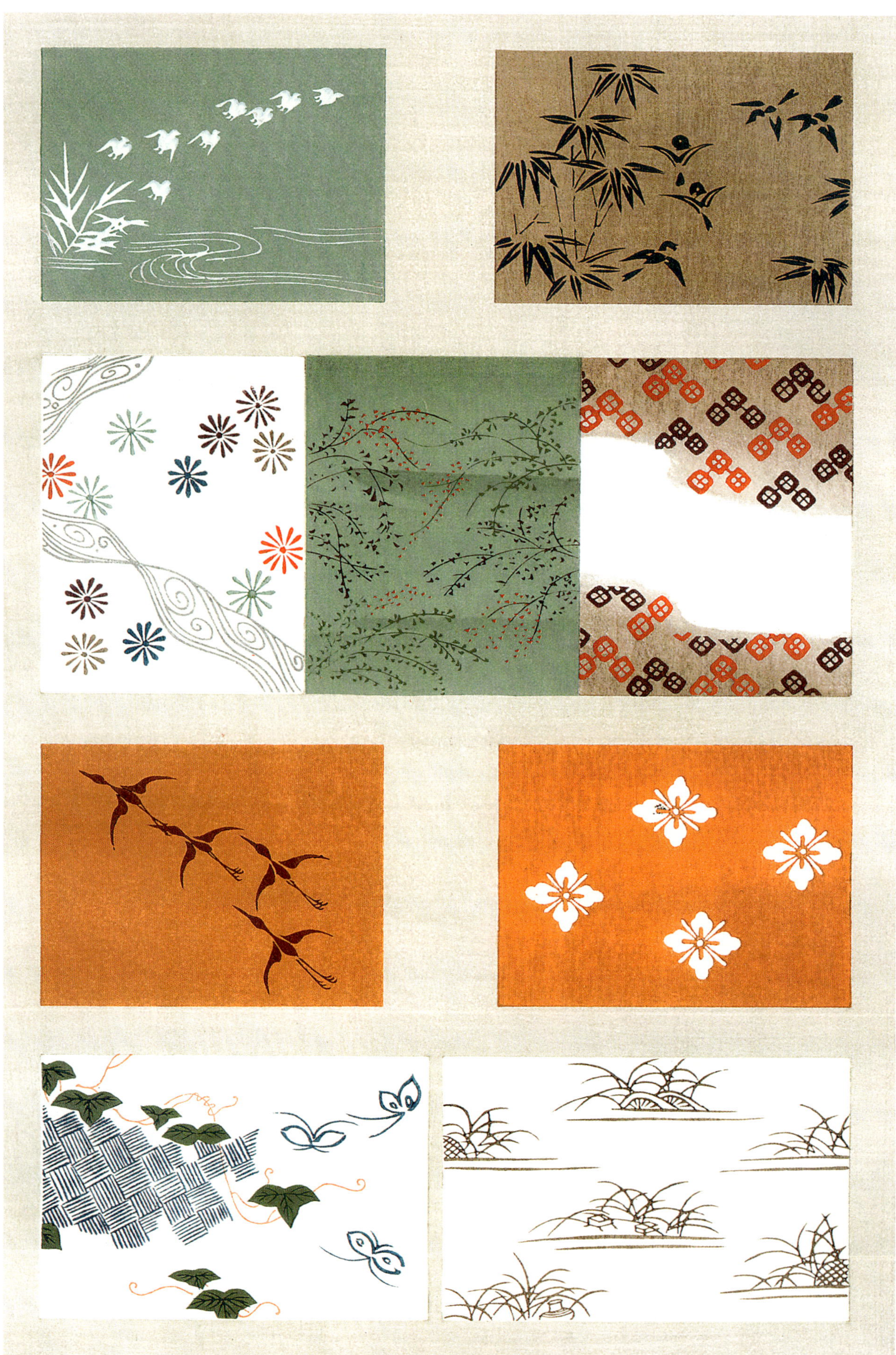

PLATE 74

Plate 75

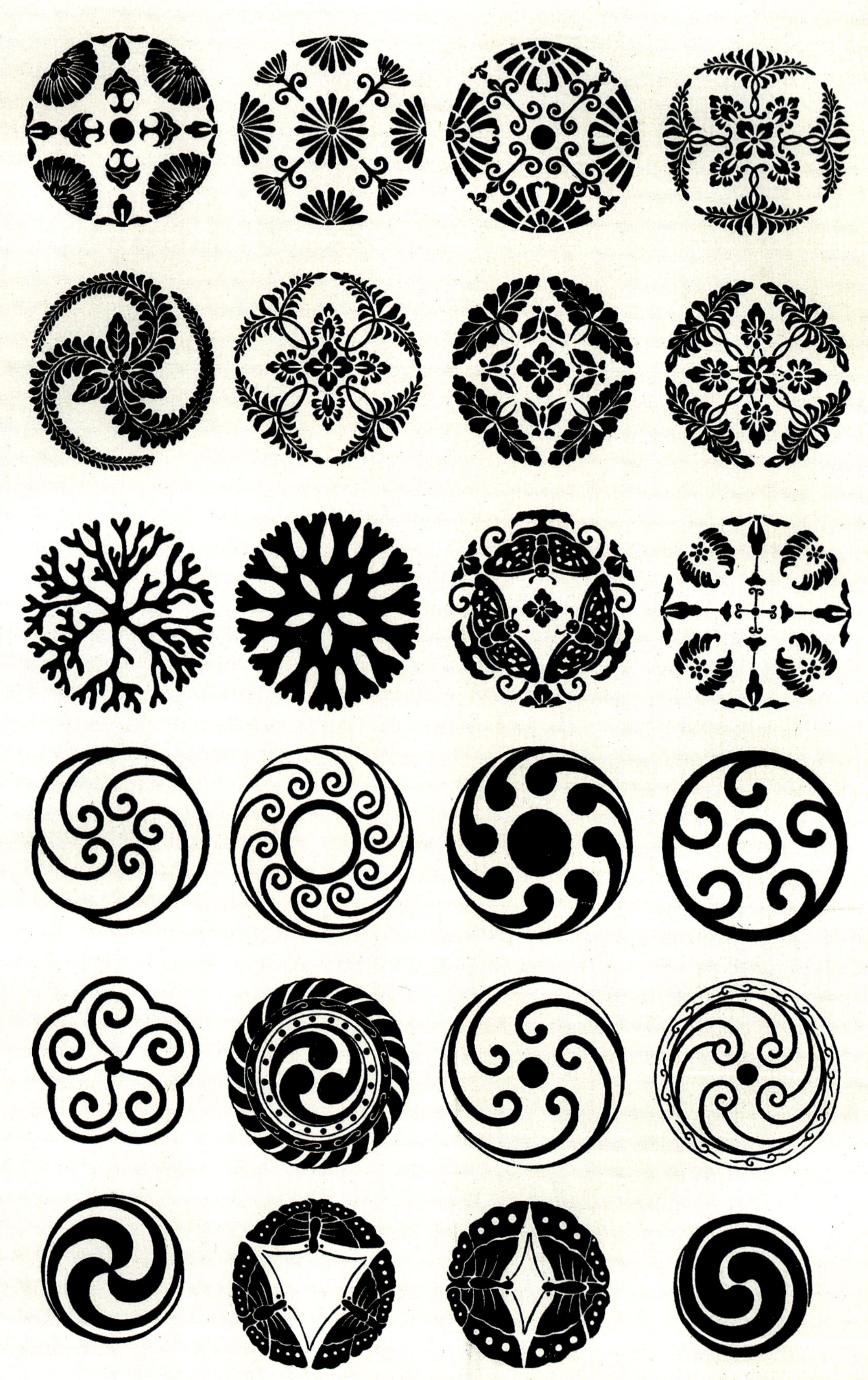

Plate 76

Plate 77

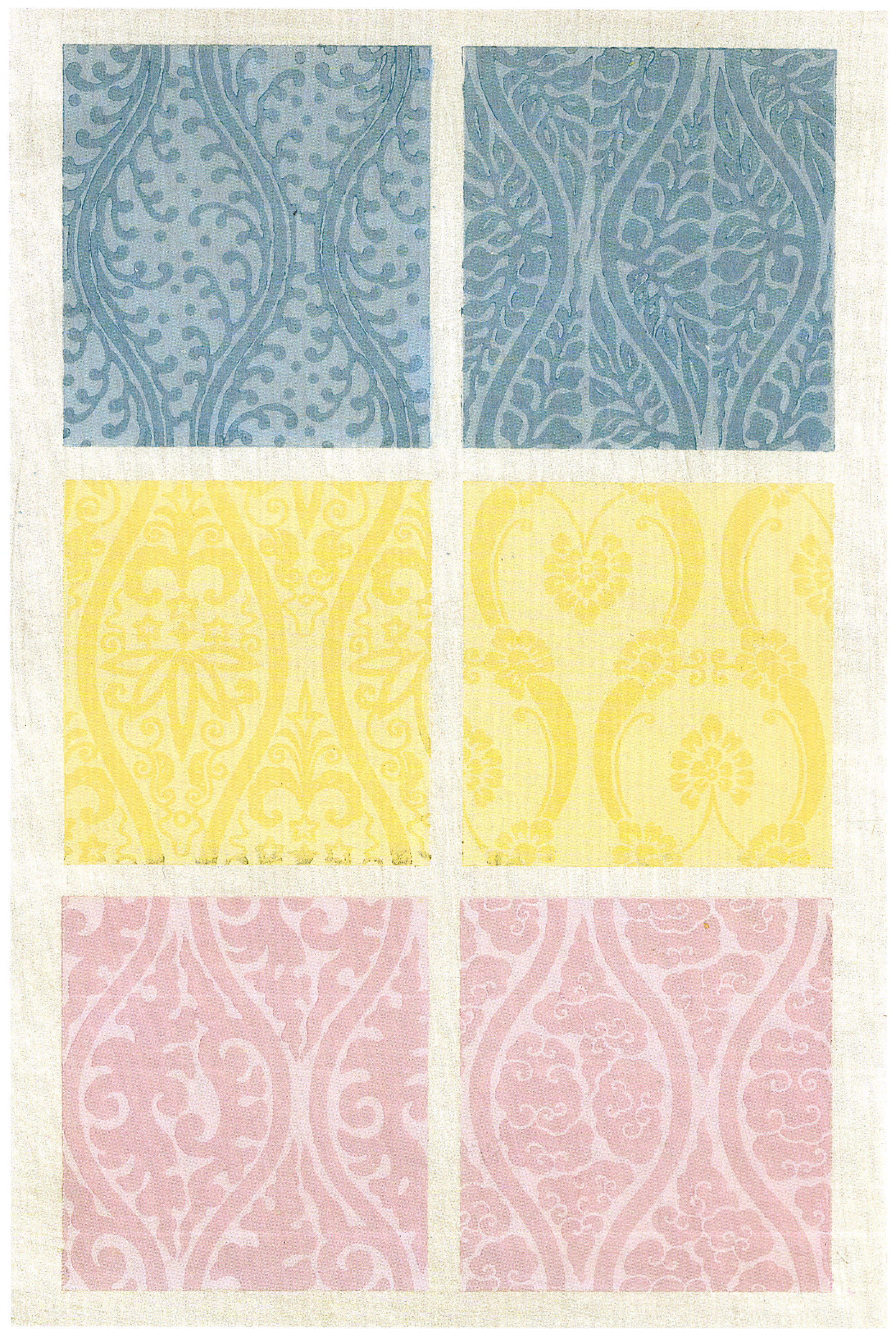

Plate 78

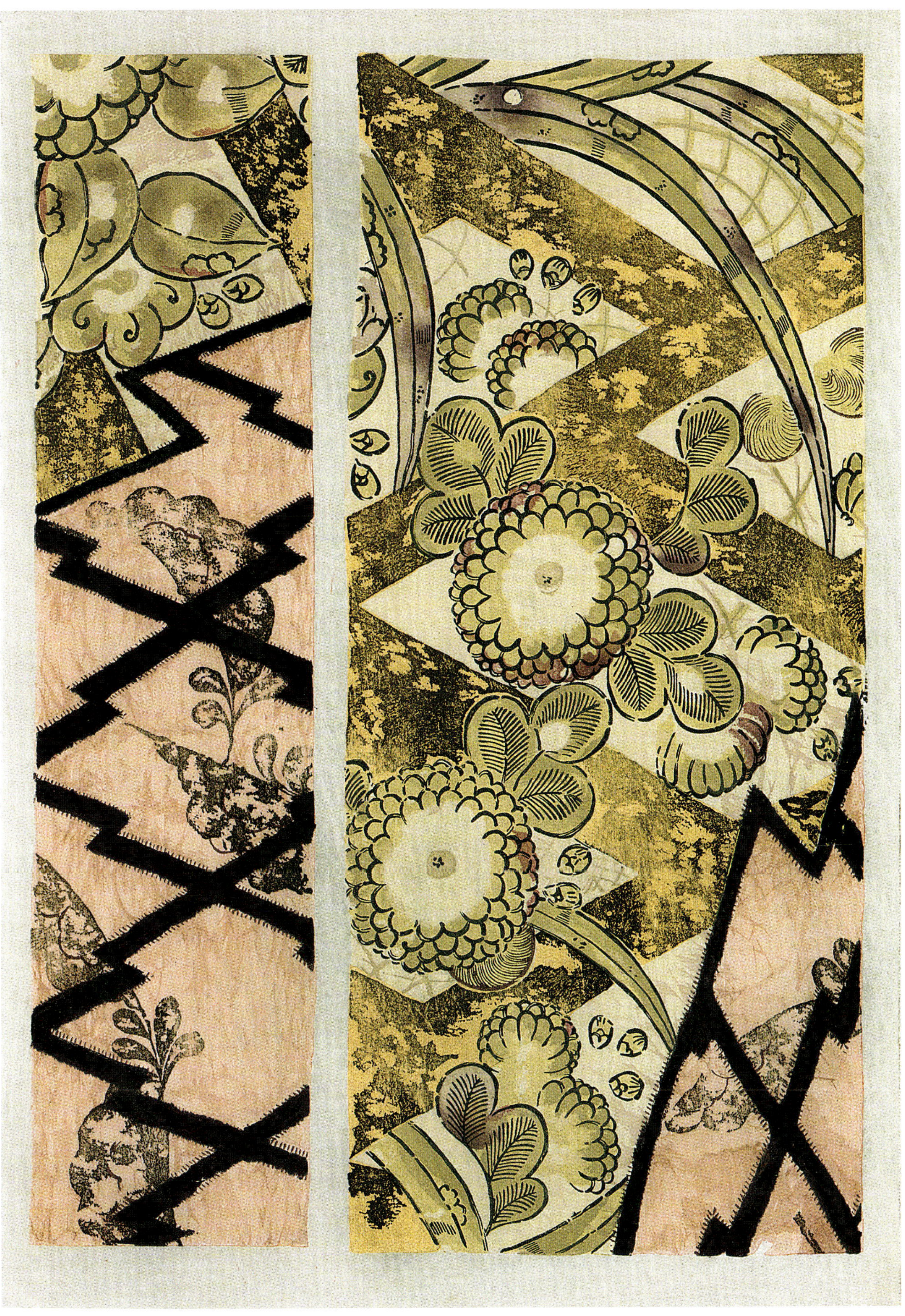

PLATE 79

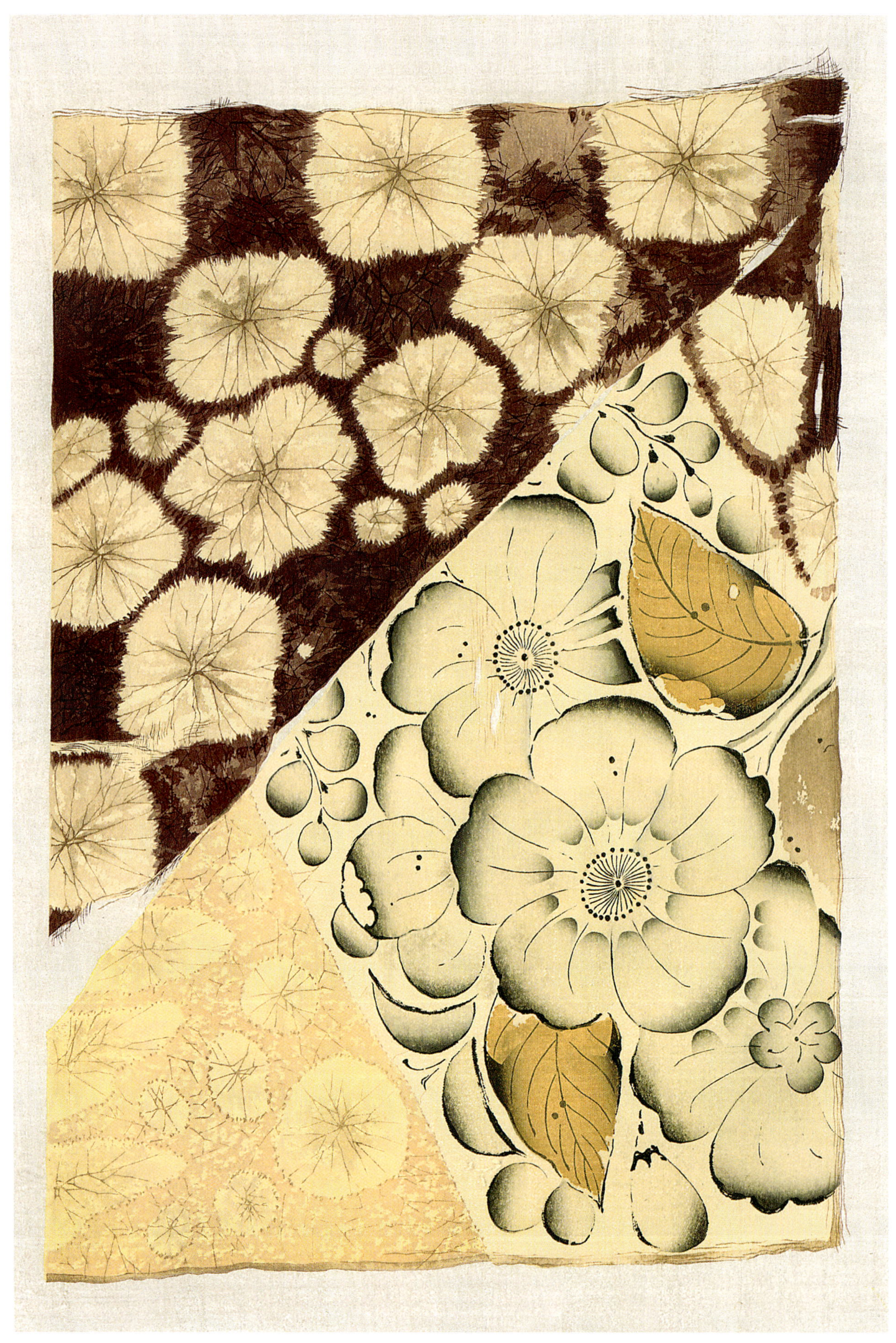

PLATE 80

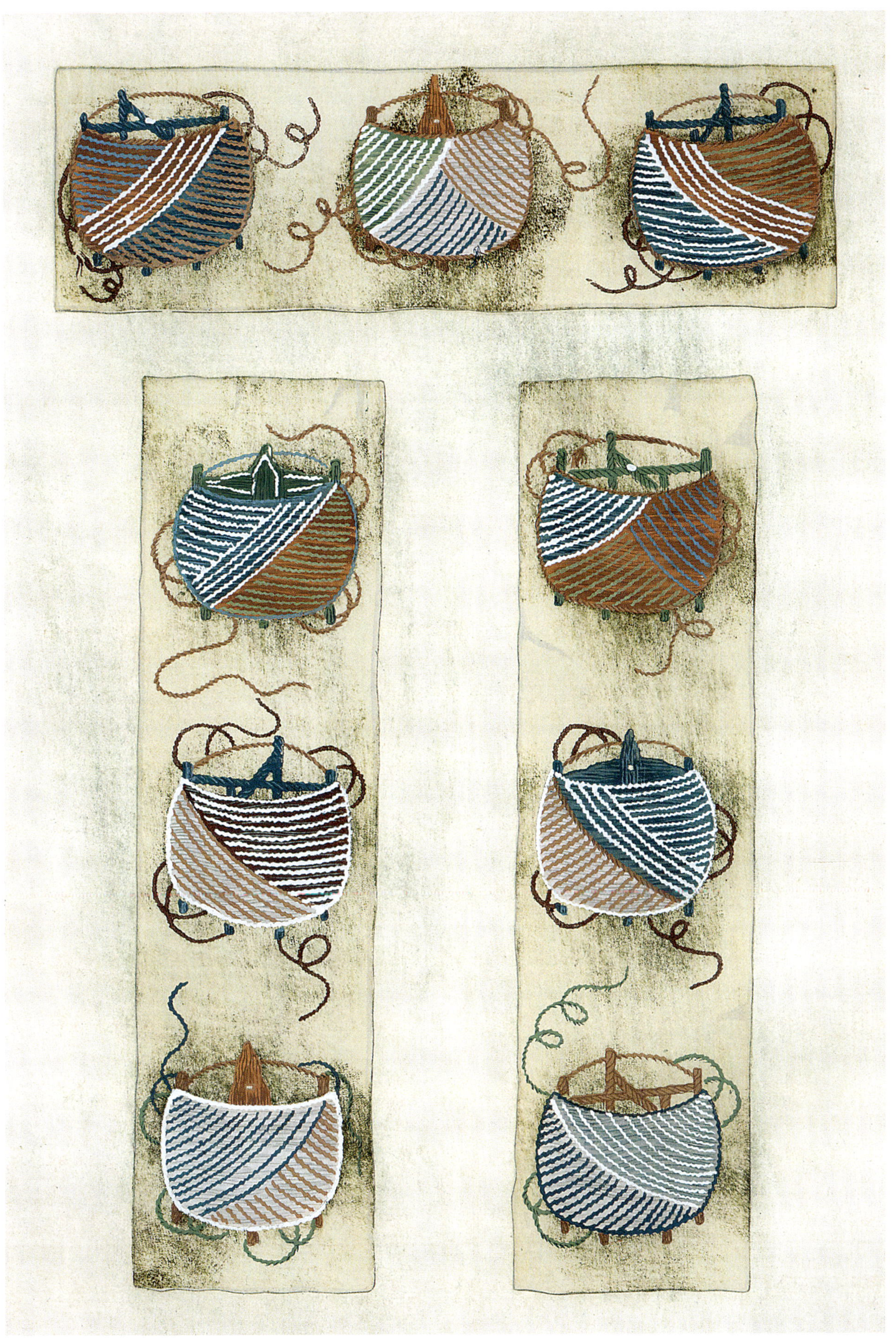

Plate 81

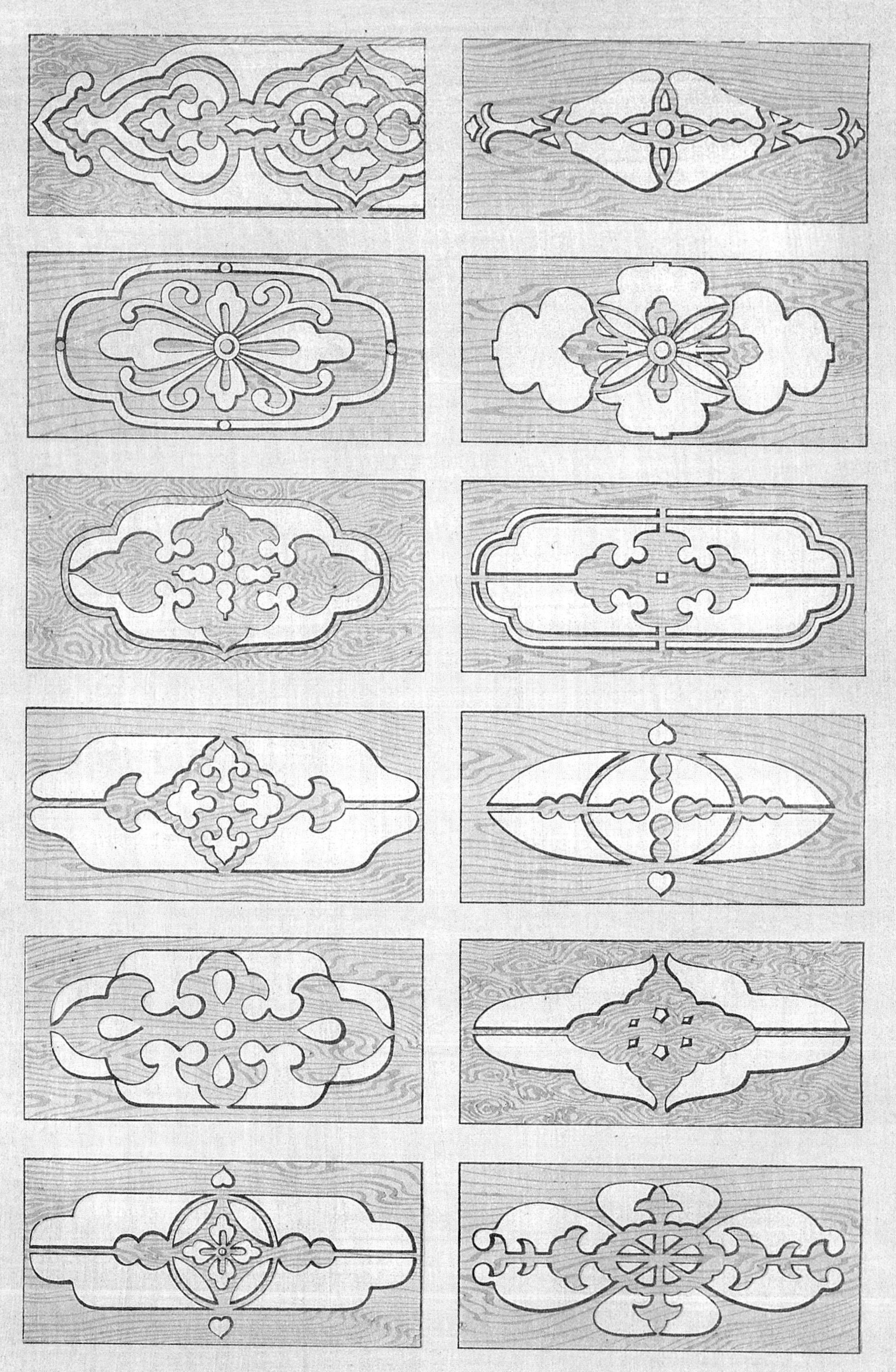

Plate 82

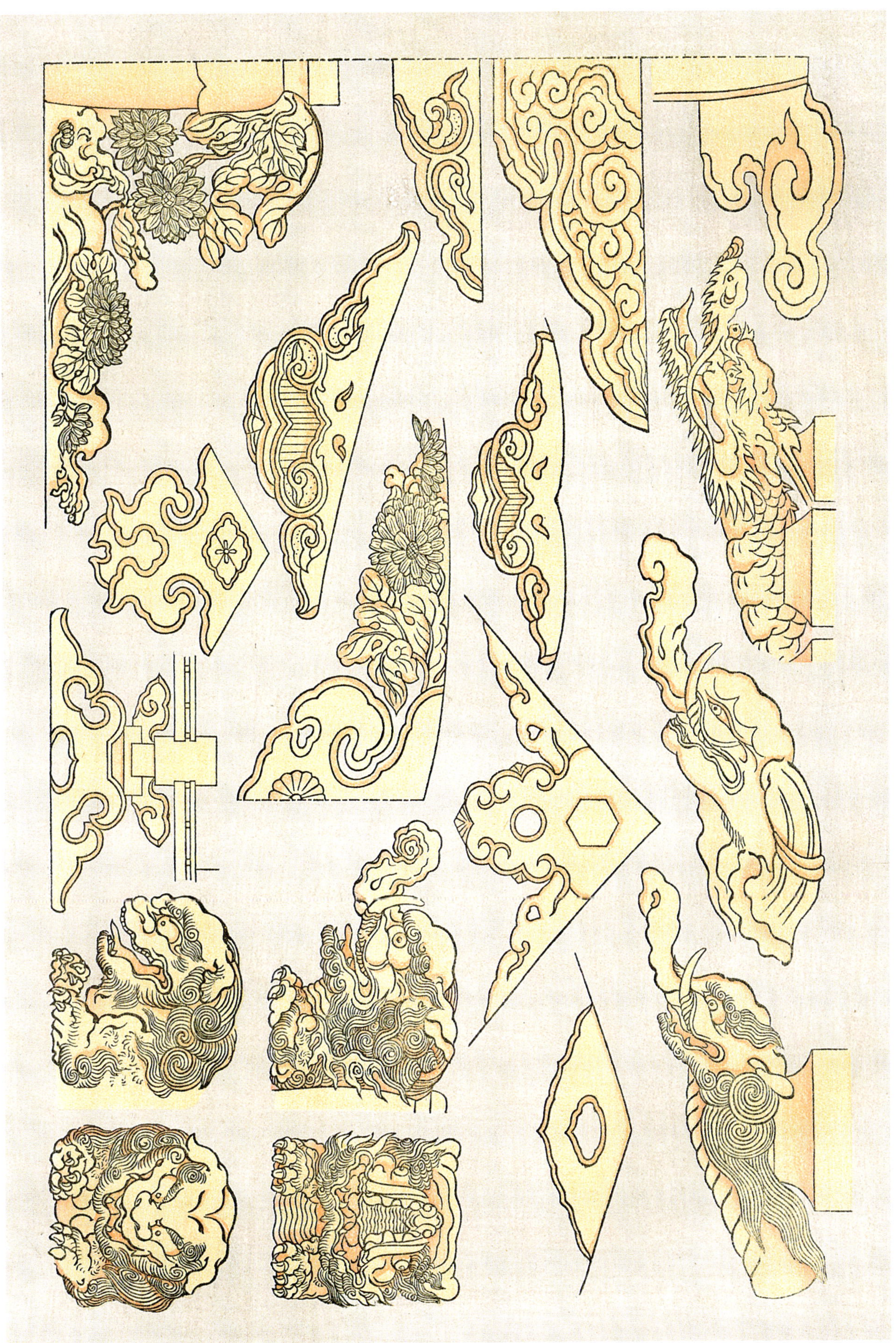

Plate 83

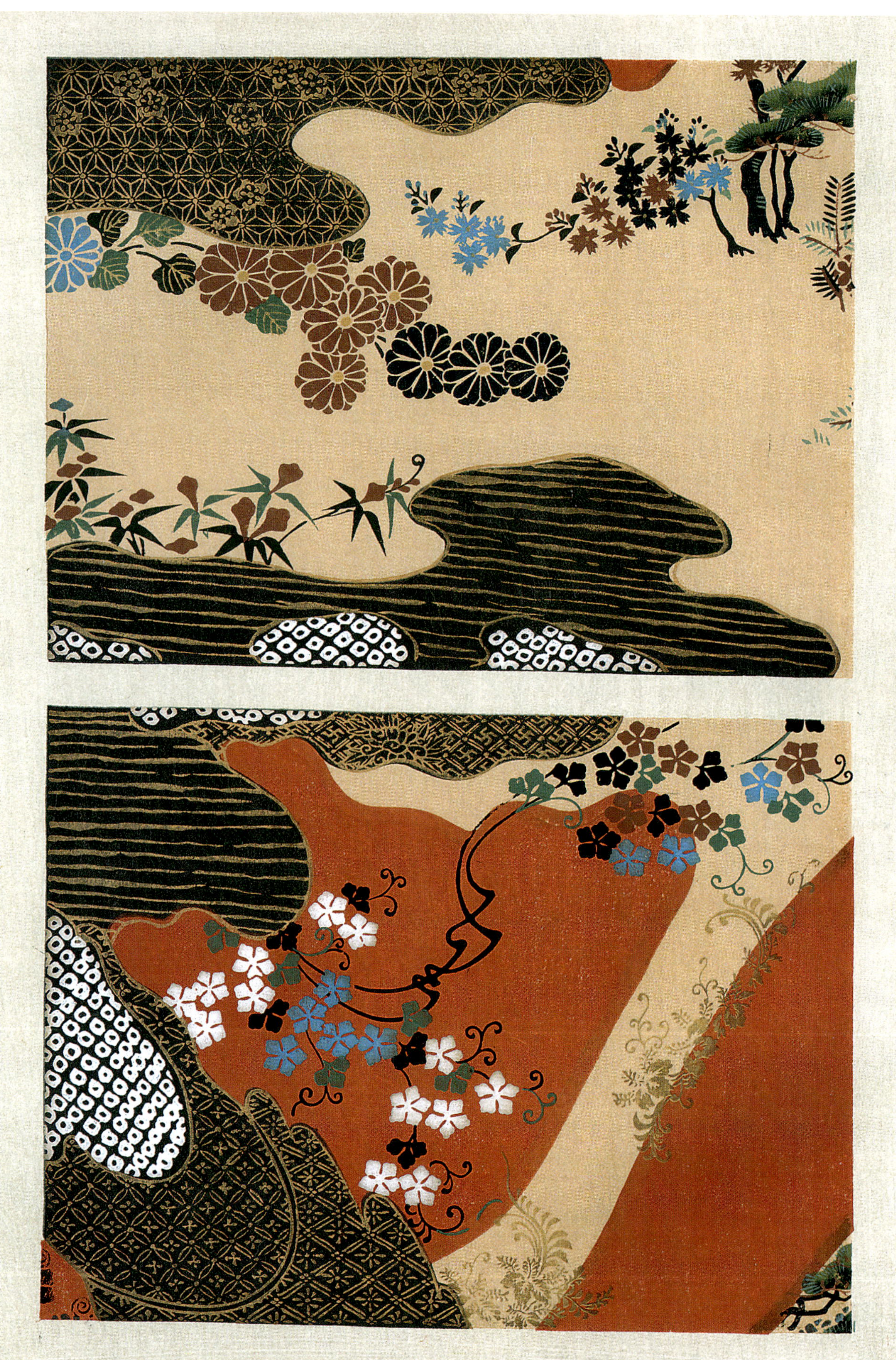

PLATE 84

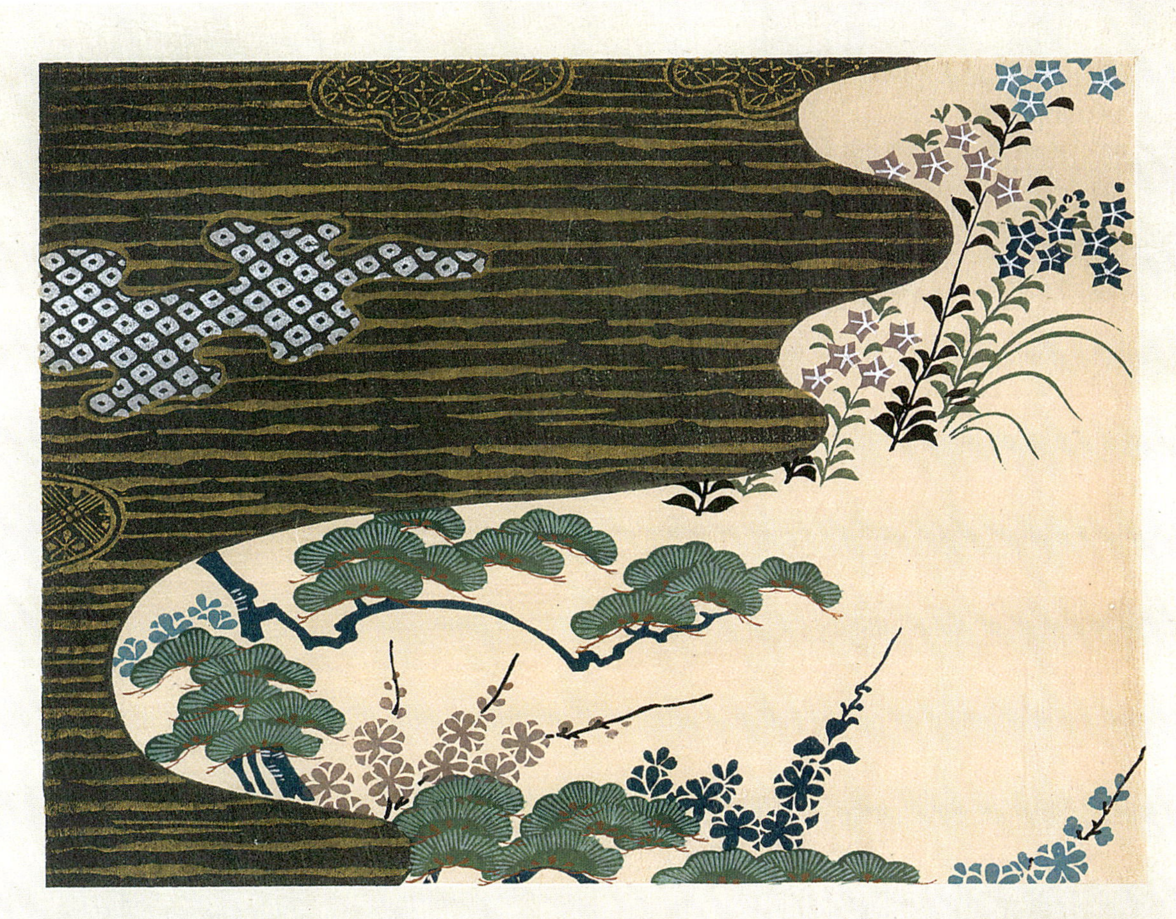

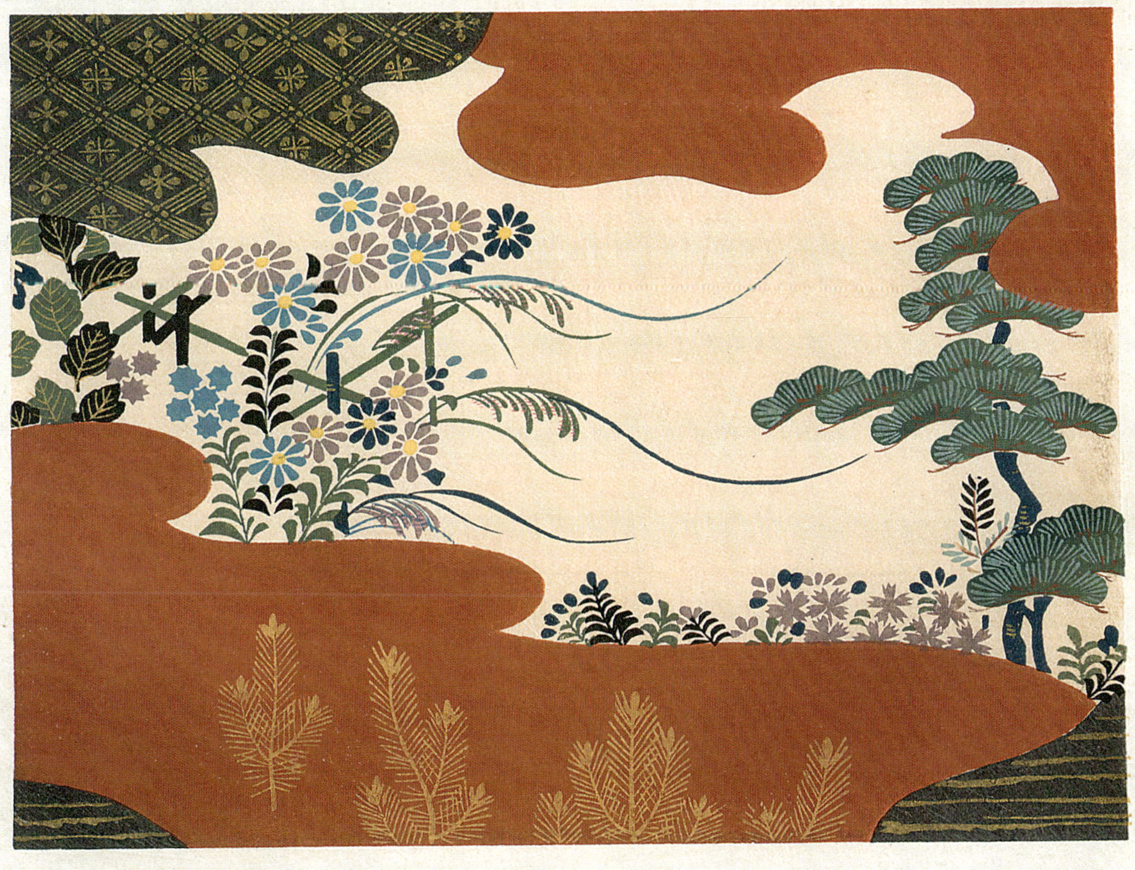

PLATE 85

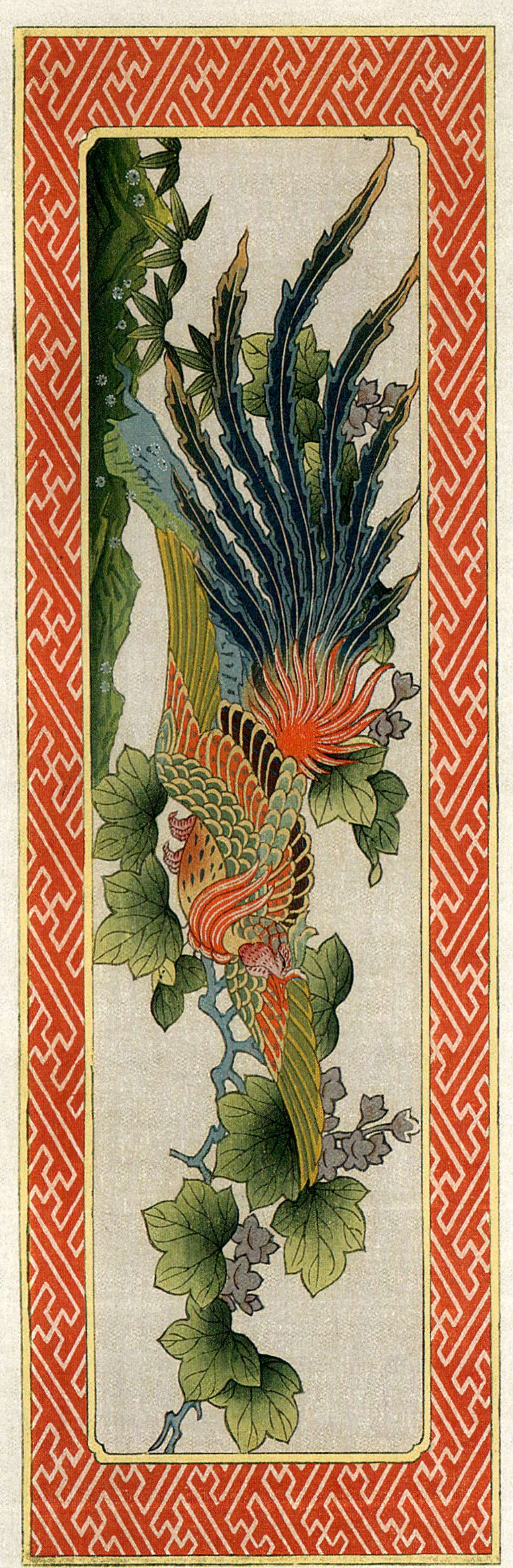

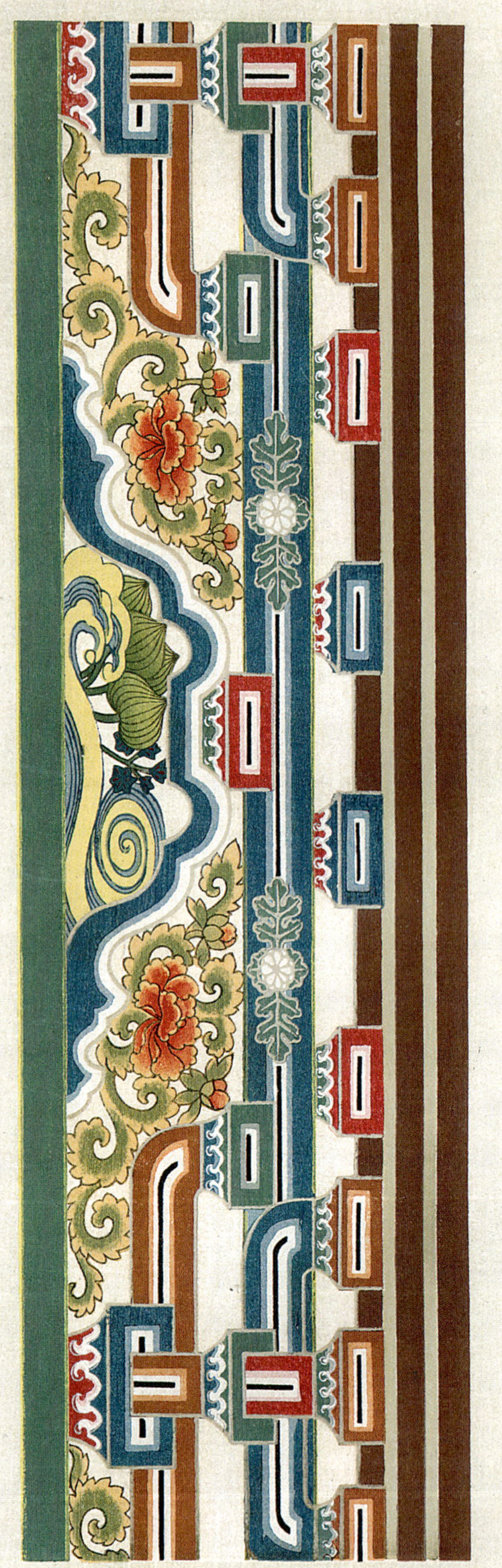

Plate 86

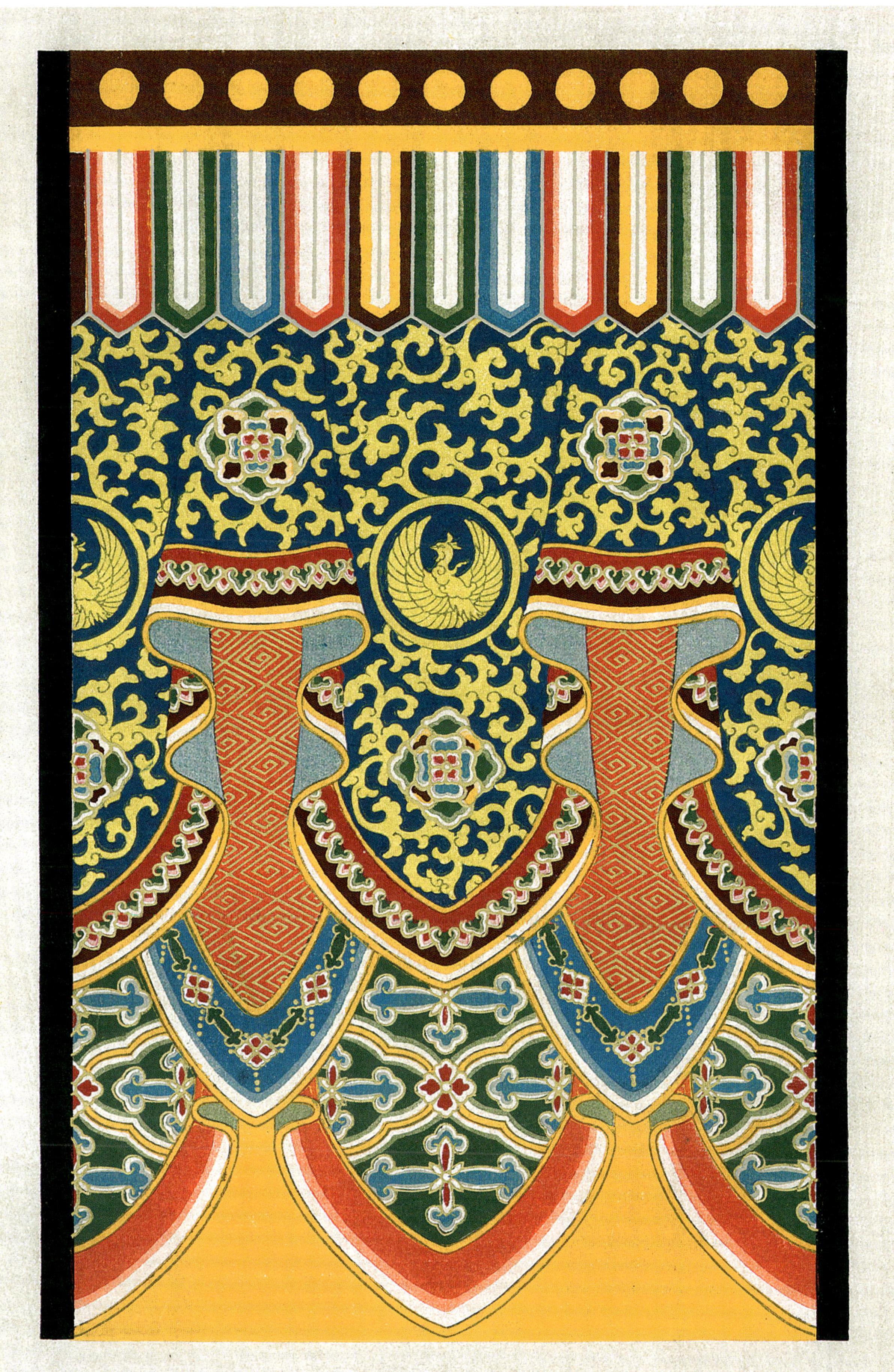

Plate 87

Plate 88

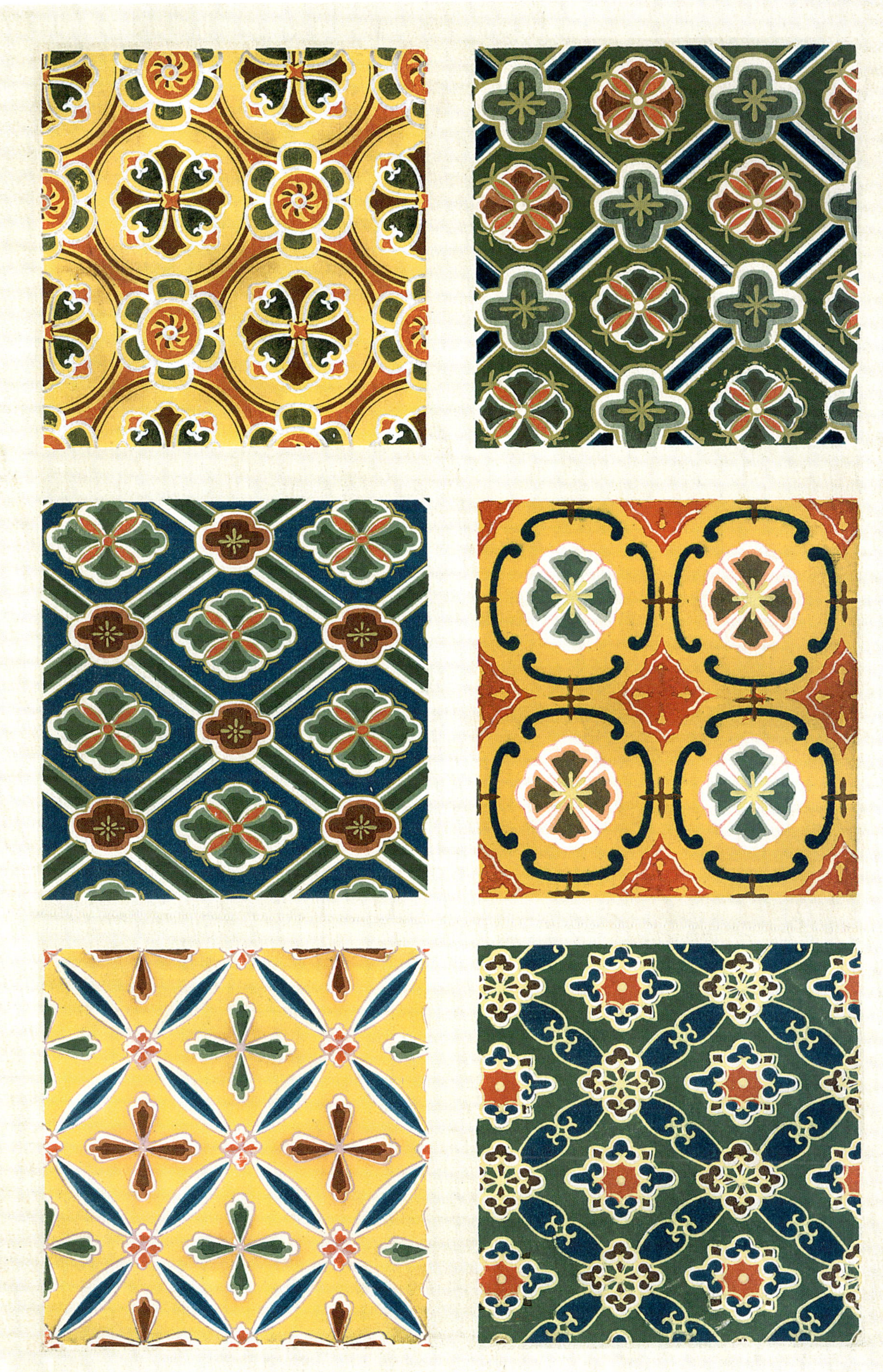

Plate 89

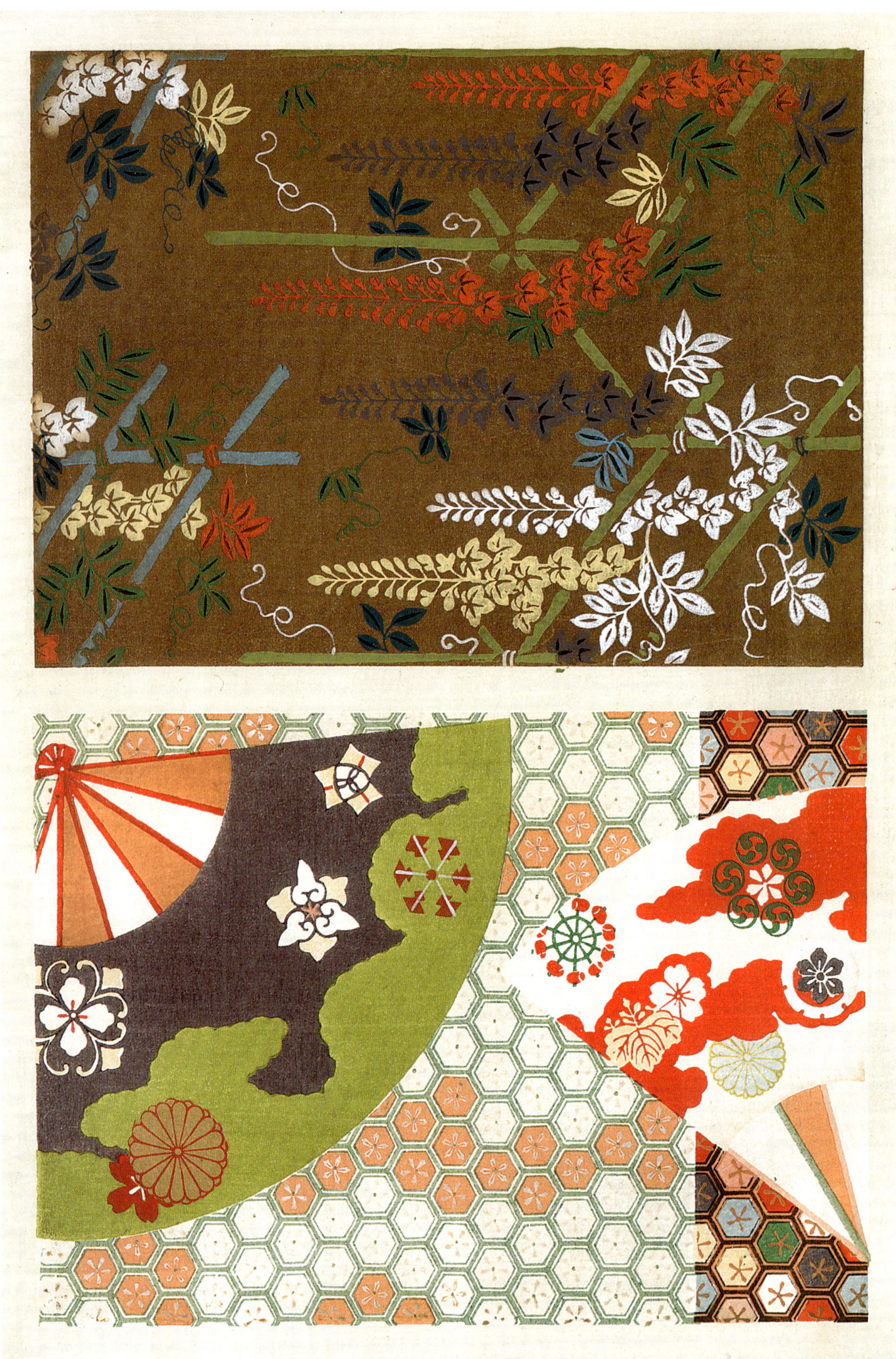

Plate 90

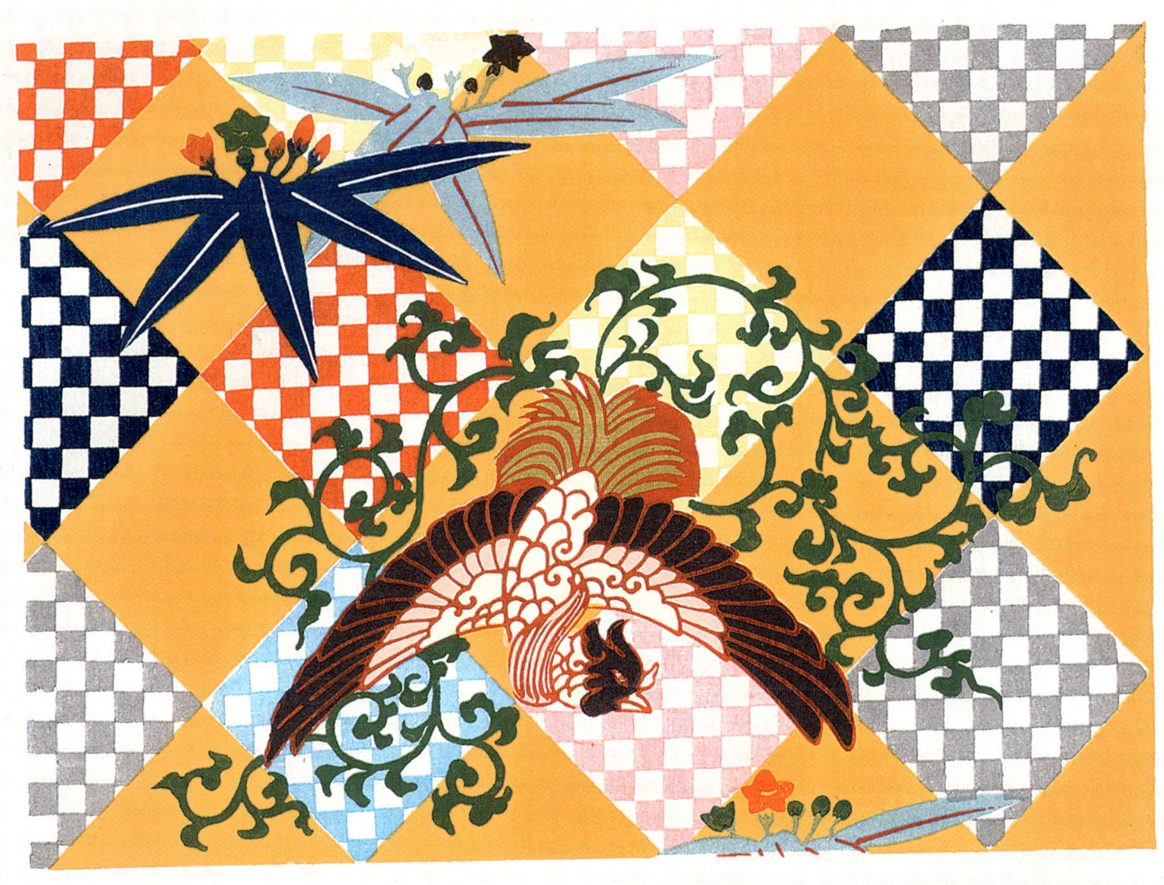

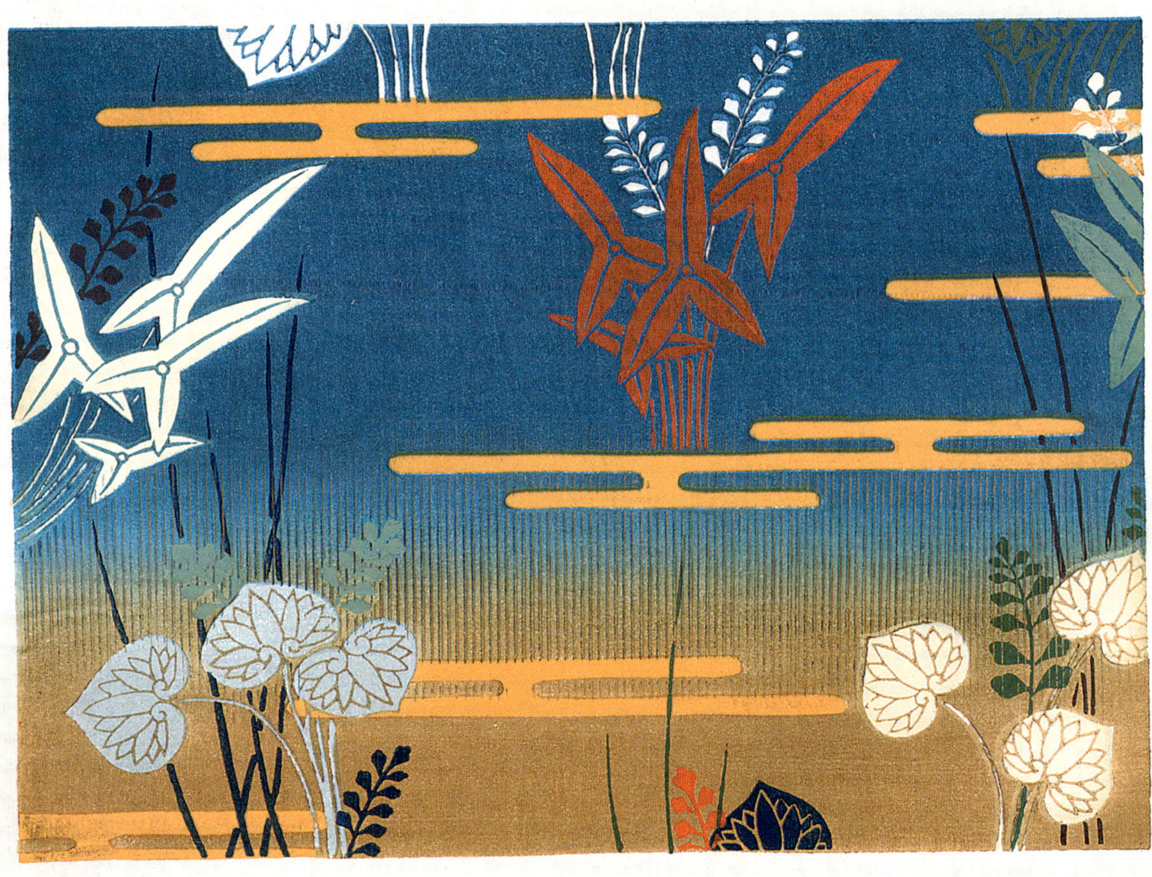

Plate 91

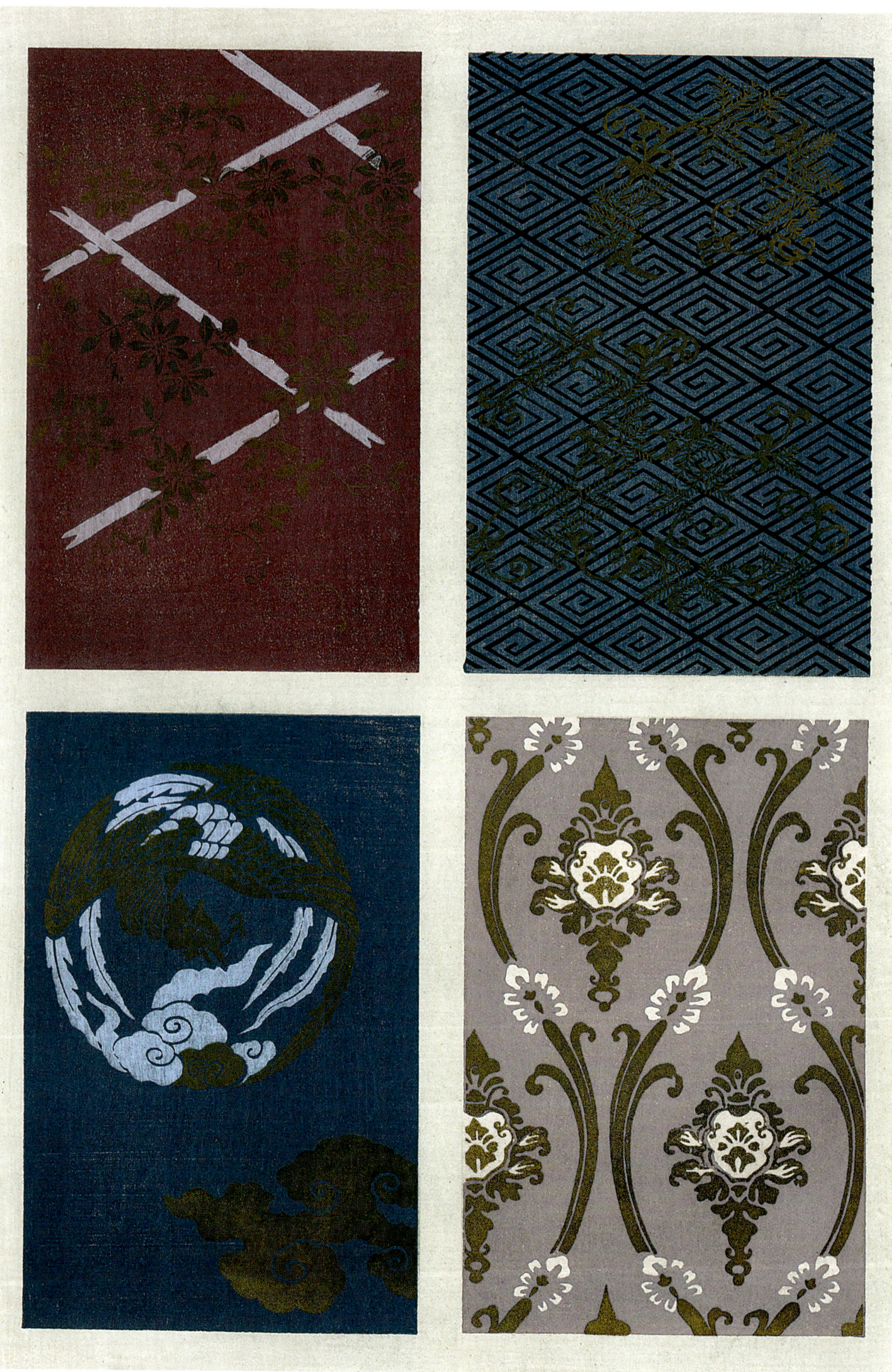

Plate 92

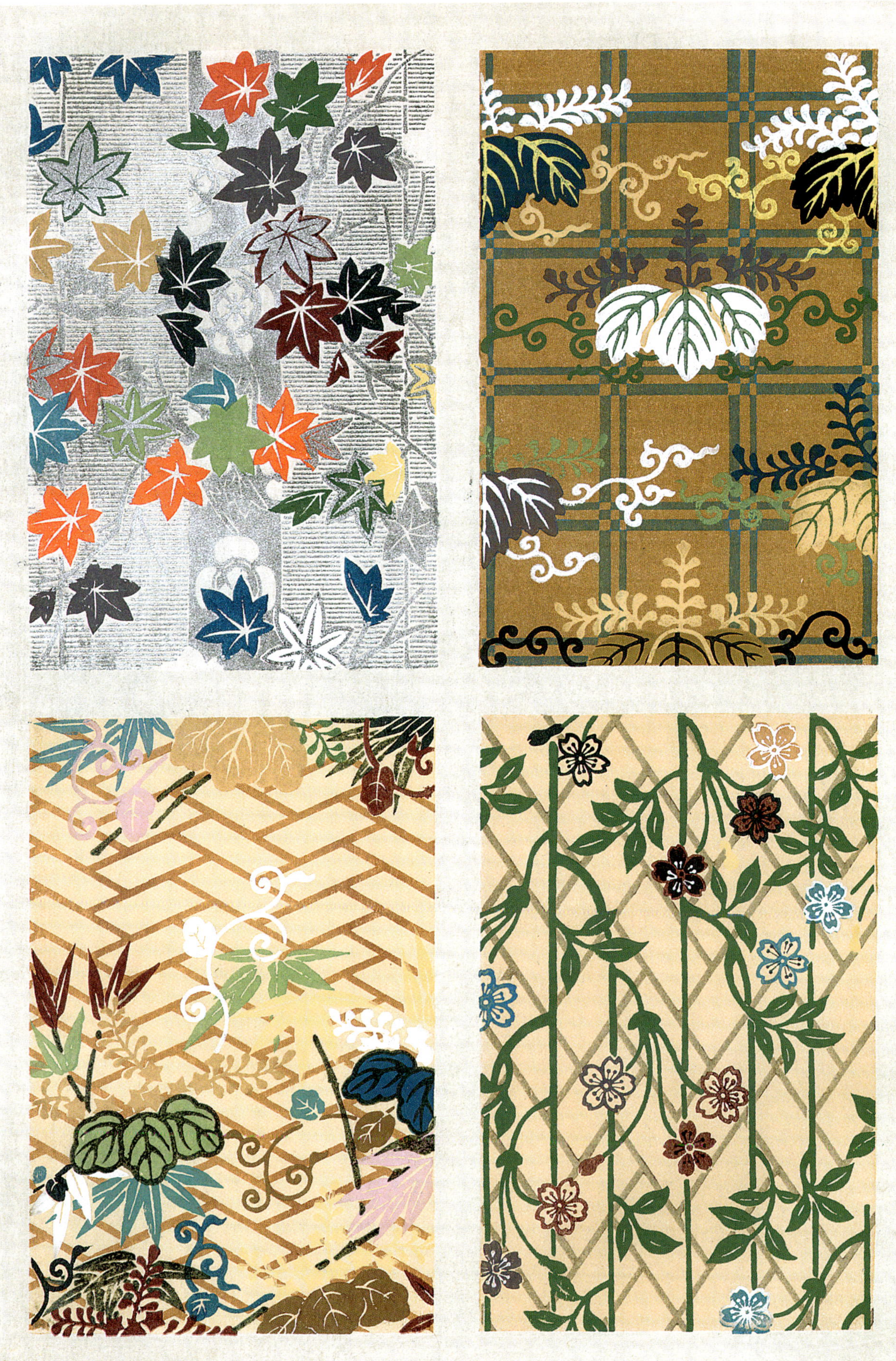

Plate 93

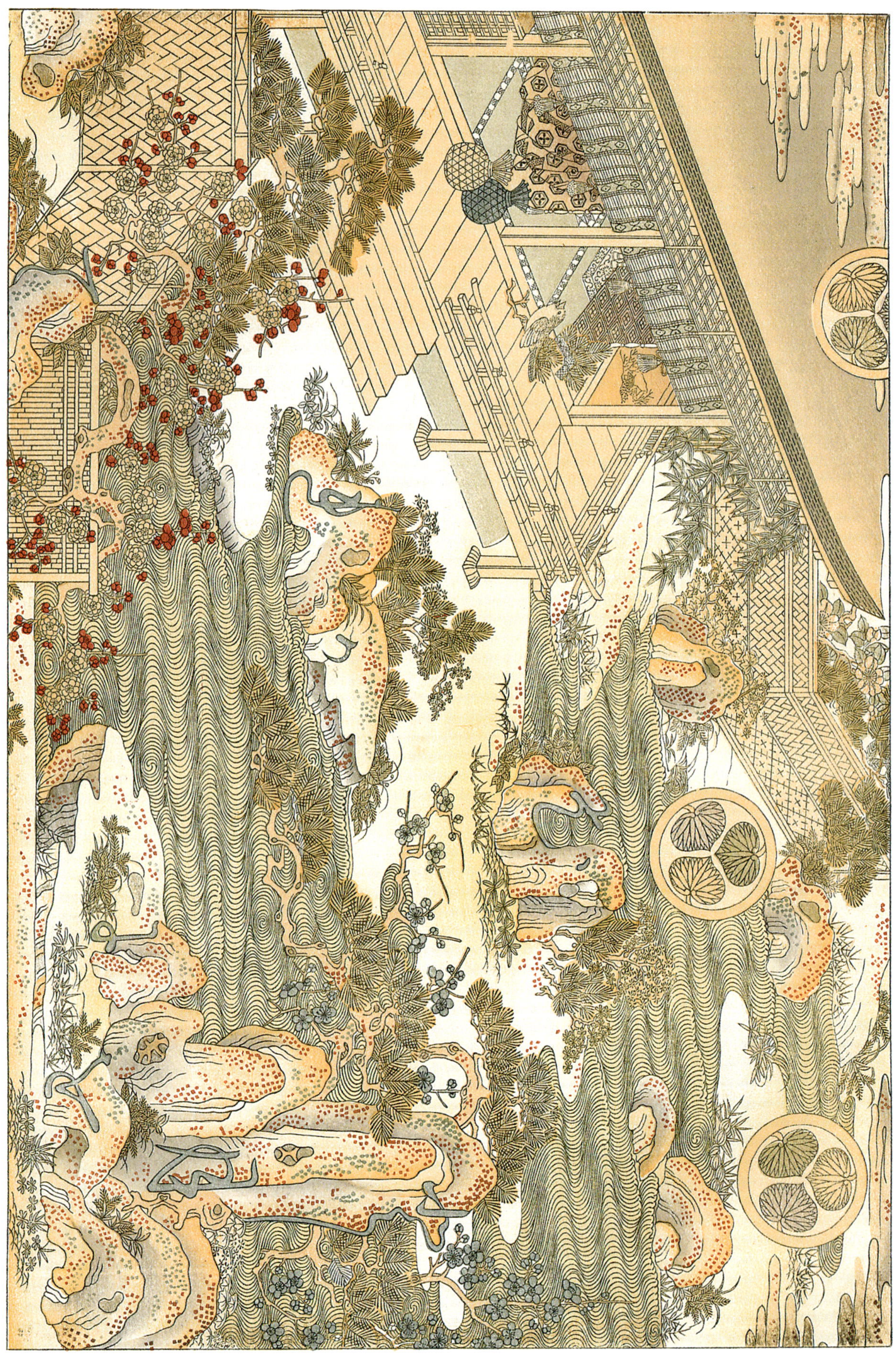

Plate 94

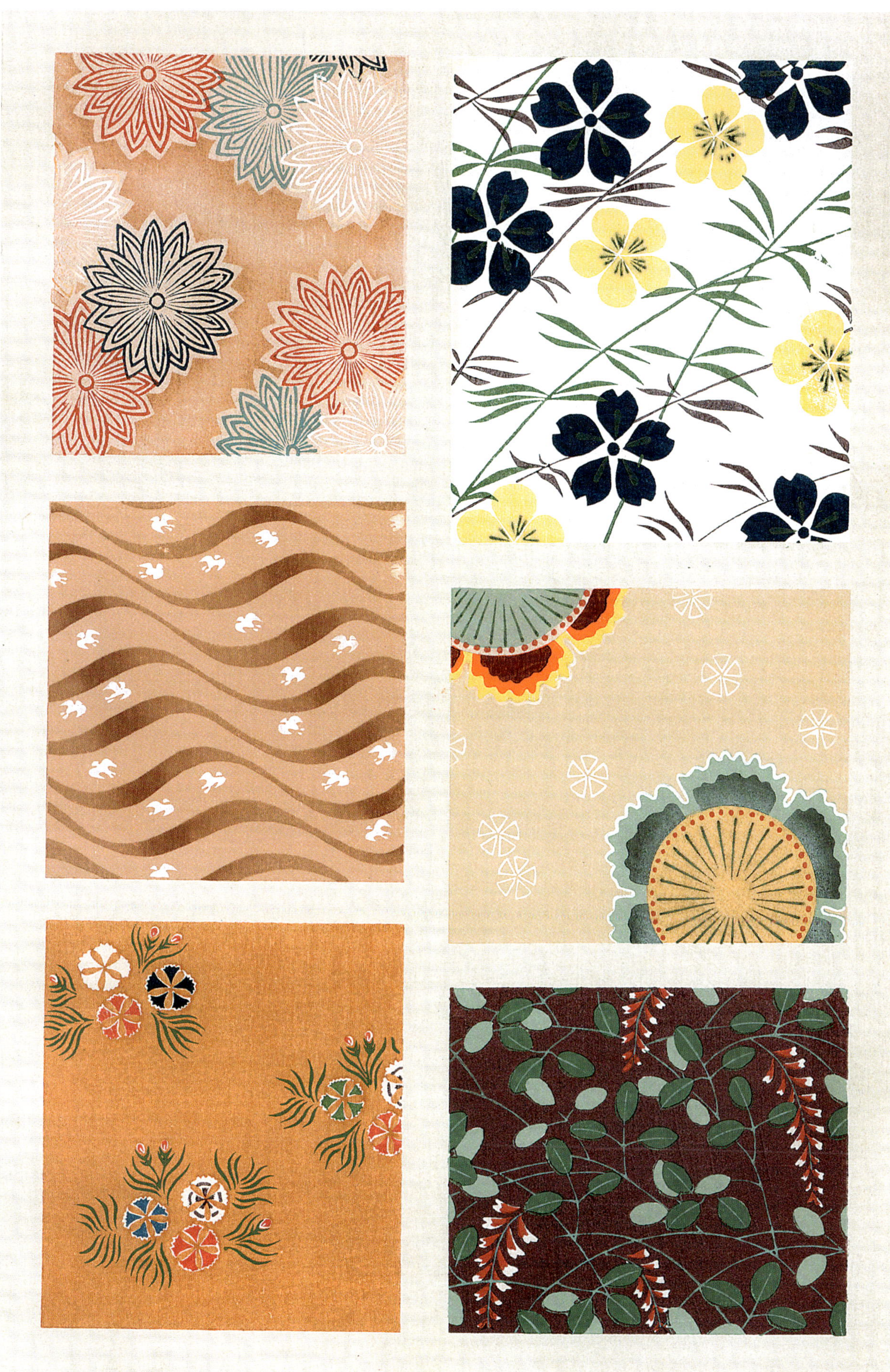

Plate 95

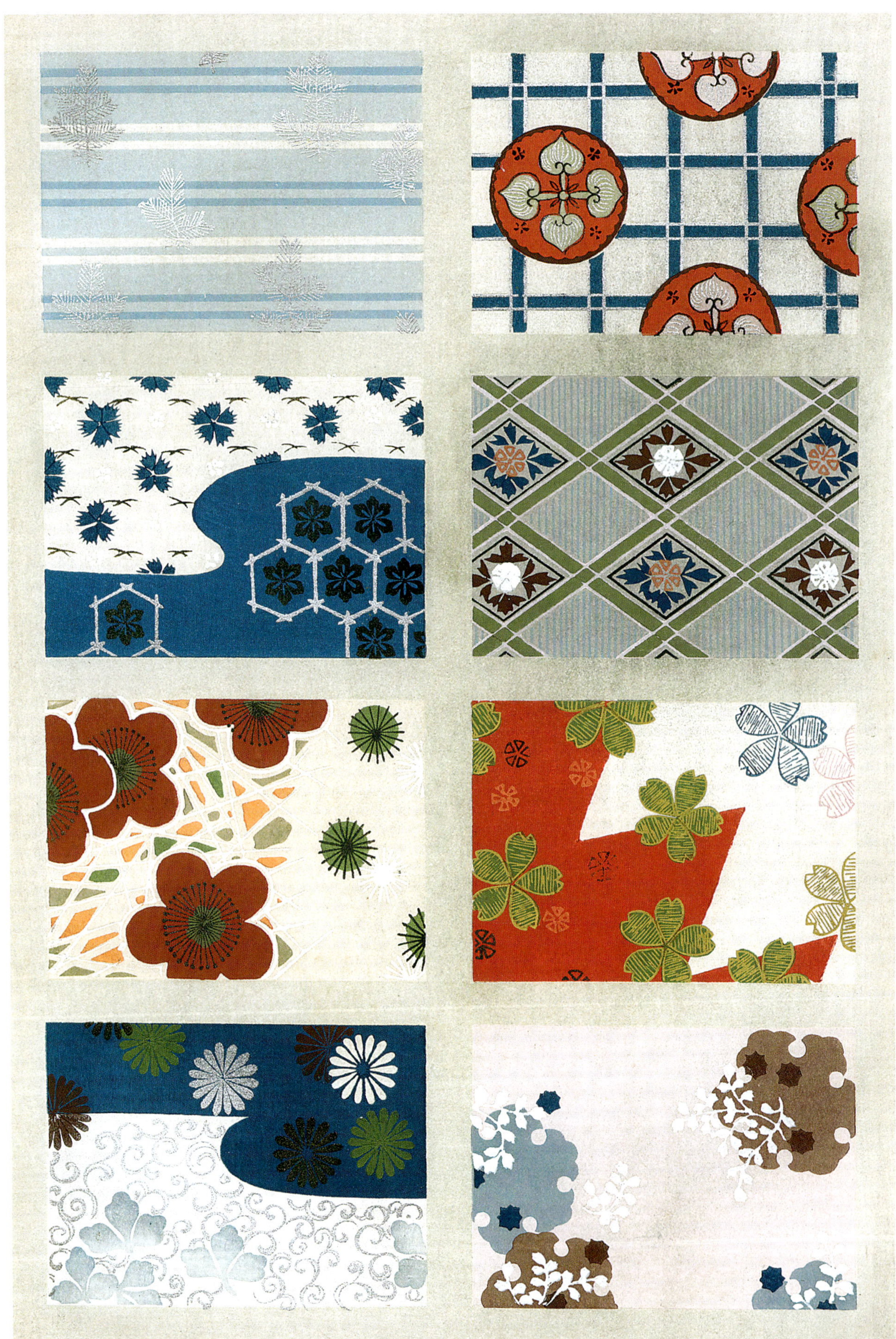

Plate 96

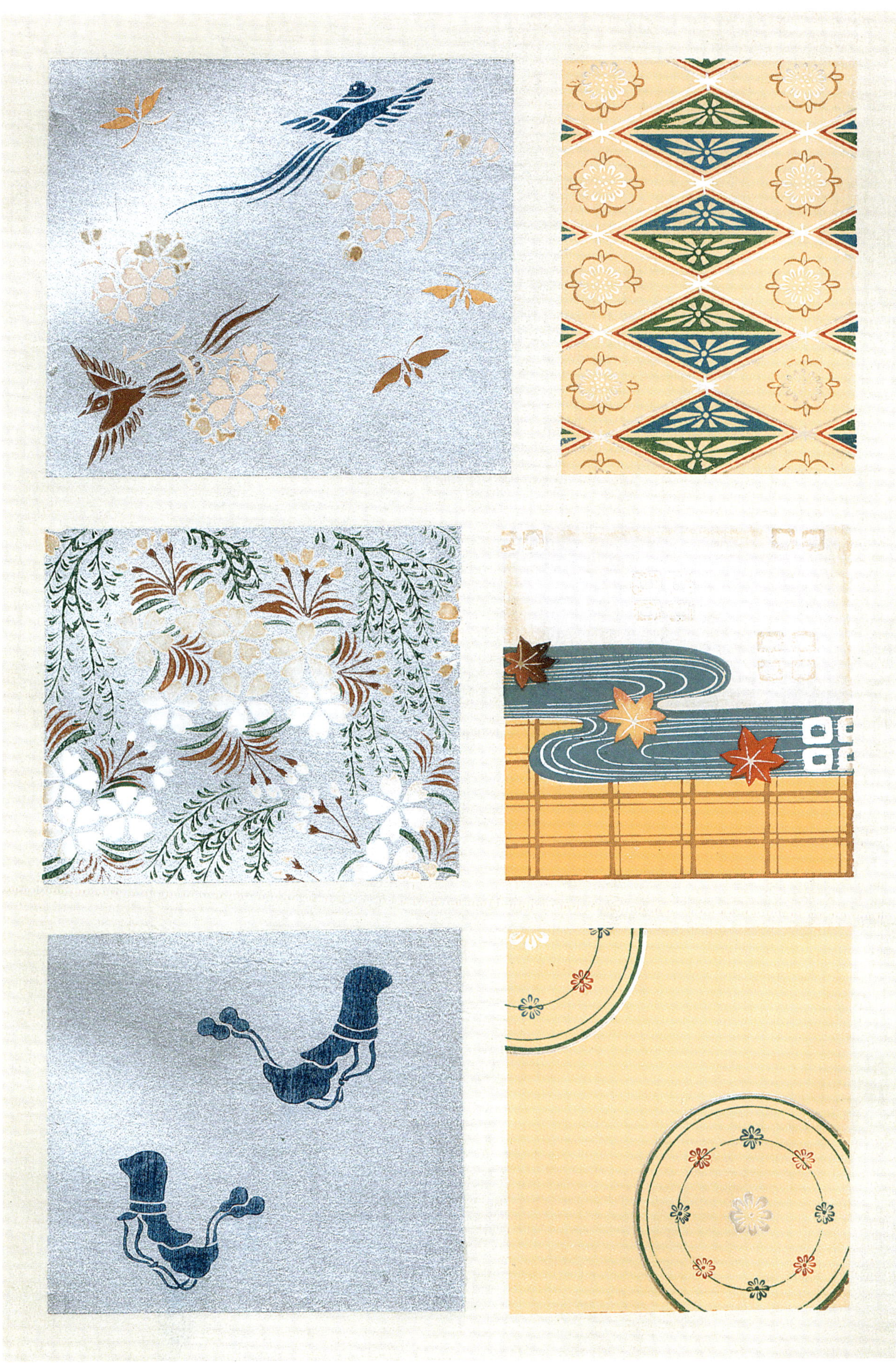

Plate 97

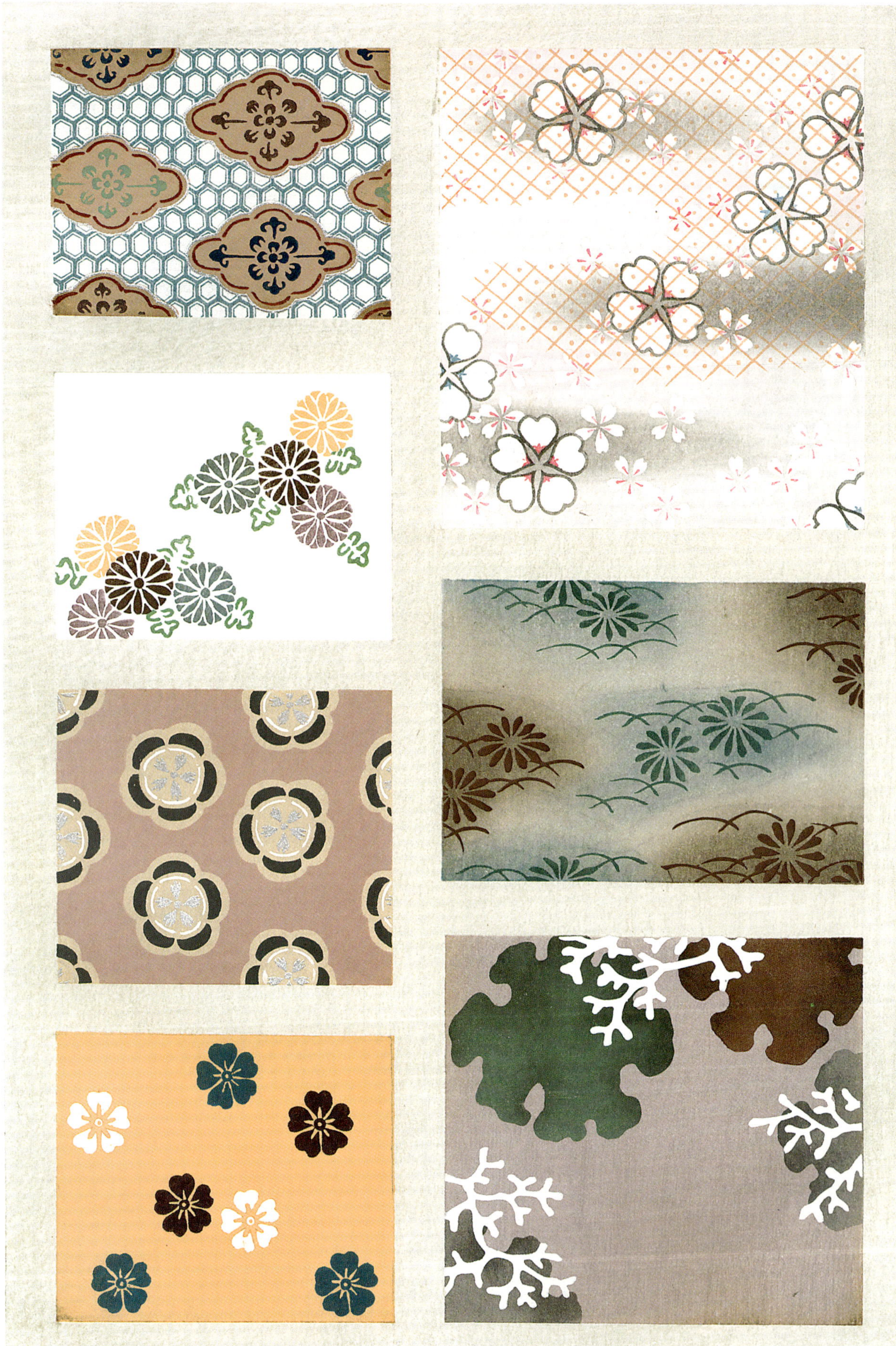

Plate 98

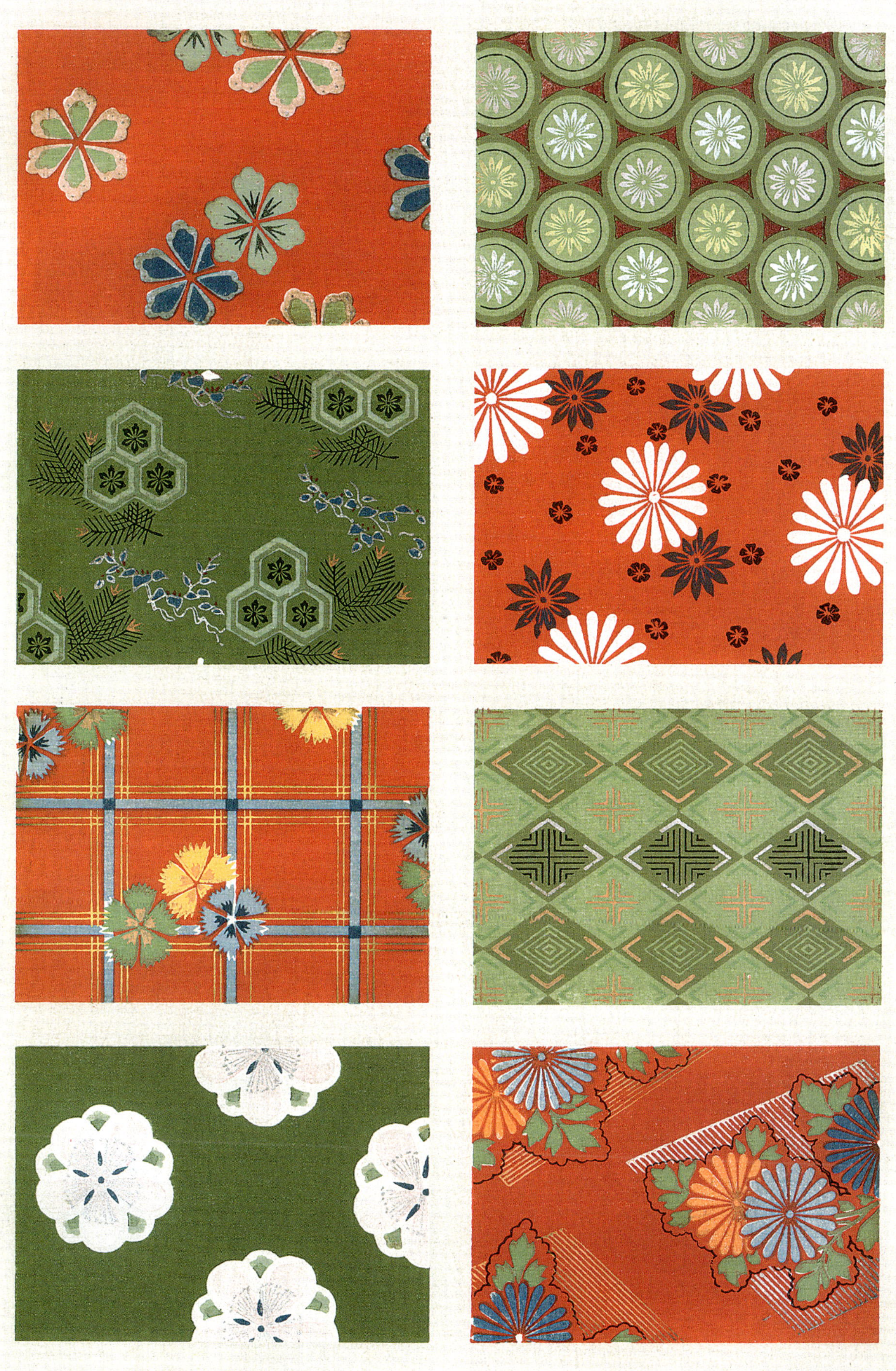

PLATE 99

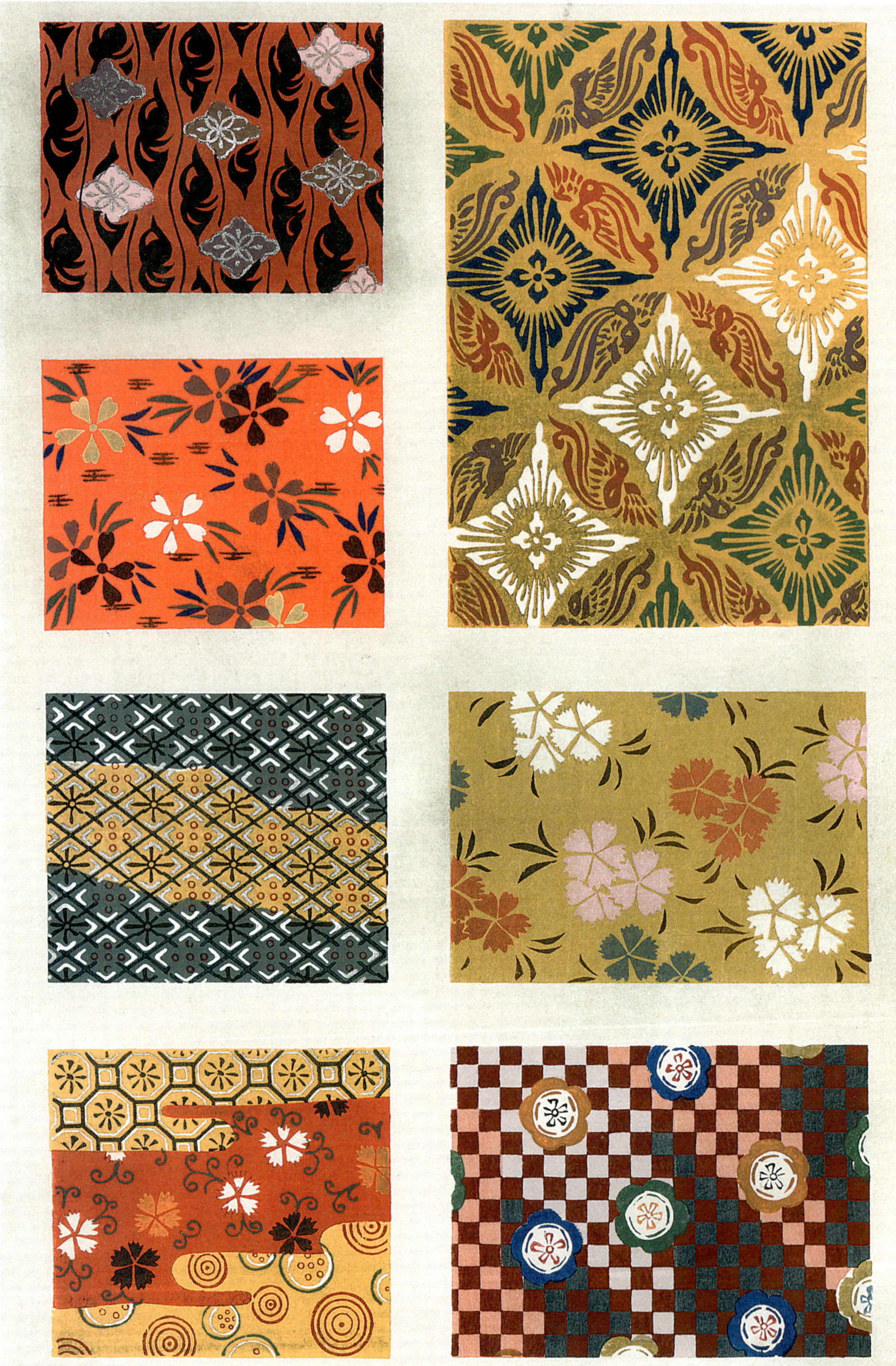

Plate 100